Becoming Cosmopolitan

Becoming Cosmopolitan

Unfolding Two Centuries of Mission at
Virginia Theological Seminary

WILLIAM L. SACHS
and WANJIRU M. GITAU

Foreword by Daniel Aleshire

PICKWICK *Publications* · Eugene, Oregon

BECOMING COSMOPOLITAN
Two Centuries of Virginia Theological Seminary in Mission

Pickwick Publications
An Imprint of Wipf and Stock Publishers
199 W. 8th Ave., Suite 3
Eugene, OR 97401

www.wipfandstock.com

PAPERBACK ISBN: 978-1-7252-8354-1
HARDCOVER ISBN: 978-1-7252-8358-9
EBOOK ISBN: 978-1-7252-8361-9

Cataloguing-in-Publication data:

Names: Sachs, William L., author. | Gitau, Wanjiru M., author. | Aleshire,
Daniel, foreword.

Title: Becoming cosmopolitan : two centuries of Virginia Theological
Seminary in mission / William L. Sachs and Wanjiru M. Gitau ; foreword by
Daniel Aleshire.

Description: Eugene, OR: Pickwick Publications, 2023. | Includes bibliographi-
cal references.

Identifiers: ISBN 978-1-7252-8354-1 (paperback). | ISBN 978-1-7252-8358-9
(hardcover). | ISBN 978-1-7252-8361-9 (ebook).

Subjects: LSCH: Virginia Theological Seminary—History. | Episcopal Church—
Missions—History.

Classification: BV3380 S23 2023 (print). | BV3380 (ebook).

01/03/23

The photos reproduced between chapters 5 and 6 are printed by permission of the
Virginia Theological Seminary Archives.

Scripture quotations are from New Revised Standard Version Bible, copyright ©
1989 National Council of the Churches of Christ in the United States of America.
Used by permission. All rights reserved worldwide.

Contents

Foreword

THEOLOGICAL SCHOOLS EMBODY INSTITUTIONAL structures and educational practices that have developed over millennia and changed substantially within those millennia. They do not exist for themselves, at least not the best of them: they exist in service to communities of faith, the religious convictions of those communities, and the scholarly renewal of those convictions. To explore the history of theological schools over two centuries entails charting their function as schools in the context of changing educational practices, and their relationship to religious communities in the context of the events that have shaped and changed those communities.

In the colonies, the education of Protestant clergy—if they were educated at any advanced level—occurred in colleges like the College of William and Mary or King's College (now Columbia University) for Anglicans, at the College of New Jersey (now Princeton University) for Presbyterians, and at Yale and Harvard for the Congregationalists. In the early decades of the nineteenth century, Protestant theological education began moving from colleges and universities to freestanding theological schools. Andover was the first of these schools, founded in 1807, and Princeton Seminary soon followed when it separated from the College of New Jersey in 1812. General Seminary was chartered by the General Convention of what is now the Episcopal Church in 1817 and occupied its first campus ten years later. Virginia Seminary held its first class in 1823. The freestanding theological school was, for the most part, an American invention.

Early American theological education focused on the interpretation of biblical texts, explication of theological commitments, ecclesiastical history, as well as preaching and liturgy. These subject areas, however, were not organized into academic disciplines. One professor could cover many. Disciplinary structures in theological education took form after they developed in higher education as a whole in the last quarter of the nineteenth century. Academic disciplines provided new canons for technical study by which the quality of academic study could be judged. The emergence of disciplinary fields influenced theological schools in two significant ways. First, it increased the number of faculty. *Becoming Cosmopolitan* notes the growth of the Virginia Theological Seminary faculty during the nineteenth and twentieth centuries. While the size of the faculty was in part due to increased enrollment, it was more a function of the increased number of disciplines. The increase in the number of disciplines continued though much of the twentieth century with the addition of areas like religious education, pastoral care, and sociology of religion. Second, the theological disciplines challenged theological education. The disciplinary study of Scripture, for example, raised questions about the historical accuracy of some biblical texts, debates over literary forms, and the authorship of the texts. These questions troubled the waters of theological schools, as was the case at Virginia Seminary. The twentieth-century ministry practice disciplines pushed theological education in the direction of professional education, which raised concerns about whether ministerial excellence would become defined more in terms of professional knowledge and skills than by priestly character, sensitivities, and piety.

The pedagogical practices of theological education changed over the centuries. Recitation was an early teaching strategy that involved assigning a text to students who were responsible for studying it so they could recite a summary of what the text said in response to a professor's question. Learning was, for the most part, by rote. This educational pattern continued in many Protestant seminaries well into the twentieth century. The twentieth century brought a new pedagogical practice called the lecture. Students were still responsible for reading particular assigned texts, but they no longer had to recite them in class. The work of the professor moved from guiding learning by asking questions for recitation to guiding learning by describing and interpreting material. The shift was controversial because it exchanged more objective textbook education for professorial explanation and interpretation that could be more subjective. As *Becoming Cosmopolitan* notes, this controversy showed itself at Virginia Seminary as professors who used recitation were perceived as less academic than the ones that were lecturing. Lectures have subsequently been supplemented with experiential learning, student presentations, and group projects—all of which have received their share of critique.

Theological schools were formed either by or for ecclesial constituencies. Andover was not directly under the control of a church, but its formation ensured trinitarian theological education for New England Congregationalists. Princeton was founded in a way that ensured church control over the seminary. The founding of General and Virginia reflected ecclesial needs as the Episcopal Church restructured itself as an American denomination. These schools were all founded as servants of a single denominational or confessional community. The nineteenth century was an era of denominational competition and few denominational seminaries enrolled students, employed faculty, or elected board members from outside the school's denomination. This tight denominational connection served the schools by supplying new students, ensuring employment for graduates, and providing financial support. It served the denomination through relationships formed among students and educational outcomes practiced by graduates to advance denominational commitments. Virginia Seminary embodied this model exceedingly well.

The relationship between seminary and denomination sometimes led to difficulties. Advances in theological scholarship often came at the expense of a settled or at least widely held conviction. Such advances raised questions about the purpose of theological study: is its goal to provide the intellectual support for existing understandings of the denomination, or is it to guide or push the denomination's theological understandings in new directions? Theological tensions in the late nineteenth century at Union Seminary in New York led to the separation of Union from the Presbyterian Church. While theological controversy at Princeton did not change the relationship with Presbyterians, some faculty members left to form a new seminary. Virginia Seminary was spared conflict that threatened its place in nineteenth- and twentieth-century Episcopalian life, but theological conflict did arise on its path to becoming cosmopolitan. Respect for other world religions raised questions about the shape of a missionary effort if it does not advocate for exclusive Christian truth claims. The theological controversies, or worries about them, often led to changes in the governing structures of the boards. The general conventions of higher education pushed college and university governance in directions intended to ensure independence and academic freedom. The conventions in theological education often pushed in the direction of theological fidelity to denominational expectations. Theological schools have one foot in higher education and the other in ecclesial communities, and governance struggles often reflect these competing identities.

In the nineteenth and first half of the twentieth centuries, most denominational schools received the majority of their funding from denominations. That pattern began to shift for mainline theological seminaries in the last half of the twentieth century. Increasing costs of a free-standing theological school and declining denominational resources led to a long-term decline in the percentage of operating revenue theological schools derived from their affiliated denomination. Seminaries had to look elsewhere for the majority of their revenue, and they tended to look in two directions. The first was to charge more tuition from existing students and expand the enrollment to new groups of students, either through offering new degree programs or recruiting students from other denominations. While these efforts yielded needed revenue, they had negative consequences for students who borrowed money to pay tuition and who then entered typically low paying first-call positions with educational debt, sometimes significant debt. The second direction was to cultivate a community of individual donors who could fund endowments sufficient to provide a significant proportion of the school's needed revenue. Virginia Seminary chose the second direction, and the result has made it possible for the seminary to serve its students, the Episcopal Church, and the broader Anglican community.

Both theological schools and denominations are affected by forces that are far removed from schools and ecclesial bodies. Virginia Seminary in part owes its founding to the outcomes of the Revolutionary War. The victory of the colonies set the stage for the establishment of an American Episcopal church. War is a radical and traumatic event that shapes everything it touches, and it would be only a few decades after the founding of the seminary that the Civil War affected nineteenth century theological schools. Some Southern schools ceased operation or closed, and Virginia Seminary's finances, nascent missionary efforts, and even its future were all threatened. Many of the constituents of the Virginia Seminary, including faculty, board members, and graduates, were enslavers. Racial prejudice and systemic racism are cultural inventions as violent as war but without the boundaries of time and territory, and the cultural legacies of prejudice and racism unfortunately remain. William Faulkner's line in *Requiem for a Nun* is as true as it is over-quoted: "The past is never dead. It's not even past."

While the trajectory of Virginia Seminary has reflected the journey of much of American theological education, some exceptions are significant. The Episcopal Church has had its share of separating factions over the years, yet the denomination has largely stayed intact. The Episcopal Church is one of the few mainline denominations that is not the result of a major twentieth-century union with another church body. The United Methodist Church, for example, was formed from a merger of the Methodists and Evangelical United Brethren; and three Lutheran denominations merged to form the Evangelical Lutheran Church. These mergers brought with them theological schools that had been associated with predecessor denominations, and most of these seminaries experienced changes in funding, governance, and constituencies. Virginia Seminary was spared the need to negotiate these changes.

Virginia Seminary is unique in the tenure of senior leadership across the past forty years. One observation from my decades working at the Association of Theological Schools is that schools that have successive long-term presidencies are able to develop strengths that schools with successive shorter-term presidencies tend not to develop. It requires, of course, the right kind of president during his or her term of office, but the benefits that accrue to successive longer-term presidencies—integrity of mission, financial capacity, and ability to contribute to broader communities—can be impressive. I have known and worked with the last three deans and presidents of Virginia Seminary—Richard Reid, Martha Horne, and Ian Markham—and each has contributed to the considerable capacity the seminary now enjoys. Chief officers are not the only persons who add strength to theological schools; it also requires faculty, administrators, and boards who are committed to the school and its mission.

Some theological schools serve their denominations prophetically from a theological distance. Others serve by protecting liturgical patterns or historical commitments. Still others serve by practicing the complex art of leadership and service from the center. Virginia Seminary is more this third kind of seminary. It has an evangelical heritage that has embodied changing Episcopal theological understandings related to liturgy, gender, and sexual orientation. It has sought to serve the broader Anglican community while embodying American Episcopal commitments that are at odds with a significant portion of worldwide Anglicanism. While serving from the center is demanding, when done over decades with theological integrity and missional competence, it is a pattern of institutional service that builds institutional capacity.

Virginia Seminary has traveled a long road in a common direction and gained strength along the way. Some schools can lose their way across many years, think their past can save their future, imagine themselves outside of the risks that other schools face, but this seminary has avoided these fault lines. As Virginia Seminary has learned to become cosmopolitan, it has had to ask what it means to be a particular institution that has been changed by the world; what it means to be an American Episcopal seminary that is a meeting place for the conflicted Anglican Communion; what it means to an institution that both teaches and learns. These are traits to celebrate as much as centuries of institutional service, perhaps more because they pave the way to the next century of service.

                                                    Daniel Aleshire

Acknowledgments

"SEEK THE TRUTH; COME whence it may, cost what it will." The words of William Sparrow, an early faculty member at Virginia Theological Seminary, are inscribed on the wall of the Bishop Payne Library. They cannot be missed unless a student is preoccupied. The campus bears various names embodying a legacy of education in the Christian faith and service in Christ's name to the church and the world. But Sparrow's words summarize the seminary's intention.

This history of Virginia Seminary pays special attention to its historic emphasis on mission, especially beyond the United States. At first, the task seemed obvious even with its arduous demands. Seminary graduates set forth to every continent to make converts to the faith and to build church life. An inordinate number succumbed to harsh conditions though an impressive number spent significant portions of their ministries in adopted contexts. Virginia Seminary's record is unmatched by any other Episcopal institution.

As they went to convince unconverted people of the Christian truth, missionaries found that they also were seekers of truth. They encountered unfamiliar languages and cultures based in complex patterns of human values and character. The truth of the Gospel was enhanced by such experience. The process of seeking truth became reciprocal and that process extended back to the seminary where it had begun. Those who went to inspire were inspired; those who went to teach also learned and brought their insights home. Mission and education became cosmopolitan. It will be shown that cosmopolitanism encompassed both the intentions of mission and what came of it. Similarly, the motivations of missionaries were refined by what they experienced as they lived out their callings. The

historic dialogue between intention and outcome, between ideals and realities, frames this analysis of Virginia Seminary's history.

The writing of this book has entailed such a dialogue. Fortunately,
the intended history reached fruition because of the encouragement
and contributions of various people. The idea of writing this book was
broached in 2019 by Robert Heaney, professor of mission and then
the director of the seminary's Center for Anglican Communion Studies (CACS). Robert's invitation grew out of prior conversation with Ian
Markham, the seminary's dean and president. I am grateful for their trust
and encouragement. I express further gratitude for their readiness to be
consulted as the writing progressed.

The Center for Anglican Communion Studies has been a constant
source of guidance and support. I value the conversations with Katherine
Grieb, CACS director, and Hartley Wensing, associate director. Warm
friendships have grown from working on this history. Administrative
coordinators Molly O'Brien and now Courtney Henderson-Adams have
responded skillfully to various requests. A vital aspect of the seminary's
work, CACS made this book possible.

The Bishop Payne Library, where Sparrow's words are prominent,
holds an impressive and varied collection that proved invaluable to this
work. The quality of library staff matches the quality of the holdings they
oversee. I am especially grateful to Mitzi Jarrett Budde, librarian, who
sets an ideal tone for all who come seeking truth. As work began on this
project, the library's archives loomed large. The archival collection was
warmly and ably explained by Chris Pote, until recently the archivist. He
knew where I could find all that I needed, and he was proactive in locat-
ing related materials. I wish Chris well in his endeavors. I also wish to
express gratitude to the staff of the Bishop Payne Library for finding and
granting permission to use the photographs in this book.

To embody the cosmopolitan spirit, the creation of this book required a colleague. Wanjiru Gitau brought the experiences of a Kenyan
upbringing and the skill of an astute student of Christian mission. She
lent perspective that balanced the narrative and gave insights that set
Virginia Seminary's history in broader contexts. I am grateful also for
the Florida hospitality she and her husband, Bryan Froehle, offered. Several friends commented on chapter drafts as they appeared. Robert Al-
len, Neal Goldsborough, and John Miller guided and corrected warmly
and clearly. Naturally, Robert Heaney also read closely with particular

attention to the history of mission and to the seminary's international links. The book is better for their attention to it.

An appreciative perspective for this book became possible because a diverse group of people agreed to be interviewed. Their experiences of Virginia Theological Seminary and the contexts in which they work vary impressively. Together their dedication and enthusiasm for the seminary is heartening. I am grateful to: Herman Browne, Joanildo Burity, Anne Fredericks-Cooper, Martha Horne, Richard Jones, Vicentia Kagbe, Sandra McCann, Troy Mendez, Hosam Naoum, Robert Prichard, Leslie Steffensen, Joseph Thompson, Joel Waweru, and John Yieh.

No manuscript can become a book without the able scrutiny of a skilled editor. Christopher Poore, a Virginia Seminary student and an alumnus of the University of Chicago Divinity School, filled this role admirably and warmly. His work is gratefully appreciated.

A book project such as this flourishes as it builds its own version of cosmopolitanism. What is intended to be expressed is refined by the process of learning that must define it. Histories often prove circular. Thus, one returns to Sparrow's maxim which proves timeless. Amid complex and discomforting truth, there is redemptive possibility as the history of Virginia Seminary continues to unfold.

William L. Sachs

1

Introduction
Becoming Cosmopolitan

JOHN PAYNE'S RESOLVE

LATE IN 1851, JOHN Payne addressed the alumni association of Virginia Theological Seminary in Alexandria, Virginia. Newly consecrated as the first bishop of the Episcopal Church in Liberia, he was an alumnus of the seminary, having graduated in 1836. Payne spoke candidly of how his motivation to become a missionary was formed while he was a seminary student. He had already served in Liberia for fourteen years and wanted to emphasize that his vocation had been shaped gradually. It was not a matter of "divine impulse." In shaping his call, Payne felt bound to use reason, his "natural powers," as much as he heeded "divine direction." While a seminary student, he concluded that "my Master's call directed me . . . to the heathen [*sic*] rather than to the Christian world, as the sphere of my labours."[1]

But, he wondered, to "what portion of the heathen world" was he called? Reflecting on the extent of the non-Christian world, he mused that "all alike [were] perishing for the bread of life." He considered service in China, where a fellow alumnus of Virginia Seminary, William J. Boone, would launch pioneering mission work as Payne went to Africa. His attention to Asia was not momentary; a sense of direction seemed to form. He resolved "by God's grace . . . to lay down my life for the

1. *Spirit of Missions* 16 (1851) 492f.

Chinese." But the "Foreign Committee" of the Episcopal Church did not endorse this conviction. The leadership of Episcopal Church mission preferred that Payne go to Africa where there was need. Payne initially resisted. He feared the African climate would prove harmful to his health. He also wondered how much good he might accomplish.

Yet Payne resolved to consider African service and became aware of the "new colony" that had been planted at Cape Palmas, Liberia, on Africa's west coast. The idea took hold and concerns about health eased. "After all, then, might not a prudent, healthy white man go to this new settlement, with a reasonable hope of living and being useful?" One further consideration shaped his motivation, more urgent even than questions about health or usefulness. "For centuries God had permitted white men to live on all parts of the west coast of Africa, whose only business it was to enslave and destroy the souls and bodies of the miserable inhabitants. Would he not preserve those whose object was to save them, even with the salvation of the Gospel!" It was a remarkable sentiment, all the more so for its passion. A generation before the Civil War, amid a Virginia culture of slavery, John Payne condemned slavery and resolved to challenge it through Christian mission. For him, mission entailed redeemed social relations as well as the salvation of individual souls. He would hardly be alone in this intention.[2]

Payne's outlook would not be lost. Over a century and a half later, a student at Virginia Theological Seminary, James Livingston, reflected on the pages of the seminary's *Journal* about his recent trip with other students to Tanzania. Mindful of the legacy of the church's opposition to injustice, he was struck by local hospitality. In a Tanzanian congregation, joining a worship service, Livingston found a notable sense of sharing with one another, "all pretenses stripped away," with the people of this locality. "In Christ we are brothers and sisters alike," he added.[3]

Such sentiments filled the pages of "Leadership and Mission," an edition of the *Journal* from the fall of 2010 devoted to mission. Article after article depicted the seminary's extensive international engagements, spanning Africa, Asia, Latin America, and the Middle East. Students and faculty described their recent pilgrimages, emphasizing the excitement of cross-cultural discovery and the building of reciprocity in the relations that resulted. Other articles noted the arrival of international students on

2. *Spirit of Missions* 16 (1851) 492f.
3. Livingston, "Reflections on Tanzania," 28.

the seminary campus, again emphasizing relations framed by discovery and mutuality. This characterization was not new, and it would not be lost in later seminary publications. Though an entire issue devoted to mission would appear only occasionally, this emphasis and the way it was characterized would surface repeatedly. There would be regular references to mission in other publications throughout the seminary's history.[4]

By the early twenty-first century, Virginia Seminary's historic emphasis on mission had acquired a certain character, which we term "cosmopolitan." A basis for this outlook could be glimpsed in John Payne's resolve to contrast slavery with the intentions of mission. Clearly Payne's vocation was shaped as a seminary student, and clearly an emphasis on mission has been historic. But how did this emphasis come about? How did Virginia Seminary influence its students, and the wider religious culture, toward the cosmopolitan sensibility? How did mission expand from basic proclamation of the gospel with the intention of reaching unconverted people to address a range of social conditions? How did mutuality and reciprocity arise as mission unfolded? Further, how was it that mission became integral to the work of theological education? Whether they would serve outside the United States or not, how were generations of students imbued with the conviction that mission was essential to their ministries and their identities?

Christian mission has long meant proclamation of the gospel and the reframing of social life, embodied in the formation of the church as religious community. The history of Virginia Theological Seminary provides unusual insight into the pursuit of these goals and their relation to theological education. More striking, there has been the rise of an emphasis in theological education upon cultivation of cross-cultural relations marked by mutual appreciation and collaboration. The cosmopolitan spirit that emerged has reflected patterns of common purpose and ongoing discovery. This narrative will not gloss over the reality of entrenched patterns of imperialism and racism reflecting presumptions of Western cultural superiority and prerogative. Granting these realities and at points adding detail to them, it will be shown that missionaries and the peoples whom they encountered forged relations in which prejudice and disparity would be challenged. Cosmopolitanism emerged among missionaries and at the seminary that trained them, gaining influences from the experience of mission in disparate contexts rather than from Western assumptions. Mission has not been one-sided, and the turn toward

4. "Leadership and Mission," *Virginia Theological Seminary Journal* (Fall 2010) 28.

cosmopolitanism in Christian mission is unfinished. The cosmopolitan perspective is focal for Virginia Seminary. It is an ideal that is unlikely to be complete. The pursuit of this ideal frames this book.

COSMOPOLITANISM AS A LENS ON MISSION

The history of Christian mission seems incontrovertible. For two millennia Christian churches have expanded the compass of their faith and the dimensions of their social influence by making converts and building indigenous expressions of faith. Modern Christian mission has been characterized by complex formal and informal links to patterns of Western influence. Yet the impact of Christian mission has not been one-sided. As the history of Virginia Theological Seminary will reveal, mission fostered reciprocal, cross-cultural relations between those who came to evangelize and those who responded affirmatively. Mission proved dialogical, for it encouraged forms of encounter and discovery that would awaken the cosmopolitan sensibility. Yet, more than a sensibility, the turn to a cosmopolitan stance in varied contextual situations increasingly framed mutual intentions and initiatives in church life. The dynamism of evangelism and building church life, of offering education and social service, was overtaken by cosmopolitan outlook and activity. The history of Virginia Seminary encompasses the emergence of cosmopolitan patterns of relation through the way this institution emphasized mission.

The essence of Christian mission is an encounter with difference. It is easily assumed that mission entails conversion, which envisions overcoming difference by the transformation of unconverted people into Christian believers. However, the dynamism of Christian mission in practice has been nuanced. As a considerable body of literature now attests, the relations built around the intention of Christian mission have featured reciprocity, socially and culturally as well as religiously. Mission cannot be understood simply as religious. Certainly, the intentions of missionaries in all ages have been religious. It is necessary to understand the faith of those who proclaimed the gospel in places previously unknown to them. Missionaries could not presume to know the outlooks and mores of those they would convert; they had to become culturally grounded. As evangelism unfolded, complex relations emerged. Missionaries were compelled to adapt to the contexts they entered. Those who came to convert first had to learn.

They could not simply preach. They had to translate and thus learn to communicate. They could not simply persuade people that fuller life was possible. They had to demonstrate in practical terms what such life would be. Pivotal to the missionary task was building a church where patterns of Christian life would be fostered. In turn the church would encourage programs designed to root it in its new contexts. Typically, missionaries gave great emphasis to education, seeking to expand the horizons of those they sought to convert and gaining recognition as a prime source for patterns of social development. Education began with familiarity with the Bible and with literacy. It would expand to encompass basic aspects of Western learning and often included such marketable skills as carpentry. The roles of women, as students and as teachers, grew profoundly with the expansion of missionary tasks. In short, missionaries intended to convey the Christian faith by making converts, building congregations, and enhancing the locales where they ministered. In time they would think in more complex terms about leadership formation and social development. In time, too, the missionary church would become an elaborate institution, often managing an array of schools, social services, and hospitals.

Given this well-recorded history, the course of mission, and its control, could seem decidedly one-way. But that firmly held idea is being challenged, and this book will deepen this conversation in several respects. First, this narrative will describe the impact of mission upon those who conducted it as well as those for whom it was intended. The lives of missionaries were changed by the experience, often profoundly and irreparably. At a basic level they were forced to translate into practice the ideals they had absorbed in their training at home. Over time, the missionaries had to adapt their approaches in ways that were designed to convince those persons they sought to persuade. The necessity of personal as well as ecclesiastical adaptation meant that missionaries had to become appreciative of host cultures. Simply put, they had to listen before they could speak. In the process, the nature of mission changed, the training required of missionaries changed, and the missionaries themselves underwent profound transformation. They learned how to live in cultures that were not their own.

One must be wary of easy and seamless generalizations. Different missionaries responded differently to diverse cultures and to the myriad of local contexts within a given culture. Indeed, part of the process of becoming cosmopolitan for missionaries was the shattering of ready and often biased generalizations in the face of encounters with actual human beings and their lived experiences. The struggles of missionaries to reconcile what they intended with the personal and social realities they found is a basic aspect of our narrative. Even as they could be slow to relinquish their presuppositions, the missionaries found that their views of culture, faith, and human nature expanded. They became cosmopolitan.

In general, "cosmopolitanism" refers to persons who become familiar with and at ease in many different countries and cultures. In contemporary parlance, being cosmopolitan suggests travel and cross-cultural immersion, though there can be hints of superficiality in such a definition. At a more substantive level, cosmopolitanism refers to persons influenced by a variety of cultures who move toward allegiance to a sense of global community. In political as well as philosophical terms, the cosmopolitan person acquires responsibility beyond local obligations toward different and distant persons and cultures. Missionaries could approach their host cultures thinly, as religious dilettantes. But in order to advance their intentions, they were compelled to move deeper, to formulate "thick" descriptions of peoples and cultures about whom they could no longer easily generalize. Becoming cosmopolitan meant deepening appreciation through ongoing interpersonal encounter in local contexts amid tasks that were both religious and social.

More than terms such as "globalization" or "multicultural," "cosmopolitan" bespeaks personal experience. In his notable book *Cosmopolitanism*, Kwame Anthony Appiah speaks of his own movement toward wider appreciation. Being cosmopolitan did not represent simply being drawn into wider or more intricate arcs of connectivity. Appiah defines cosmopolitanism as building wider obligations to other people, especially those who are different from one's own origins. Cosmopolitanism also entails serious regard to particular human lives and the beliefs and practices that lend them significance.[5] By this definition, missionaries were compelled to become cosmopolitan. They may have rendered critical judgments about those they sought to convert. Yet they could not proceed without cultivating serious regard. Even single-minded evangelism required no less. In fact, most missionaries developed sufficient regard to reframe their task. Our narrative will describe what this has meant and how it has happened.

---

5. Appiah, *Cosmopolitanism*.

Analysis of cosmopolitanism in terms of mission can be confined neither to any one context or era, nor to the impact created by missionaries alone. The missionary experience echoed through the church at home. To assess cosmopolitanism expansively, our narrative frame is the history of one particular American theological seminary, albeit one with a history of focusing on mission and being influenced by it. From its inception in 1823, Virginia Theological Seminary made mission an organizing principle of its approach to educating clergy and church workers. Mission also became Virginia Seminary's priority as it built influence across the Episcopal Church and beyond. The seminary became notable as a gathering place for continuing education, for informing broad adult audiences, and for shaping consideration of the church's role in modern life. This institution became a bellwether for shifts in theology and pedagogy across mainstream Protestantism. The experiences of Virginia Seminary alumni in mission settings have continuously revised inherited assumptions about not only theological education but also the shape of American religious life and the nature of its influence upon diverse peoples. The rise of a cosmopolitan sensibility took place at home as well as abroad.

An emphasis on mission had practical expression early in the seminary's life. Within a decade of its founding, a graduate in the class of 1830, John Hill, went to Greece where he and his wife, Frances, would spend over fifty years running schools for girls. In the 1830s, Virginia graduates founded the Episcopal churches in Liberia and in China. In 1859, seminary alumni founded the Episcopal Church in Japan. Subsequently, in 1890, recent graduates launched the Episcopal Church in Brazil. As these new branches of the Episcopal Church and global Anglicanism took root, they established schools, social service agencies, and hospitals, casting an emphasis on service and not simply conversion. As they launched such initiatives, complex patterns of religious development, interpersonal encounter, and cross-cultural relations resulted. In each case, Episcopal mission looked to form new generations of leaders and to inject what they saw as redemptive possibility into a largely non-Christian ethos. Such emphasis extended to the seminary's work in East Africa and in Jerusalem from the mid-twentieth century onward. The role of Virginia Seminary proved influential amid other influences from the Anglican world.

All the while, foreign mission efforts by seminary graduates multiplied, especially in Latin America and the Philippines. Domestic mission also grew with particular focus on work in Alaska, Appalachia, and among

Native American peoples. This narrative will give particular attention to a few key sites, while noting the breadth of initiative and considering what was learned in mission experience and brought back to Alexandria in the classrooms and in special gatherings. The relation between mission and theological education is a formative theme for this book. In that sense, cosmopolitanism represents a deepening of appreciative ties across cultural lines. It reflected ongoing reconsideration of Christian faith and its appropriate forms of expression. As mission moved outward, it also returned home to transform those who had envisioned it.

Recent literature on cross-cultural relations, Western influence, and mission shapes our investigation of cosmopolitanism and theological education. Here it is sufficient to allude briefly to certain authors whose works inform this analysis. The history of Virginia Theological Seminary will be treated extensively. It was given virtually exhaustive attention by William Archer Rutherfoord Goodwin in a two-volume, multiauthored work at the time of the seminary's centennial in 1923. The volumes consider every facet of the institution's development, including detailed accounts of mission efforts from the seminary's earliest years.[6] A later history by John Booty traces institutional developments toward the end of the twentieth century. He gives particular attention to conflicts over social justice and changes in church life which reshaped theological education.[7]

Histories of the Episcopal Church, of American evangelicalism, and of mission work launched by various denominations also shape this narrative. The writing of Robert Prichard, emeritus faculty member of Virginia Seminary, looms large.[8] Also notable, the works of Mark Noll depict evangelicalism, theology, and mission. Noll points beyond an older generation of histories that either extolled Christian mission or criticized it as constrained by American cultural assumptions.[9] Both religious intention and social outcome must be represented in histories of mission. Themes of contextuality and indigenous church life, perhaps termed "enculturation" in the dynamism of mission, loom large. In his publications, Robert Schreiter has discussed "local theology" as well as a globalized religious sensibility, what he terms "the new catholicity."[10]

6. Goodwin, *History of the Theological Seminary in Virginia*.

7. Booty, *Mission and Ministry*.

8. Prichard, *History of the Episcopal Church*; Prichard, *Hail, Holy Hill*.

9. Noll, *America's God*; Noll, *History of Christianity in the United States and Canada*; Kidd, *America's Religious History*.

10. Schreiter, *Constructing Local Theologies*; Schreiter, *New Catholicity*.

A number of recent studies join earlier literature to frame the significance of the work we propose. Chief among them is David A. Hollinger's *Protestants Abroad: How Missionaries Tried to Change the World but Changed America*. Hollinger shows how the missionary project set out to make the world look more like the West, and instead, changed the West. Missionaries were transformed by their experience of people of distant lands, and reflexively, they brought the American population into contact with a great range of peoples. In the process, they challenged many presumed home truths, broadened the perspectives of the American public, and influenced operations of institutions, including churches, foundations, and advocacy organizations. In a word, missionaries were bearers of an enlarging cosmopolitanism, one in which they pushed their fellow Americans to renounce the provinciality of their own society.[11]

Derek Peterson's *Ethnic Patriotism and the East Africa Revival* includes a chapter entitled "The Infrastructure of Cosmopolitanism." Peterson discusses how people were dislodged from their native provinces and propelled into linguistic and cultural encounters with people they had never met.[12] Converts were exposed to new role models, new clothes, cuisine, and modes of work, new shops, roads, and consumer goods. Tangible newness reflected new aspirations, new forms of social capital, new life disciplines, and new ways of communication. These dynamics represented the infrastructure of cosmopolitanism. While new social classes emerged around religious identity, missionaries brought influences from afar back to home communities. They faced their own parochialism as they influenced mission agencies and educational institutions. In *Facing West: American Evangelicals in an Age of World Christianity*, David Swartz describes how American evangelicalism has nurtured a networked connectivity, a cosmopolitanism around shared mission goals despite cultural cleavages. While American agency is often overplayed, this work shows how global religious imaginaries have pushed back. In mission as in other global initiatives, transnational networks have been pluralistic, participatory, and multidirectional. Relationships feature negotiation and exchange in ways that produce hybrid identities of a cosmopolitan nature. Transnational encounters inspired by mission do not always follow American cultural categories. New categories emerge, such as the theme of cosmopolitanism itself, which appeared early in the missionary movement.[13]

11. Hollinger, *Protestants Abroad*.

12. Peterson, *Ethnic Patriotism*, 37–49.

13. Swartz, *Facing West*.

Other recent works on cosmopolitanism, such as *The Global Bourgeoisie: The Rise of the Middle Classes in the Age of Empire*, also inform these chapters. This collection of essays on the rise of the middle classes reveals the pivotal role played by Christian mission, a role that often is omitted in cultural studies which focus on the formation of global society.[14] Christianity has facilitated a value system that contested imperial conquest and exploitation by forming a contrasting sense of community. Virginia Seminary has embodied this intention and the outcomes of its approach. Similarly, the arguments of Pippa Norris and Ronald Inglehart's *Cosmopolitan Communications: Cultural Diversity in a Globalized World* prove informative.[15] Contemporary networks of interdependence, electronic communication, and swift global transport make global consciousness seem like a new thing. While *Cosmopolitan Communications* has nothing to do with Christian mission, it helps the reader of missionary documents frame cultural diversity in missionary contexts. "Kosmopolites" (citizens of the world) refers to the idea that all humans interact within a single global community, not simply within a single polity or nation state. Christian faith has facilitated global connectedness in any given era. This "kosmopolites" identity need to be recovered and placed in creative tension with local and indigenous identity.

CHAPTER OUTLINE

Following this introduction, chapter 2, "American Awakenings," gives an overview of the state of religious life, particularly that of the Episcopal Church, from the colonial era in North America to the early decades of political independence from Britain. More than other religious groups in the new nation, the Episcopal Church faced severe adaptive challenges. In much of colonial America, it had been the Church of England and had enjoyed the advantages accorded the church of the colonial power. Shorn of such influence and stigmatized as the church of the king, the Episcopal Church was forced to articulate its identity and to secure its own resources if it was to survive in the newly independent nation. Mission became inherent in Episcopal identity, and mission entailed not only proclamation of the gospel but building a compelling vision of the church. Chapter 3, "Ideals and Outcomes," locates the founding of

---

14. Dejung et al., *Global Bourgeoisie*.

15. Pippa and Inglehart, *Cosmopolitan Communications*.

Virginia Theological Seminary in the context of American evangelical religion, in particular the appearance of what would be known as the Second Great Awakening. The earlier First Great Awakening focused upon personal faith and the remaking of the nature of the church. The second awakening sought to align revitalized personal faith with the development of commitment to mission in the new nation and abroad. This chapter traces the origins of mission and links its development to the founding of Andover Seminary, the first theological seminary. The ideal of cosmopolitanism surfaced amid early encounters between missionaries and peoples they intended to convert.

Chapter 4, "Navigating Sociocultural Difference," depicts Episcopal missionaries as they break ground in new worlds and introduce values that are vastly different. Their encounters with imperial and colonizing forces on the one hand, and traditional societies and indigenous religions on the other, encouraged a broader confessional identity and created a variety of outcomes. Missionaries could find themselves becoming intermediaries in complex situations of cultural contact. Local situations might produce conflict, complementarity, or collaboration, all of which contributed to the shape of the new Christian community and new social classes attached to it. Within such dynamism, a cosmopolitan consciousness evolved. Chapter 5, "Fostering Social Aspirations," explores changing societies as the mission work adapted to new social realities from the late nineteenth century into the twentieth. Missionaries contributed to the building of institutions devoted to knowledge production, medical work, industrial mission, and theological training. The aspirational class nurtured by missionaries morphed into a middle class, the members of which staffed emerging state bureaucracies, bringing wage labor to new economies and populating cities. The church took a primary role in the formation of differentiated social identities that rejected secularized enlightenment as interpreted in the new nations. As nationalism and localization acquired import, the concept of cosmopolitanism became compelling. Questions surfaced about the relationship between mission and such moral ills as racism and imperialism.

Chapter 6, "Into All the World," begins with the formation of the Episcopal Church in Brazil by recent graduates of Virginia Seminary late in the nineteenth century. As this chapter also explores, the idea of cosmopolitanism was taking shape as patterns of formal and informal international networks developed, with Alexandria, Virginia, serving as an important nexus. The seminary devoted new attention to the study

of world religions as well as mission. The focus will be upon local realities in several settings where Episcopal missionaries educated at Virginia
Seminary functioned. Thus, we show how situational realities exerted
pressures to ameliorate injustice. There were also shifts in the educational
sensibilities at the seminary and across the Episcopal Church, as cosmopolitan awareness became a basis for confrontation with injustices.

In chapter 7, "Mission amid Social Upheaval," Virginia Theological Seminary appears in the context of twentieth-century social trends at
home and abroad. Developments such as liberal evangelicalism, higher
biblical criticism, and the socially progressive tenor of the era amid civil
rights struggles became part of the seminary's ebb and flow in its fluctu-
ating engagement in mission. New initiatives influenced thinking about
mission, for instance the lecture series given by Virginia Seminary faculty
at Washington Cathedral under the title "Christianity and Modern Man."
Chapter 8, "Renewing the Church's Mission," engages a central theme of
this book—namely, the influence of mission upon the life of the church.
In the last quarter of the twentieth century, across the Anglican world,
unprecedented discussions on mission and leadership took shape. This
level of exchange represented a decided change from the years of colonialism and displayed a new Anglican cosmopolitanism. A key aspect
of these discussions was their focus on Anglian worship and spirituality.
Virginia Seminary became a significant participant in these discussions,
providing leadership and a meeting site in Alexandria.

Chapter 9, "Mission and Global Society," considers the impact of
division among Anglicans, notably furor over the ordination of women
and acceptance of homosexual persons in the church, including as clergy.
Amid such tensions, Virginia Seminary worked to expand cosmopolitan sensibility, notably by founding the Center for Anglican Communion Studies. This chapter considers the recent impact of mission and
international church leaders and students upon Virginia Seminary and
its environs. There was an acceleration of mutual exchange through the
seminary's engagement in mission. There was also indigenous exchange
with Virginia Seminary as students from mission sites came to study and
returned commissioned or ordained to their nations. The transnational
perspectives of incoming and outgoing missionaries influenced the curriculum, relations with churches, and perspectives about mission in
emerging nations.

Chapter 10, "Toward Mutual Benefit," describes the flowering
of a cosmopolitan emphasis in the twenty-first century. More than a

sensibility, cosmopolitanism in the life of Virginia Seminary has brought a practical emphasis on human flourishing. The seminary not only had become a prominent gathering place; it had become a catalyst for gatherings that intended to transcend difference. This historic turn of theological education now reflects an approach to mission notable for mutuality across church life. The legacy of an emphasis on mission is intact even as the intentions and outcomes of mission have shifted. Mutual regard and mutual benefit now frame Virginia Seminary's historic commitments and its emerging ones.

2

American Awakenings

AN INHERENT FOCUS ON MISSION

BY 1823, WHEN VIRGINIA Theological Seminary was founded, it had become apparent that religious life in the United States had been confronted with the necessity of mission. In the colonial era, this reality had not been as apparent for the Church of England as it had been for other religious confessions. In certain of the North American colonies, especially Virginia, the Church of England had been established. That is, as the extension of the church of the throne, the colonial English church enjoyed legal and social advantages in certain colonies. Such advantages included, for instance, ownership of land parcels, the income from which helped to support the church's life. Outside these pockets of establishment, however, the colonial church was compelled to adopt mission strategies to secure its presence.

This was apparent in New England where the Church of England challenged the Congregationalist establishment. The rise of the Society for the Propagation of the Gospel (SPG) early in the eighteenth century in England helped to secure the church in New England.[1] A notable example of rising influence came in 1722 at Yale College, a Congregationalist bastion. Seven faculty members and recent graduates of the college expressed doubts about the validity of clerical ordinations not performed by bishops. Four of the seven—Daniel Brown, Timothy Cutler, Samuel Johnson, and James Wetmore—sailed to England for reordination.

1. Woolverton, *Colonial Anglicanism*, 88.

14

Although Brown soon died, the others would serve American parishes under SPG guidance. Johnson would also become president of King's College in New York. It was a sign of challenge to Puritan control and a striking example of SPG influence on behalf of the English church. Mission was becoming prominent in American religious life.

The extent of religious need was clear. By general consensus, no more than twenty percent of the colonial population belonged to a religious institution. There was widespread disregard for the Church of England in the middle colonies and the Carolinas, as well as New England. The SPG sent missionaries to North America beginning with George Keith in 1702. He launched his work by making a tour of the colonies to assess need.[2] In New England, Keith surfaced long enough to engage in theological debates with Puritan leaders. In time, his successors as SPG missionaries would fan out across the colonies, even extending their ministries to African Americans and Native Americans. The basis for later Episcopal Church mission was being laid, however modestly. The SPG style of mission reflected both English devotional life and the latitudinarian theology that was prominent. SPG missionaries predicated their work on appeals to natural reason and an innate conscience. They worked to persuade their hearers of the nature and truth of revelation and of the Bible as its supreme expression. Reason blended with revelation to compel those who heard the message to embrace the Christian faith. If converts became religiously rooted in the Church of England, they entered a tradition rich not only in reasoned faith but in its commitment to pastoral care. The church's offices, centered on the Book of Common Prayer, offered guidance along life's journey toward God's eternal embrace.

Yet, even in colonies where the English church managed to create a semblance of religious establishment, or otherwise to make religious inroads, it could not replicate English circumstances. Religious establishment in North America was incomplete at best. Religious pluralism was the defining reality, and its extent steadily increased. Further, the church could not assume its accustomed identity and governance. Public opposition to the presence of a bishop could not be overcome. Yet dependence upon the English church was required. Prospective clergy had to travel to England for ordination. Though there was recurrent consideration of having colonial bishops in America, there was insufficient support for such a step. Bishops were abhorrent symbols of royal authority, thus, of control from afar. The church's defining office was entirely absent during

2. Woolverton, *Colonial Anglicanism*, 181–82.

the colonial period. Instead, governance was rooted in parish vestries and in the novel office of commissary—in effect, a church administrator in a colony where establishment had emerged. The colonial church in North America adapted in various ways to its novel circumstances. In the "highly laicized environment that was Virginia's Anglican church," there was an impressive level of Christian devotion that followed the Book of Common Prayer and centered on the home.[3] The focus was upon religious practices, especially regular prayer, familiarity with the Bible, and rites of passage. A grassroots culture of Christian life pervaded the colonial church, notably in Virginia. Religion provided social glue, a reasonable faith, and a vivid sense of community, even in the absence of a bishop and inconsistent clergy leadership.

The emphasis on social order—and religion's integration into it—had moral limits. Laity and clergy debated the wisdom of baptizing enslaved people, for example. In part, there was an instinct to save the souls of Native Americans and Africans held in servitude. Yet the prospect of baptizing them raised the question of whether the rite would grant them freedom. In 1667, the Virginia legislature passed an act which prohibited such an interpretation. However, colonial gentry continued to worry about "a kind of social, cultural, and religious leveling, and they did not like it."[4] A different opinion, especially held by clergy, was that baptism would encourage enslaved people to be more obedient and diligent in their prescribed duties. They "would be more reliable and better equipped for the tasks they were expected to discharge." In the end, relatively few enslaved persons affiliated with the established church. Patterns of African spirituality persisted, usually quietly. When they became Christian, enslaved persons were more drawn to evangelical religion, especially in the eighteenth century as the impact of the First Great Awakening spread.

There had been little consideration of the spiritual needs of enslaved persons, much less their material needs, by the colonial church during the seventeenth century. In the eighteenth century, there was some clerical initiative to offer the church's ministries to enslaved people, especially in light of the fact that they made up a significant part of the population. By one estimate, enslaved people accounted for forty percent of Virginia's population by 1780.[5] As their numbers grew, the question of their re-

3. Winner, *Cheerful and Comfortable Faith*, 2.

4. Winner, *Cheerful and Comfortable Faith*, 38–44.

5. Nelson, *Blessed Company*, 263.

lation to the church surfaced. Early in the century, Edmund Gibson, bishop of London and nominal head of colonial ministries, encouraged the conversion of African American persons. Commissary James Blair echoed Gibson's sense of purpose. The result was fresh emphasis on religious instruction preparatory to baptism. There also was evidence of enslaved people attending worship, typically set apart in a gallery. At the prominent Virginia parish of Bruton, eighteenth-century clergy generally "encouraged slaveowners in and around Williamsburg to support the instruction and baptism of their slaves."[6]

The tendency of colonial clergy to advocate for including enslaved persons in the church, at least marginally, was tepid at best. In no sense did the clergy promote freedom and equality. If Virginia Seminary's emphasis on mission later gave rise to cosmopolitanism, such cosmopolitanism was lacking in colonial America. The logic of the clergy followed the theology of the day, i.e., that baptism promised eternal salvation to those who received it. The clergy's theological position also represented an assertion of their sense of prerogative. They alone could perform the sacraments. As much as the colonial religious world centered on lay initiative and religious life in the home, the Virginia clergy would not be overlooked. Just as there were debates about the baptism of enslaved people, so there were debates about whether baptisms should be conducted in the home or in the local parish church, and these debates were even fiercer if the children being baptized were members of elite families. The conscientious intentions of the clergy should not be discounted. Yet their ministries reflected endorsement of the existing social order.

Virginia's clergy had a particular stake in the religious life of their colony. Through the eighteenth century, the percentage of native-born clergy in Virginia rose. By 1776, one-third of the Church of England clergy in Virginia had been born there. They still had to travel to England for ordination, but that voyage had become more dependable and affordable during the eighteenth century. Some aspirants to the ministry came from affluent families who could offer their sons education at Oxford or Cambridge. For others, clerical education had to be found closer to home. The extent and quality of training varied greatly. For example, only two-fifths of Virginia's clergy in the eighteenth century had some measure of college education.[7] Many had read various theological and pastoral texts, often

6. Nelson, *Blessed Company*, 265.

7. Nelson, *Blessed Company*, 104.

self-directed, at times with the aid of a tutor, usually a local parson. For those who found an American college, some—even from Virginia—received training at King's College (later, Columbia) or Philadelphia (later, University of Pennsylvania), in addition to Yale and Harvard.

The closest to an affiliated college for the church was William and Mary. After 1720, it figured prominently in Virginia. At least thirty-one of Virginia's colonial parsons studied in Williamsburg. Virginia commissary James Blair exerted a formative influence on the college and on training for ministry. Blair envisioned three schools of study at the college: a grammar school teaching Latin, Greek, and some classical authors; a philosophy school offering such liberal arts as rhetoric, ethics, logic, mathematics, and metaphysics; and a divinity school to prepare some bachelor's degree graduates for ordination. In the mid-eighteenth century, William and Mary adopted a four-year course of study for the BA and an additional three years for the MA degree. As one historian observes, the "projected divinity school most likely represented little more than the appointment of one or two professors of divinity to supervise the post-baccalaureate reading of students preparing for ordination."[8]

Thus, preparation for ordination remained varied, informal, and vague about the educational standards expected. Ultimately the successful candidate for ordination relied heavily upon testimonials, that is, letters of recommendation from notable persons, especially the colonial commissary. Letters typically addressed "the candidate's knowledge and moral fitness."[9] Inevitably recommendations came from local clergy and laity, as well as William and Mary faculty if such a connection existed. Some commissaries also sought public declaration of a candidate's intention to seek ordination. Once in England, candidates were examined on their knowledge of the Bible, the Articles of Religion, and the Ordinal, as well as Latin and Greek. Aspects of pastoral practice were likely to surface.[10] Ultimately the varied paths to ordination converged before an English bishop. Otherwise, the process proved extended and elusive.

However, the American revolution and political independence made this reality moot. As one historian comments, the American Revolution "broke many of the intimate ties that had traditionally linked

8. Nelson, *Blessed Company*, 110.

9. Nelson, *Blessed Company*, 114.

10. Nelson, *Blessed Company*, 117.

religion and government, especially with the Anglican Church."[11] Political upheaval and independence meant the ending of religious establishment and the continuing advance of religious pluralism. All religious groups were thrust upon their own resources and capacity to organize themselves. With political connection gone, social advantage eroded. The church's links to aristocracy weakened. The former church of the crown was forced to compete with other religious groups for allegiance. In effect, it had to embark on mission.

Although the church's situation was dire, it launched a process of self-organization that began to chart its American future. In some ways the Episcopal Church emerged along lines that followed the example of the new democratic nation. This adaptation of the former colonial church began swiftly. Legislatures in Maryland, North Carolina, and Virginia had suspended the salaries of Anglican clergy in 1776. Prayers for the king were replaced by prayers for the new nation, and in 1779 the Virginia legislature eliminated the chair of theology at the College of William and Mary. In 1786, the legislature adopted the Virginia Statute for Religious Freedom. Drafted by Thomas Jefferson—an achievement he considered one of his finest—the statute articulated the separation of church and state and became a basis for the First Amendment. Disestablishment entailed reorganization more than dissolution. The Episcopal Church organized through the creation of diocesan assemblies of clergy and laity. This initiative was taken first in Maryland, where the new church's name was announced. In 1780, the Protestant Episcopal Church was declared at a church assembly in Chestertown.[12] Diocesan conventions adopting this denominational name soon appeared across the new nation. They not only preceded the election of bishops; they were the means by which such elections became possible. The church absorbed the forms and ideals of the new American democracy, as did all historic religious groups. The democratic instinct was especially striking for what had been the English established church.

In 1782, William White's pamphlet, *The Case of the Episcopal Churches in the United States Considered*, advanced this organizational instinct.[13] The result was not only the adoption of democratic assemblies to govern each diocese, but also the creation of a General Convention to

11. Wood, *Empire of Liberty*, 576.

12. Hein and Shattuck, *Episcopalians*, 3.

13. Prichard, *History of the Episcopal Church*, 116.

unify and govern the Episcopal Church as a whole. The General Convention met once in 1785 and twice in 1786. One of its early tasks was the
preparation and adoption of the first American version of the Book of
Common Prayer, which was published in 1786. Meanwhile, diocese by
diocese, the first American bishops were elected. Samuel Seabury of Connecticut was consecrated to the episcopate in Scotland in 1784. In 1787,
William White of Pennsylvania and Samuel Provoost of New York were
consecrated in England. In 1790, James Madison became the first bishop
of Virginia. He would also continue to serve as president of William and
Mary, a post he had held since 1780.[14]

It is notable that Madison had been professor of philosophy and
classics before becoming William and Mary's president and then bishop.
He embodied the rational character of the age and its influence on the
church. In the wake of the American Revolution, as adherence to religious identity faltered, America's founders proposed the emergence of
a new, public faith. In their own ways, the Virginians Washington, Jefferson, and James Madison—cousin of the bishop—followed the example
of Benjamin Franklin. Hesitant about revealed religion and confessional
identity, they advanced a faith grounded in reason, a universal creed that
would serve as a broad tent under which diverse Americans could gather.
Remaining nominal church members and respecting the Bible, the nation's founders tended to speak of God as distant. They respected Jesus as
a remarkable person but not likely the Son of God. They dismissed stories
of miracles in the Bible and looked past doctrines of eternal punishment
or salvation. Instead, they were intent on shaping earthly life, especially
its social coherence.

America's founders applied the Enlightenment's rationalism in their
search for a public creed. Jefferson made this pursuit more militant.[15]
While Washington praised religion's public role, even advocating for it
in his Farewell Address, and mobilized chaplains to serve in the military,
Jefferson resisted any hint of support for religious expression. When he
organized the University of Virginia, Jefferson allowed no religious allegiance, especially among faculty. Insisting that he believed in the de-
ity, Jefferson distanced himself from sympathy for religious institutions
and all they entailed. Few could match the idiosyncrasy of Jefferson's
views, but many shared the practical implications of his outlook. Church

14. Prichard, *History of the Episcopal Church*, 120; Hein and Shattuck, *Episcopalians*, 55.

15. Wood, *Empire of Liberty*, 577.

membership, never widespread, declined precipitously following the American Revolution. The erosion of allegiance to religion and the influence of rationalism did not represent secularism. Criticism was directed at religious organizations more than at religion's premises.

The ground of religious life was shifting to the grassroots. The energies that prompted organization of new Episcopal dioceses proved illustrative. The church's nature, as well as its form, was being reconsidered. This process was more than an emblematic embrace of democratic assembly. Once disadvantaged, such religious groups as Baptists and Methodists surged as religious freedom and the separation of church and state appeared. In part, Baptists and Methodists modeled a new approach to mission, growing rapidly as the new nation expanded westward. Even more, they embodied a form of religious life that would become in striking ways definitive of American religious life. They were the leading edge of evangelicalism, and this evangelicalism would prove influential for the Episcopal Church in general and Virginia Episcopalians in particular. We cannot understand the history of Virginia Theological Seminary and its commitment to mission without consideration of the nature and impact of evangelicalism.

THE NEW RELIGIOUS SENSIBILITY

The organization of the Episcopal Church could not ensure its vitality much less its survival. Even as the church emulated the forms of American democracy, it required emphasis on mission that was reflective of revitalized Christian faith. Organizational innovation—including the eventual creation of Virginia Theological Seminary—would embody the energies of religious awakening as well as the necessity of adaptation to the American social environment. The energies required for these tasks gained impetus from fresh forms of proclamation of the faith and expansion of the church. Spiritual awakening fueled religious organization and became the hallmark of Episcopal theological education, especially at the seminary founded in Virginia.

It was a surprising conjuncture for Episcopalians. In the first half of the eighteenth century, when the spiritual fires of awakening swept North America and the British Isles, the Church of England and its colonial offspring largely remained aloof. The notable transatlantic progenitor of awakening, John Wesley, was a priest of the Church of England and remained so, by his own definition. He had served the church in Savannah, Georgia, until he was forced to return to England in disgrace. After attending a prayer meeting in the Aldersgate section of London in 1738, he recorded in his diary that he felt his heart had been "strangely warmed."[16] It was the first tremor of religious upheaval, and its energies would soon attract scores of followers. It was not Wesley alone, though he would leave the largest imprint. His experience, his organizational ability, and his theological insights would infuse a movement that became the Methodist Church. Wesley had notable contemporaries. A transatlantic revivalist who had been Wesley's fellow student at Oxford and became a deacon in the Church of England, George Whitefield, regularly preached in public venues across the colonies and Britain. His message was elaborated from a New England pulpit by Jonathan Edwards. The differences between Wesley, Whitefield, and Edwards were significant. But the convictions they shared proved lasting.[17]

These key figures of the First Great Awakening agreed on a basic point: the public need for an enlivened, personal Christian faith. There had been periodic revivals of religious energies in western Massachusetts from the late seventeenth century, especially under the influence of Congregational pastor Solomon Stoddard.[18] The roots of what would be known as evangelicalism were becoming secure. Commitment to the Christian faith required emotive as well as rational assent. Awakening to faith required a conscious experience of being born again, following the words of Jesus in the New Testament. Sin must be rejected, repentance leading to a life of holiness must be pursued. Whitefield, the revivalist preacher, conveyed this message to public masses. Edwards probed the meaning of religious "affections" and linked them to God's plan of salvation. Wesley guided enlivened persons toward a new fellowship of the redeemed and charted the path toward sanctification, i.e., personal holiness.

The colonial Church of England tended to resist these religious energies and the innovation they promised. As soon as his movement gained public notice, Wesley would be derided for "enthusiasm," seen as unruly emotionalism suggesting social as well as religious upheaval. In North America as early as 1740, the church's commissary in South Carolina, Alexander Garden, confronted George Whitefield when he

---

16. Marty, *Pilgrims in Their Own Land*, 118; Noll, *Old Religion*, 48–49.

17. Heitzenrater, *Wesley and the People Called Methodists*, 88.

18. Noll, *America's God*, 41.

began a revival campaign in Charleston. Forbidden from preaching in churches of the colonial establishment, Whitefield delivered his sermons in public venues where he was seemingly more comfortable and more productive.[19] Those who had scarcely been touched by the ministries of the established church were struck and transformed by the evangelical message, which promised that God's grace could immediately lift the weight of personal sin.

It would be unfair to dismiss the colonial Church of England and especially its clergy as indolent and ineffectual. A generation after Whitefield challenged Garden, a tradition-minded cleric of the established church named Charles Woodmason launched a peripatetic ministry through the backcountry of the Carolinas. His journey suggested that of an evangelical circuit rider of the later Methodist sort. He was intent on baptizing, and his diary records that he welcomed dozens of persons to the faith. In the process, his comments on rural life and religious practice revealed evident biases in regards to class and religion. On September 21, 1766, he wrote that most of those he met and even those who heard him preach were "Rude—Ignorant—Void of Manners, Education, or good breeding—No genteel or polite person among them." A few days later, on September 28, 1766, he commented that the "people all new settlers, extremely poor—live in log cabins like hogs and their living and behaviour as rude or more so than the Savages." He added that he had taken quarters "in a tavern and [been] exposed to the rudeness of the mob. People continually drunk."[20]

Summarizing his travels and ministrations in 1766, he added thoughts about the religious pluralism of northeastern South Carolina and southeastern North Carolina. "Among this medley of religions— True Christianity is not to be found . . . These sects are eternally jarring among themselves—The Presbyterians hate the Baptists far more than they do the Episcopalians, and so of the rest." He added that "'Tis These roving teachers that stir up the minds of the people against the established church, and her ministers and make the situation of any gentleman extremely uneasy, vexatious, and disagreeable. . . . Some few of these itinerants have encountered me, I find them a set of Rhapsodists, Enthusiasts, Bigots, Pedantic, illiterate, impudent hypocrites." He did attract large crowds to his sermons, but noted, with both amazement and disgust, that

19. Woolverton, *Colonial Anglicanism*, 193.
20. Woodmason, *Journal*.

in one "great multitude," he was the first "Episcopal Minister they had seen since their being in the province. They complained of being eaten up by itinerant teachers, preachers and imposters from New England and Pennsylvania—Baptists, New Lights, Presbyterians, Independents, and a hundred other sects."[21] Nevertheless, Woodmason's ministry emulated the roving style of these itinerant teachers and extended to Native Americans. On January 25, 1767, he noted: "A congregation at the Cheraws of about 500 people. Baptized about 60 children." Thus, he persisted, and in the process he gave a vivid image of mission in rural America. The extent of dissenting identities combined with the fact of religious and social disorganization. Life on the frontier was framed by uncertainty and fragility which became too much for him. Woodmason returned to Virginia and then Maryland, where he seemingly found a suitable haven. But he was vocal in his prayers for the English king, emphasizing authority and obedience as revolution neared. In 1776 he was urged to return to England for his own safety, and he promptly did so.

Woodmason would have been horrified at the suggestion that his ministry fit into the patterns of the First Great Awakening. Yet its influence on his life was undeniable. Wesley, Edwards, and Whitefield ensured that the importance of personal awakening never disappeared from American religious culture. America now bore the imprint of a new theological language, one which foregrounded immediate salvation from sin through the acceptance of God's grace and which stressed the importance of biblical allegiance and moral observance. Evangelical religion had been born, touching individual lives and transcending denominational distinctions. It could not be attributed to some social classes more than others. Woodmason's distinction faded as evangelical influence expanded in the United States during the nineteenth century.

As the first wave of awakening seemed to wane, a second wave began. It proved more socially and religiously definitive through its insistent emphasis on mission, an emphasis which Episcopalians absorbed. In part, the Second Great Awakening began as Woodmason would have feared. Sparked by Presbyterian itinerant preacher James McGready, a period of religious revival began in the early 1800s and was centered in Kentucky. Religious assemblies of increasing size and energy marked this outburst. Soon, a founder of the "Christian" movement which would include the Disciples of Christ denomination, Presbyterian minister Barton

21. Woodmason, *Journal*.

Stone took initiative to organize a mass meeting at Cane Ridge, Kentucky, in August 1801. For weeks constant preaching by scores of Presbyterian, Baptist, and Methodist clergy produced thousands of converts. By some estimates, twenty thousand people attended. Accounts of the event feature descriptions of people caught up in religious ecstasy. Crying and dancing by some were matched by trances and stupors in others. External religious energies vied with internal, personal withdrawal. In each case, religious experience was stamped by the experience of conversion.[22]

Before McGready and Stone began their exertions on the American frontier, Methodists had already arrived. Arguably Methodism became the first religious movement to mark American frontier life. In 1784, John Wesley had named Thomas Coke as "superintendent" for his American church. He soon was joined by Francis Asbury, who displayed remarkable energy and thoughtful innovation.[23] Methodism had not had a distinguished American beginning because of Wesley's vigorous calls for loyalty to the king. After political independence was secured, Asbury distinguished his approach to mission and church growth from that of Wesley. Like Wesley he traveled continuously, perhaps as many as three hundred thousand miles, constantly preaching and organizing. Unlike Wesley he intended to instill a religious sensibility that matched the new nation's westward march. Evangelical religion became integrated into American life. As the frontier became settled, Methodism adapted again, eventually becoming at home in influential business and social circles. Methodism also became noteworthy for its efforts to found colleges and universities, some of which remain as leading educational institutions. This link between evangelical religion, education, and mission became the hallmark of the Second Great Awakening. Social and moral initiative arose from deep religious experience. Indeed, mission arose out of a fierce commitment to change the world and not merely to convert it.

The Second Great Awakening differed significantly from its precursor in the first half of the eighteenth century. The nature of religious experience and the nature of salvation framed debates about what it meant to awaken in the First Great Awakening. Wesley's theological leaning toward Arminianism, a way of making room for human effort in the pursuit of the sanctified life, contrasted with the Calvinism many awakeners and older line Protestants held. Jonathan Edwards, for example, advanced a

---

22. Kidd, *American Religious History*, 74.
23. Heitzenrater, *Wesley and the People Called Methodists*, 314.

strong sense of God's providence, or direction of the world's activities. Yet, even in the midst of theological divergence, there was an emphasis on the need for personal recognition of sin and acceptance of God's grace through faith.

In the Second Great Awakening, on the other hand, the emphasis continued to be on salvation through awakening. However, the ground of faith and the Christian life expanded from personal salvation and recon-figuration of the church toward a broadly public emphasis. The drama of salvation was played out through the dynamics of social life. In a sense, this should have been no surprise. The second awakening began amid political revolution in America and France, rather than the political equi-poise that marked English colonial society. But awakening was no mere reaction against the age of revolution. In fact, leading voices of religious awakening built distinctive theological positions that reflected principles of democratic revolution. Thus, New England cleric Samuel Hopkins in the late eighteenth century advanced the idea of "disinterested benevo-lence" as a key to faith in daily life.[24] Yet more striking, Hopkins became a proponent of abolition, declaring slavery to be immoral. His position was challenged by old-line Calvinists less for its opposition to slavery than for its allowance of human moral initiative, a seeming challenge to God's providence. Hopkins's qualified Calvinism was refined in the nineteenth century by theologian Nathanael W. Taylor and given further expression by Congregationalist pastor Lyman Beecher. Both were iden-tified with the "New Haven Theology." They retained emphasis on divine sovereignty while endorsing the necessity of moral agency.

The emphasis on moral agency was a theological beacon. Formally and informally, in congregations, in large assemblies, and in the increas-ing number of "societies" devoted to aspects of religious and social reform, the theme of agency was the foundation. Slavery would be the banner issue. In time, as the Second Great Awakening became varied, evangelicalism developed revivalist and abolitionist wings, the two often overlapping. The great revivalist of the early nineteenth century Charles G. Finney inspired a cluster of younger evangelical activists such as Theo-dore Dwight Weld and William Lloyd Garrison. They elevated the idea of moral agency to the level of social urgency.[25] There was no greater confirmation of the ties between religious awakening and democratic

---

24. Noll, *America's God*, 135.
25. Block, *Nation of Agents*, 378.

revolution. As one historian has explained, agency embodied the shift from carrying out specific duties in a stratified society to "individuals participating actively in shaping the worldly means to be employed for realizing divine and collective purposes."[26] Empowered by evangelicalism, American Protestantism turned to the task of creating the moral infrastructure of the nation. Thus, Donald G. Mathews defined the Second Great Awakening as an "organizing process."[27] Its fruits were apparent in the creation of new kinds of organizations, starting with denominational structures but moving beyond them. Sunday schools, education societies, societies to spread the Bible, and even the American Colonization Society to transport freed slaves to Africa reflected theological and moral purpose. Mission, for the Episcopal Church, reflected this purpose and the influence of the Second Awakening.

Mission is more than an idea. Mission embodies the encounter of religious ideals with social realities, the necessity that religious intention finds appropriate expression. In all eras, mission has entailed evangelism and the addition of converts to the Christian faith. Mission also has meant enlivening the faith of nominally professed Christians. Yet the moment of religious awakening has never been the whole of mission. The ongoing life of the newly awakened and the nature of an awakened church become primary considerations. During the early decades of American independence, the church's social role extended religious awakening. American religion became personally intense and publicly expansive. We shall find that mission acquired cross-cultural breadth that introduced the first hints of cosmopolitanism. A new appreciation of cultural difference reflected the Second Awakening's theology and organizational energy.

Thomas Kidd explains that the missionary emphasis of the Second Great Awakening had a symbolic beginning at the "Haystack Prayer Meeting" at Williams College in Massachusetts. In the summer of 1806, five students who had gathered for prayer hid under a haystack when a storm arose. Whether it was the inclement weather or the fact of being more intensely together, the students resolved to devote their lives to the cause of mission.[28] The idea spread widely, even to some of American Christianity's most influential voices. In 1813, Yale College president Timothy Dwight dared to imagine that American missionaries heralded

26. Block, *Nation of Agents*, 22.
27. Mathews, "Second Great Awakening."
28. Kidd, *American Religious History*, 99.

the day "when the Popish, Mohammedan, Hindoo, and Chinesian worlds shall be created anew."[29] Mission quickly became wed to social reform and was not to be confined to North America.[30]

As a result, Kidd describes how the triumvirate of mission, evangelism, and reform "ballooned after 1810."[31] The American West and America's burgeoning cities had evident needs, for which there seemed to be obvious solutions. Congregationalists Samuel Mills and Daniel Smith were alarmed at the absence of the Bible in new American locales. Among the flurry of societies created to promote religious and social reform, the American Bible Society, founded in 1816, loomed large. Possession and study of the Bible would spread the Christian faith and encourage moral governance in society. Lyman Beecher illustrated the new link between religion and reform. He helped to launch a temperance society in 1826 reflecting a concern with drinking. In 1832, he became president of Lane Seminary in Cincinnati, where his goal was to ensure that the West was evangelized by Protestants, not Catholics. But in 1834, a majority of the Lane student body withdrew, most transferring to the new Oberlin Institute, also in Ohio. At Oberlin there was resolute support for the abolition of slavery, a stance on which Beecher had not been vigorous. He did not grasp the motives of the "Lane Rebels" nor the implications of their withdrawal. Lines of division were appearing in American life.

American religious life has relied upon the power of consensus. Authority arises from below, more from the popular level than from hierarchical authority. Even as conflict loomed over slavery, a powerful religious consensus arose over the necessity of mission. In part, as we have seen, mission was the condition of social survival in the new nation. Its apparent features were organizational and theological. Not only did denominational structures arise; their work was abetted by voluntary societies which advanced mission initiatives in response to social needs. At the same time, the theology of moral agency secured mission's rationale. Mission reflected the energies of national expansion and political consolidation. The extent of this approach to Christian mission became astonishing. For the first time, concerted mission to non-white peoples, at home and abroad, seized the religious imagination. The founding of Virginia Seminary with its emphasis on mission reflected earlier

29. Kidd, *American Religious History*, 92.
30. Kidd, *American Religious History*, 94.
31. Kidd, *American Religious History*, 93.

precedent. As mission by American churches built cosmopolitan sensibility, Virginia Seminary would be in the forefront.

Among the types of societies created by the Second Great Awakening was the mission society. The first substantial and lasting example was the American Board of Commissioners for Foreign Missions (ABCFM), founded in 1810, spurred by the "Haystack Prayer Meeting" in 1806. The students who gathered for shelter and felt moved to act also resolved that mission should be unbounded. They gave particular attention to foreign missions and drew most of their support from Congregationalists and Presbyterians. While the ABCFM created more extensive missions to Native Americans than had been the case before, they quickly looked overseas. The Indian subcontinent was a special focus. Adoniram Judson, the first ABCFM missionary, went to India via London in 1811. The ABCFM also developed mission stations in such disparate locations as the Middle East, western and southern Africa, the Hawaiian Islands, and even in Greece. The earliest missionaries were expected to spend their entire lives in their assigned sites. In addition, they were directed to focus entirely on evangelism while paying little attention to "fulfilling other basic needs of the people they were serving." The ABCFM believed that the gospel offered the only adequate relief for human suffering. Yet the numbers of those serving as ABCFM missionaries grew steadily. By 1860, Brooks Holifield notes, the ABCFM had sent 567 men and 691 women as missionaries overseas. That number mushroomed to five thousand by 1961.[32]

We will have occasion to cite various aspects of the mission program developed by the ABCFM. There will be striking parallels with the mission emphasis of Virginia Seminary and with the Episcopal Church as a whole. This should not be surprising. The theological framework of mission that arose was widely shared, reflecting the religious and social circumstances all American Protestants faced. The result was comparable approaches to proclaiming the gospel and building the church. The most apparent tie between Episcopalians and the Second Great Awakening centered on theological education and encouraged the centrality of mission in church life. When Virginia Seminary cemented this tie, it followed abundant precedent.

32. Holifield, *God's Ambassadors*, 108.

MISSION AND EDUCATION

As he looked back on the organization of the Episcopal Church after the American Revolution, William Meade admitted that the church in Virginia was in the doldrums. Not only was there "defective preaching," but "evil living among the clergy," as well. There were some "who were discarded from the English Church yet obtained livings in Virginia."[33] It was not surprising to Meade that religious dissent—in the form of Baptists, Methodists, and Presbyterians—had spread across the former colonies. More glaring still, at the time of revolution there had been ninety-one clergy functioning in some 164 churches and chapels. At the war's conclusion, there were only twenty-eight clergy. In other words, few clergy were left in Virginia, and most of this remnant did not distinguish themselves.

Born in 1789 in Clarke County, Virginia, Meade became one of a coterie of Episcopal leaders who experienced the church's dolor after the revolution, but brought fresh faith and vision to its life. Meade was ordained in 1811 by Bishop Madison and would recall the sparse attendance on the occasion. He also noted the lack of churches in Richmond. St. John's Church there continued from the colonial era, but only opened its doors for Sunday worship and often shared its space with a Presbyterian gathering. Meade was forgiving toward Madison, blaming "the want of zeal and infidelity in many of the ministers as one of the causes of the low condition of the church." In Meade's view, Madison's "hopes of the revival of the Church evidently sank," and he put his energies into the administration of William and Mary.[34]

After Madison's death in 1812, church life in Virginia reached its nadir, according to historian John Booty. The convention to choose Madison's successor as bishop attracted only fourteen laity and fourteen clergy. John Bracken, rector of Bruton Parish, Williamsburg, was elected but declined to accept the office. Instead, surprisingly, Richard Channing Moore of New York was chosen and accepted his election. For over ten years he would serve as bishop of Virginia, succeeded in 1829 by William Meade. The generation of church leaders that had been hamstrung by revolutionary change was being succeeded by a new generation intent on religious invigoration. As they helped to forge the birth of an evangelical party among Episcopalians, these Episcopal leaders would reveal the influences of the Second Great Awakening.

33. Meade, *Old Churches*, 1:16.
34. Meade, *Old Churches*, 1:29.

Ironically, the energies of awakening were absorbed by both the nascent evangelical cluster in the Episcopal Church and by the emerging high-church party. The imprint of the Second Awakening was evident in Meade's ministry. He articulated its theology of moral agency and devoted much of his ministry to the creation of new congregations in Virginia. He joined other prominent Americans in supporting the creation of the American Colonization Society, helping to create a link to what would be Liberia, an early site for mission effort by graduates of Virginia Seminary. Meade would be one of a group of clergy who helped to make the Washington area a center of evangelical Episcopal identity. They would generate fresh emphasis on the Bible's authority and the importance of mission, then solidify this witness in Episcopal life. This evangelical imprint would live on at the seminary founded in Alexandria.

The core of evangelical faith has been the need for each person to be born again, and evangelical Episcopalians readily endorsed this conviction. The spiritual new birth would remake one's heart and mind, and then the momentous process of rebuilding one's life would begin. Episcopal evangelicals believed that this focus, and the grounding of Christian life in the Bible and moral agency, embodied the essence of the Church of England's founding at the Protestant Reformation. In this assertion, Meade and such colleagues as Richard Channing Moore and William H. Wilmer were in good company. They were aware of an evangelical coterie in the Church of England centered on the activist politician and opponent of slavery, William Wilberforce. A layman in the Church of England, Wilberforce exemplified the English version of the American Second Great Awakening.

Evangelicals in the Episcopal Church paralleled their English counterparts in various ways, especially in holding a modified Calvinism that affirmed the church's offices while endorsing the necessity of the experience of new birth.[35] Like Wilberforce, they were hesitant about the public excesses of religious awakening in emotive outbursts and claims of instant and perfect salvation. But the Episcopal version should not be seen simply as an extension of the initiative shown by Wilberforce and his colleagues, known as the Clapham Sect. Evangelicals on both sides of the Atlantic Ocean relied upon voluntary societies to address particular issues in church and society. Both were intent on energizing the church's mission. Wilberforce and his associates launched the Church

35. Booty, *Mission and Ministry*, 14.

Missionary Society in 1799, where they were joined by the noted clerics Charles Simeon and John Venn. Otherwise, the initiative, and Clapham efforts generally, were led mostly by lay persons. The Episcopal evangelical movement, on the other hand, would attract influential lay support, but its key leadership remained clerical.

Moreover, the American form of this evangelical movement revealed parallels with the Episcopal high-church party that were hardly the case in England. High-church Episcopalians placed an emphasis on the sacred efficacy of the sacraments and tended to look askance at the experience of new birth, especially if it was deemed central to personal and church life. This tension would result in intramural church divisions in America and England when the movement known as ritualism arose later in the nineteenth century. In the early part of the century, however, fascinating similarities can be noted in the leadership style and goals of William Meade as bishop of Virginia (1829–1862) and John Henry Hobart as bishop of New York (1816–1830). Although their episcopates barely overlapped, their approaches reflected similar responses to American circumstances. Hobart traveled ceaselessly, visiting existing parishes and starting new ones. He encouraged the creation of Sunday schools and supported mission work among the Oneida Indians. In 1817, Hobart also was one of the founders of General Theological Seminary, the first seminary of the Episcopal Church. For a time, he served as its dean as well as teacher of pastoral theology. He would inspire the creation of what would become Hobart College in upstate New York, founded in 1822 and renamed for its patron in 1852.[36] Thus, the parallels between two otherwise theologically distinct leaders, Meade and Hobart, are striking.

Like Hobart, Meade knew that the church's growth required increasing the number and the quality of the clergy. Already the General Convention of the Episcopal Church had encouraged the development of a theological course of study which was produced in 1804. The "Course of Ecclesiastical Studies" consisted of three parts: first, readings from Scripture, church history, theology, homiletics, liturgy, pastoral care, and the church's constitution and canons. Second, there was a list of essential books, followed by, third, a detailed "Library for a Parish Minister." Booty comments that Protestant reformers were omitted including such English divines as Cranmer and Jewel.[37] The list, therefore, had its shortcomings.

36. Mullin, *Episcopal Vision*, 100.
37. Booty, *Mission and Ministry*, 8.

Yet it opened the door to a more substantial program of preparation for ordained ministry.

The first American theological seminary was founded in 1807 by Congregationalists at Andover, Massachusetts, near Boston. Andover Seminary arose in part as a reaction against developments at Harvard, which seemed to be turning toward Unitarian principles and so away from historic Christian orthodoxy. At its founding, Andover combined traditionalist Calvinists and those who were more receptive to the revivalism of the Second Great Awakening. Early and notable faculty included Leonard Woods and Moses Stuart. Woods had been a founder of the ABCFM and was Andover's first professor of theology. Stuart, educated first as a lawyer and then becoming a pastor, taught biblical languages and interpretation. He was one of the first American biblical scholars to engage German theological works sympathetically.[38]

Early Virginia Seminary faculty members Reuel Keith and Joseph Packard were Andover graduates. Packard credited Andover with providing an example of gathering students for three years of intense theological and biblical study grounded in "orthodox Christianity."[39] While Andover's founders believed they were defending the faith from theological error and social evil, they also declared the possibility of new birth and eternal salvation for all who would receive Jesus Christ as their Savior. The possibility had practical import. The church's life and work would be judged by the extent to which it encouraged salvation. Thus, Andover Seminary's theological and practical affirmations provided a ready basis for Christian mission.

The need for an educated clergy with a primary focus on mission was apparent to Richard Channing Moore as he prepared to leave New York for Virginia. William Meade described a meeting between Moore and Augustine Smith, who was about to become president of William and Mary.[40] Upon assuming the office of bishop, Moore pursued the creation of a theological program in Williamsburg. Of course, it was not a new idea and, once more, it came to naught. At this time, however, the conversation created momentum for the birth of a seminary. As the new General Seminary took shape, leading evangelical Episcopalians envisioned a theological institution at Alexandria. William H. Wilmer, rector

38. Noll, *America's God*, 253.

39. Packard, *Recollections*, 53–62.

40. Meade, *Old Churches*, 1:140.

of St. Paul's Church, Alexandria, from 1812 to 1826, was a key figure. He became the first editor of the *Washington Theological Repertory*, a journal founded in 1819 that embodied the convictions of the Education Society, established in the previous year to raise funds for the education of young men for the ordained ministry. Almost immediately, Wilmer and his colleagues, including Meade, created a board of trustees and began to plan the creation of a seminary. The failure of efforts to create an institution at Williamsburg shifted attention to Alexandria. Once this direction was clear, concrete steps were taken quickly. Virginia Theological Seminary began instruction on October 15, 1823, using the facilities of St. Paul's Church, Alexandria. William H. Wilmer, St. Paul's rector, and Reuel Keith were the first faculty. Keith drew upon his teacher at Andover, Moses Stuart. By May 1824, there were eleven students, and by 1825 there were twenty-one enrolled.

3

Ideals and Outcomes

BUILDING THE SEMINARY

IN THE SPRING OF 1836, when he was teaching at Bristol College, in Pennsylvania, Joseph Packard was elected Professor of Sacred Literature at Virginia Theological Seminary. A native of New England, Packard reckoned that the number of Virginians at Bristol, and at Andover Seminary where he had studied, opened the door for his appointment. He became a seminary fixture, serving until 1895. At his death in 1902, the year in which his memoirs were published, Packard could claim to have known almost all of the students and faculty despite arriving thirteen years after the seminary's founding. His *Recollections* are as much a tracing of personal connection as a record of institutional history. The result is an intimate and adoring narrative.[1]

He recalled arriving at the seminary in October 1836, first traveling from Baltimore to Washington by rail which was a new mode of transportation. Then Packard took a steamer which ran twice daily across the Potomac River from Washington to Alexandria. A pleasant chat with an Episcopal clergyman on board enhanced his transit.[2] Then he hired a carriage to bring him up the hill to the seminary. He discovered a young campus, "embosomed deep in lofty woods, which stretched nearly all the way from Alexandria, with paths and roads through them." Upon his arrival there were twenty-two students and three faculty, Packard

1. Packard, *Recollections*, 68.
2. Packard, *Recollections*, 76.

becoming the third. He joined Reuel Keith and Edward R. Lippitt. Keith was an original faculty member with William Wilmer, who left in 1826 for William and Mary. Keith would serve until his death in 1842.

The seminary began in what was the town of Alexandria utilizing the facilities of St. Paul's Church. In the fall of 1827, the seminary moved to what was then Fairfax County, the site being chosen "on account of the healthiness of its atmosphere, the beauty of its prospect, and its many conveniences." The "Hill," as it was already known, cost $5,000 and occupied sixty acres, only half of it cleared when it was acquired. A brick building was built and would become the south wing of the early seminary building. The north wing would be added in 1832, before Packard arrived. He extolled the site as "unsurpassed for beauty and extent of prospect." Packard felt the hand of divine guidance in the seminary's founding and in the unfolding of its life.[3]

The need for Virginia Seminary was apparent to Packard. "By its situation in the South, and its accommodation to the habits and manners of that section, it attracted without injury to the General Seminary a support and attendance which otherwise would have been lost to the Church. Many of its students would have attended no seminary, and would doubtless have never entered the ministry." Packard's knowledge of early graduates gave him a deeply personal view. He recalled William F. Lee of the class of 1825, whose energies were applied to the church in Virginia. "He laid the foundation anew of the churches in Goochland, Powhatan, Amelia, and Chesterfield, and lived to see them all supplied by ministers."[4] Before Lee's health failed, he also served churches in Richmond and in the Shenandoah Valley. Further, Lee became the founding editor of the *Southern Churchman*, a leading Episcopal publication for over a century. William Meade recalled, and Joseph Packard recorded, that Lee became a valued advisor to Bishop Richard Channing Moore as the church in Virginia regrouped. Lee embodied the intention of Virginia Seminary to build the church in the mid-Atlantic region.

Packard recited the contributions of a few other early graduates. In addition to Lee from the class of 1825, he named William L. Marshall, ordained by Bishop Meade at the same time as William Lee. For a time, Marshall was rector of a church in Anne Arundel County, Maryland, before studying the law and becoming an eminent judge. Of graduates in

3. Packard, *Recollections*, 88.

4. Packard, *Recollections*, 80.

1827 and 1828, Packard observed that George L. Mackenheimer "never failed to speak a word for Jesus" and served his ministry in Maryland. John Grammer was a native of Virginia and served churches there entirely. Ebenezer Boyden was rector of Walker's parish, Albemarle County, Virginia, for forty-three years. His two sons entered the ministry, Packard added.[5] These summaries reveal that before 1830, seminary graduates consistently entered ordained, parochial ministries in Virginia and Maryland. Many stayed in the same locale for most of their careers. The sensibility of engaging distant cultures was yet to surface. Mission was understood in a local sense. But the instinct to evangelize and to build the church was apparent.

The plan of instruction by which early graduates were trained was described by Packard and echoed by Booty in his history. The emphasis throughout was biblical and included studies of the Gospels and Acts in Greek, and Genesis and Psalms in Hebrew. "Systematic Divinity" and church history were presented as well. Students were expected to prepare a thesis and a sermon, and to read the liturgy. While teaching was by exposition and students were expected to recite the lessons presented, there was opportunity for "criticisms and remarks on the performances, which must have made things lively and interesting."[6]

At a board meeting in May 1825, there was a description of the curriculum "reflecting the influence of the House of Bishops' syllabus and of the curriculum of Andover Seminary but with a larger number of departments." Added to biblical interpretation and languages, church history, and systematic divinity, there were "Evidences of Revealed Religion," "The Nature, Ministry, and Polity of the Church," and "Pastoral Theology and Pulpit eloquence," emphasizing sermon preparation and delivery. Booty notes that "there was nothing peculiar about this course of study, nor was it devised without faculty involvement."[7] His comment suggests an environment in which discussion and negotiation were emerging. This thought is bolstered by evidence that students were expected to meet once each week with their professors for worship, including the delivery of sermons. It is also worth emphasizing that the board's statement linked theological learning to the advancement of personal piety. Each student was expected to be "assiduous in the cultivation of evangelical

---

5. Packard, *Recollections*, 86.

6. Packard, *Recollections*, 79.

7. Booty, *Mission and Ministry*, 38–41.

faith, and a sound practical piety; neither contenting himself with mere formality, nor running into fanaticism." Study blended with daily times of "meditation and devotion, having due regard to the ways and seasons recommended for this purpose by the Church."[8]

The seminary grew steadily during its first decades and its evangelical character became indelible. Following Packard's arrival, William Sparrow came in 1841 and soon inherited Reuel Keith's classes in systematic divinity as the latter's health declined. Sparrow had been ordained in the Episcopal Church by Bishop Philander Chase in Ohio, a key figure in the church's growth westward. He taught at Kenyon College before joining the Virginia faculty. His evangelical piety was enhanced by his continuing intellectual inquiry. This blend of faith and reason stamped Sparrow's career. He would be the seminary's guiding star in its early years and again in its reconvening after the Civil War. His influence endures in the phrase he coined that has marked Virginia Seminary's life: "Seek the truth, come whence it may, cost what it will."[9]

In the same year that William Sparrow arrived, William Meade became president of the seminary and chairman of its board of trustees, Richard Channing Moore having died. Meade began to offer lectures in pastoral theology to the senior class even as he managed the demands of being bishop of Virginia. Meade's imprint reflected the evangelical convictions of other faculty but added important distinctions. He conveyed guidance for the application of evangelical conviction that was characterized by pastoral intent. Wisdom, moderation, and charity were words Meade pointedly invoked.[10] He depicted the church lovingly, to be held by its clergy responsibly and invitingly. This approach set a tone that portrayed ministry transcending dogma. Like Sparrow's search for truth, Meade's pastoral emphasis became foundational for graduates and channeled energies for mission. Through his presence and style, Meade linked seminary life to the Diocese of Virginia. Of course, various church currents flowed through the "Holy Hill," and seminarians represented many different Episcopal dioceses. Yet the Diocese of Virginia assumed a first among equals role in seminary life. We shall see repeated examples of such influence that proved to be both formal and informal.

8. Goodwin, *History of the Theological Seminary*, 2:597–98.

9. Goodwin, *History of the Theological Seminary*, 1:234.

10. Booty, *Mission and Ministry*, 79–80.

It is worth noting that William Meade was a founding member of the American Colonization Society, which was launched in 1816 and centered in Washington. The society proposed to transport freed slaves to the west coast of Africa.[11] It succeeded to the extent that Liberia was founded, creating circumstances that we shall describe as we consider the rise of Episcopal mission there. For a time, the society offered a middle ground between the defense of slavery and the gradual amelioration of it. Notable Americans who endorsed colonization included Thomas Jefferson, James Madison, and Francis Scott Key. An Episcopalian, Key was an early supporter of Virginia Seminary. Like other endorsers of colonization, Key and Meade were troubled by slavery and fearful of its social impact. Such concern extended to opposition to the slave trade, a stance consistent with the moderate appeal of colonization. However, moral questioning did not challenge racist outlooks or impel measures to abolish slavery; rather, colonization proved attractive to those white Americans who sought to adopt a rhetoric of moderation and deliberation in the face of human enslavement. This stance proved untenable as Americans chose sides between abolition and avowed defense of slavery. There was no apparent influence from the colonization initiative upon the development of mission from Virginia Seminary. Yet colonization signaled American interest in overseas initiative and the invoking of moral criteria, however flawed, by some who were integral to the seminary's life.

By the twenty-first century it had become commonplace to speak of "formation" as an apt description of the training of clergy. The term encompasses both formal education and personal, spiritual preparation. Formation hints at engagement with, and appropriation of, lived religious tradition. Formation also portends contextual expression of religious faith and tradition in lived circumstances. Thus, to invoke another contemporary term, "vocation" is the intended outcome of processes of formation. Vocation implies a personal calling which is shaped by one's years in a seminary. The seminary intends to align personal direction and capability with the church's needs, equipping students for ministry. The character of Virginia Seminary was evangelical and the academic emphasis was substantive. The task seemed apparent: to build the church as the nation expanded. Although it is anachronistic to apply such terms as "formation" and "vocation," the intentions of these later terms could be

---

11. Howe, *What Hath God Wrought*, 261.

discerned in the seminary's early years. They pointed beyond the classroom and became the basis of a cosmopolitan approach to mission.

A PARTICULAR ETHOS

The cosmopolitan outlook has been described as a demand for attachment to distant and different people. Kwame Anthony Appiah recalled that his father urged him and his siblings to remember that they were "citizens of the world."[12] It was a value that centered on the cultivation of mutual obligations that need not be deterred by distance but would lead one increasingly outward. Appiah's own journey began with the recognition of difference in the vicinity of his hometown in Ghana. It was signaled by an openness to multiple forms of particularity, apart from one's own particular identity. New experience of different peoples and contexts provides the basis of a cosmopolitan outlook. Thomas Bender attributes the dynamism of cosmopolitanism to a process of inquiry and discovery. For the person who is becoming cosmopolitan, new experience can be unsettling. Yet newness and difference prompt introspection. "The cosmopolitan is open to the unease of forming a new understanding of both oneself and of the world when invited by the confrontation of difference." It is a recognition of particular identity encountering alternatives.[13]

Bender cites the work of Jane Addams with immigrants at Hull House in Chicago early in the twentieth century. As Addams described in *Democracy and Social Ethics* in 1907, "The transformative moment begins with a sense of unease, or, as she put it, 'maladjustment' in the world surrounding oneself."[14] A new standard of ethics is achieved, she wrote, and it "is not attained by travelling a sequestered byway but by mixing in the thronged and common road."[15] Wide social experience prompts "a wide reading of human life" and enables "a new affinity for all men, which probably never existed in the world before."[16] Bender adds that cosmopolitanism reflects searching inquiry into oneself and negotiation with others for shared identity and shared space. Noting the work of Clifford Geertz, Bender further highlights the achievement of seeing oneself

12. Appiah, *Cosmopolitanism*, 18.

13. Bender, "Cosmopolitan Experience," 117.

14. Bender, "Cosmopolitan Experience," 117.

15. Addams, *Democracy and Social Ethics*, 6.

16. Addams, *Democracy and Social Ethics*, 9.

as local among various local others, that is, "a world among worlds." One does not abandon who one is, but discovers oneself in the midst of others, honoring both self and other.[17]

At Virginia Seminary, cosmopolitan sensibility had its first glimmers as much in the student societies that arose as in the classroom. We have noted that the Second Great Awakening was characterized by societies focused on specific tasks, such as the distribution of Bibles and the creation of Sunday schools, and these societies left a lasting imprint on American life. The American Board of Commissioners for Foreign Mission (ABCFM) was a prime illustration of how evangelical religion translated its convictions into the practical demands of organizing Christian mission. The ABCFM, and other mission efforts which it inspired, possessed an expansive horizon.[18] This outlook spoke to the nature and energy of evangelical religion, which placed no limitations on the scope of the gospel. Indeed, the breadth of evangelicalism augured for its truth, which was presumed to be universal. Mission could not be confined lest its compelling truth somehow be diminished. This breadth embodied not merely truth but urgency. There was an immediate need to include all people in the truth, however different or distant they may be. This outlook and its urgency became hallmarks of the culture evangelicalism sought to impart across America and beyond. The influence of such an evangelical culture was apparent as Virginia Seminary grew and built an emphasis upon mission.

There was resonance between evangelical Episcopalians and the high-church movement spearheaded by Bishop Hobart in New York. The General Theological Seminary encouraged high-church theology and practice among Episcopalians. Yet the high-church party acted in ways that reflected broader influences of religion in America. Hobart traveled constantly to unite his congregations and to found new ones. He could be compared favorably to John Wesley and to later, peripatetic evangelists. Hobart disapproved of Episcopalians affiliating with the pan-Protestant American Bible Society. Yet he created an Episcopal Bible and Prayer Book society to reinforce what high-church Episcopalians saw as the distinctive features of their identity.[19] Despite such similarities, however, the culture of the high-church party differed from that of evangelical

---

17. Bender, "Cosmopolitan Experience," 117–18.

18. Putney and Burlin, *Role of the American Board in the World.*

19. Mullin, *Episcopal Vision.*

Episcopalians in a crucial way. High-church piety as a rule lacked the social dynamic of contemporary evangelical life. Evangelicalism possessed a central emphasis upon "disinterested benevolence" that drew it toward social reform. Similarly, evangelicalism believed that mission involved spreading the Christian faith in such a way that it instigated social enhancement. Evangelicals intended to create cultures of faith that would transform entire societies. High-church Episcopalians focused upon enhancement of the church's worship and ordained ministries. In time, graduates of General Seminary would join Episcopal mission efforts. When they did, their mission prioritized extension of the church over those goals so precious to graduates of Virginia Seminary—evangelism and social reform. Virginia graduates would also build the church overseas. But they would arrive at this intention by utilizing a different strategy. Cosmopolitanism had diverse sources.

In contrasting high-church and evangelical Episcopalians, we have used the term "culture." Broad and defined disparately, culture describes generally accepted patterns of individual and group behavior in organizations and larger societies. Culture encompasses knowledge, beliefs, customs, and expressions, often distinguishing what is idealized and intended from what is discouraged. The religiously inspired societies that arose in the early nineteenth century intended to heighten religion's influence on American life in specific ways. They were reflections of the culture of evangelicalism, for religious movements also develop cultures specific to their convictions and intentions. Even before the founding of Virginia Seminary, mission had already begun to be prominent in the culture of the Episcopal Church. The Church's General Convention of 1820 passed a resolution that would have constituted a Missionary Society for Foreign and Domestic Missions (MSFDM) in the Episcopal Church. The resolution had been hastily prepared and passed, requiring further consideration at a Special General Convention in 1821. The Missionary Society's board of directors, consisting of bishops and other clergy, included Meade and Wilmer from Virginia. The Church Missionary Society in the Church of England and the American Colonization Society were influential examples. Soon auxiliary societies arose in various parishes, including women's auxiliaries. Mission framed the church's life, and soon the Episcopal Church was legally renamed the Domestic and Foreign Missionary Society.

Virginia Seminary began to build an institutional culture on the basis of English religious tradition, Episcopal identity, and American evangelicalism.[20] Like any new institution, the culture of the seminary emerged as it faced internal and external challenges and opportunities. Culture in such situations also reflects an intention to instill values and shape wider worlds. The rise of student societies manifested the evangelicalism that was shaping seminary life, creating a culture that was focused on mission. It could be said that the creation of Virginia Seminary itself was an expression of the emphasis on societies, an emphasis so typical of nineteenth-century church life. The seminary grew out of the work of the Society for the Education of Pious Young Men for the Ministry of the Protestant Episcopal Church in Maryland and Virginia, known more familiarly as the Education Society.[21] Founded in 1818 in Washington, DC, the Education Society, as we have noted, advanced the idea of theological instruction at the College of William and Mary in order to supply the church's need for clergy in the mid-Atlantic region. As the prospect at Williamsburg faltered, trustees of the Education Society shifted their attention to Alexandria. This fact demonstrates that religiously motivated societies combined an ability to focus on specific goals while adopting innovative strategies to achieve them. Cast in this light, mission would be portrayed at the seminary as an end whose achievement required adaptation to disparate contextual realities.

By 1839, there were four student societies representing different priorities of ministry. Newly organized in that year was the Society for the Moral and Religious Improvement of the Neighborhood of the Seminary. Its object was to establish Sunday schools and Bible classes, to distribute religious tracts, and "to use such other means as prudence may dictate to exert a healthy moral influence in the surrounding neighborhood." A few years earlier, in 1834, a Temperance Society appeared on campus following the creation of the Rhetorical Society in 1830. The latter met weekly to promote "Improvement in Extemporaneous Speaking."[22] Yet the first society, launched in 1824, was the Missionary Society of Inquiry. It met on the first Monday evening of each month when the seminary was in session. The Missionary Society's purpose was to acquire "missionary intelligence," that is, information on aspects of current mission, and to "collect funds for missionary enterprises." It also sponsored an annual sermon preached before the society in the month of July. Thus,

20. Booty, *Mission and Ministry*, 14.

21. Goodwin, *History of the Theological Seminary*, 1:120–21.

22. Goodwin, *History of the Theological Seminary*, 1:410; Booty, *Mission and Ministry*, 66.

the society took the first step toward cosmopolitanism: inquiry into the nature of difference. On June 25, 1835, for example, the society's standing committee met in the room of its chairman. Committee members reviewed questions they had selected to be sent in a new round of correspondence. Letters were mailed to various church leaders to ascertain the state of the Episcopal Church in relation to others.

Three questions were discussed for a new round of correspondence. They reveal an impressive curiosity yet also a surprising restraint:

1. What are the influences & prospects of the Episcopal Church compared with those of other sects in your diocese? Number of ministers of each sect?

2. What are the wants of the Episcopal Church? The number of vacant parishes? Is there a church edifice or not? What salary would be allowed a minister? What is the population of the town, village or county is or near which said parishes are situated, or with which they are connected?

3. What is the influence of the Unitarians? Of the Roman Catholics? Of the Campbellites?[23]

Thus, the questions were confined to Episcopal Church life and were posed in a comparative, perhaps even competitive way. Yet too much should not be made of what questions were posed. The fact that they were posed at all is what matters. A culture of mission was taking shape, and dedication to it was evident. The minutes for June 25, 1835, further record adoption of a motion to have the Missionary Society pay all postage associated with gathering information. Dr. Thomas Savage made the motion.[24] Already a physician and then a student, he would soon become one of a trio of Episcopal missionaries to Liberia. All from the seminary's 1836 class, Savage, Launcelot Minor, and John Payne were motivated not simply by meetings of the Missionary Society. Joseph Packard recalled that "they used to have a praying circle which met once a week at six o'clock in the morning for prayer and converse as to the duty of going to preach the gospel to the heathen." Packard added that Payne was moved by the urging of another student, William J. Boone, who would embark on mission to China and become the first Episcopal bishop there.[25] Boone was a forceful presence. Packard recorded that "seventeen men offered

23. Missionary Society Minutes, June 25, 1835.

24. Missionary Society Minutes, June 25, 1835.

25. Packard, *Recollections*, 140.

themselves from this Seminary to go with him to China and he raised twenty thousand dollars for the mission."[26]

A missionary society, prayer circles, avid discussions, forceful personalities—all this pointed to the culture of mission that was taking shape at Virginia Seminary. On the "Holy Hill," this culture of mission entered its first stage in the 1830s as interest in China and Liberia surfaced. The cosmopolitan nature of the culture was incipient; references to "the heathen" extended little further than the urgency of seeking their salvation through proclaiming the gospel to them in their own lands. But before Payne, Minor, Savage, or Boone, a missionary from the seminary had begun foreign service. His choice of venue and the manner of his mission evinced a cosmopolitan instinct that would become characteristic of Episcopal mission.

MISSION SETS SAIL

In 1830 the first group of Episcopal missionaries left for foreign service. The group consisted of the clergymen J. J. Robertson of Maryland and John Hill of Virginia, their spouses, and a Mr. Bingham, a printer. Hill had just graduated from Virginia Seminary. In 1832 they were joined by Elizabeth Milligan, Frances Hill's sister and the first single woman appointed as an Episcopal missionary.[27] Curiously, they sailed to Greece, a Christian nation and an unlikely destination given its place in Christian life. But by 1830, the idea of mission in Greece engaged the energies of American religious life and political nationalism. Although the Episcopal initiative seems daring, Episcopalians were late in joining mission to the eastern Mediterranean.

Episcopal foreign mission might have begun in 1822 and not in Greece. In that year Ephraim Bacon, who had been an agent of the American Colonization Society in Liberia, severed that connection and offered himself and his wife to the new Domestic and Foreign Missionary Society. The Bacons intended to return to the west coast of Africa not as agents but as missionaries. The society's board accepted them and sent them forth to raise funds and elicit interest. As Julia Emery recorded in her history of Episcopal mission up to 1921, Bacon made three trips in eleven months, ranging as far north as Massachusetts and as far south as

26. Packard, *Recollections*, 140.
27. Rollins, "Mission to Greece," 252–70.

Georgia.[28] He recorded varied expressions of interest, even from members of the Congregationalist and Methodist churches. Bacon appears to have raised sufficient funds, but the Colonization Society refused to allow his return in a new guise. The Episcopal Church at the time could not move past this obstacle. The beginning of Episcopal foreign mission awaited 1830 and the launch of work in Greece. John Hill's role in forming and sustaining that work also represented the opening of Virginia Seminary's path to international initiatives and ties.

The Domestic and Foreign Missionary Society had already embarked on domestic mission, sending its first missionaries in 1825–26 to Florida, Missouri, Detroit, and Green Bay, then considered part of the Michigan territory.[29] There was continued discussion of Liberia and even of South America. But a lack of "men and means" stymied efforts. Then, in 1828, J. J. Robertson offered himself for service in Greece, and the society granted initial approval. Robertson went on a fact-finding trip to study prospects in the region. He carried tracts and Bibles from American societies and money for charitable gifts. What Robertson found proved sufficient to organize the mission party and to fund their departure in 1830.[30]

The choice of Greece as a locus of Christian mission is readily explained by the public image of Greece at that time. In 1821, a popular revolt began in Greece against the Ottoman Empire, the ruling power since 1453. By 1823, as the revolt had become full-scale revolution, Americans widely embraced the cause. Public events raised financial support for the Greek revolutionaries. One historian writes that dress balls and special church services were held in New York, Boston, Washington, and, notably, Alexandria, Virginia.[31] Thus, as Virginia Seminary was founded, Americans were seized by the vision of an independent, democratic Greece. Over forty years before, American independence had been achieved. Greece, seen as the fountainhead of Western civilization and a principal site for the rise of Christianity, had been under the sway of the major Muslim empire for over 350 years. American newspapers named the outpouring of support as "the Greek Fire." A campaign of astonishing energy and enthusiasm unfolded.

28. Emery, *Century of Endeavor*, 36.

29. Emery, *Century of Endeavor*, 48.

30. Emery, *Century of Endeavor*, 50.

31. Santelli, *Greek Fire*, 1, 77.

Although there had been an American presence in the Ottoman Empire, public zeal was not linked to economic or policy goals. In the public imagination, this was a battle between good and evil, democracy struggling to be born and tyrannical power bent on crushing it. The Greek Fire was a noble cause that seized public imagination. America was not the only nation where such enthusiasm erupted. "The philhellenic movement originated as a transatlantic phenomenon that gained momentum from the poetry and activism of Lord Byron."[32] In America and Great Britain, the cause of a free Greece fueled efforts to end slavery. Britain had already ended its slave trade, and in 1833 it abolished slavery in all its territories by an act of Parliament. The image of Greek independence fueled hopes of various sorts, including visions of Christian mission.

The extent of public support for Greek independence arose from a broad coalition of "reformers and merchants." As the Greek revolution continued, finally resulting in independence in 1828, the nature of support shifted from bolstering the war efforts to building an independent Greece. "By appealing to a range of social reform groups, the Greek cause enjoyed widespread support beyond the conclusion of the Greek Revolution."[33] Visions of social and economic reform that would secure independence were widely discussed. Into such talks came Christian organizations. Though they invoked the obvious distinction between Muslim Turks and Christian Greeks, much more than prejudice was involved. One issue that arose was women's rights, a nascent American cause that, like the abolition of slavery, was fueled by events in Greece. In effect, the emerging Greece was seen as a laboratory for democratic reform. Christian mission broadly, and Episcopal mission specifically, adopted this point of view.

In 1819, Pliny Fisk and Levi Parsons, graduates of Andover Seminary, were chosen by the American Board of Commissioners of Foreign Missions (ABCFM) to lead what they called the "Palestine Mission," the first American effort to the Holy Land. There was no lack of ambition. Fisk and Parsons were directed to travel across the region to assess the prospects there for conversion.[34] Their work drew public interest even before the outbreak of revolution in Greece. They sent vivid reports that idealized the classical culture that had arisen in the region. They sensed

32. Santelli, *Greek Fire*, 4.
33. Santelli, *Greek Fire*, 8.
34. Santelli, *Greek Fire*, 44.

an ancient cultural purity that could be "rediscovered by the modern Greeks if they were properly educated and evangelized."[35] These dual goals became the fixation of missionary efforts. Missionaries believed that an energetic, modern Christianity in Greece could infuse fresh energy into historic churches, thereby bringing about the conversion of Muslim lands. Greece was seen as the jumping-off point, a conviction strengthened when revolution overthrew Ottoman rule in 1828.

It was not surprising that there would be an instinct toward mission in Greece. The Greek Committee of Philadelphia, illustrative of the shape of support organized in major cities, called upon Gregory T. Bedell, rector of St. Andrew's Episcopal Church, to address the cause in a sermon. A noted evangelical voice, Bedell compared contemporary Greece to ancient Israel. Rather than fleeing Egypt, the Greeks were claiming their own land for freedom and faith. Support for Greece also was evident in the state of Virginia by 1824. One newspaper report summarized that "in a variety of places, resolutions [were] adopted and contributions made for the Holiest of causes."[36] The Greek revolution was seen as "the cause of the whole human race."[37]

Those words were meant both literally and reciprocally. The Greek cause elicited impressive involvement by American women, who were sensitive to the plight of women in Greece. In part, such a focus was easily explained. Amid the upheaval, it appeared that Greek woman and children suffered the most. The Greek situation drew humanitarian efforts. American women took leading roles in calling for donations, especially through churches as well as relief agencies. "Greek committees recruited female supporters on the basis of their supposed natural inclination toward faith, community, and family."[38] The result was that participation in charitable and social reform efforts by women expanded and was not seen as flight from presumed domestic duties. Rather, the capacity of women to care gained credibility and opened talk of equality for women. As Episcopal mission work in Greece began, this idea would strengthen.

Episcopal missionaries would learn another valuable lesson from the experience of others. In 1822, after his colleague Levi Parsons died, Pliny Fisk joined another missionary, Daniel Temple, on Malta. Temple

---

35. Santelli, *Greek Fire*, 45.

36. Santelli, *Greek Fire*, 81.

37. Santelli, *Greek Fire*, 81.

38. Santelli, *Greek Fire*, 105.

had brought a printing press there, and Fisk used it to produce religious literature, which he distributed across the eastern Mediterranean. The printing press and literature moved missionary work toward education. Already in 1817, the ABCFM had launched a school for children from overseas in Cornwall, Connecticut. Fisk linked the Palestine Mission to recruiting students for the school. Interest in drawing Greek students soon extended to such colleges as Amherst and Yale. Missionaries and others who rallied to the Greek cause "believed that through the attainment of knowledge, a society could be lifted up from ignorance and achieve greatness."[39] The plan envisioned that youth educated through ABCFM would return home as leaders. The ideal was emulated. Once the Episcopal Church began mission work in Greece, the design of its work was obvious. Education would be the emphasis.

But such emphasis was not immediately apparent. Sheer evangelism, and not necessarily in Greece, was the prior consideration. The mission began with high hopes. By 1832, though still small, the Episcopal mission in Greece had purchased land that was reported to have an arresting view of Athens. However, the intention was not to limit the mission to that city, nor to Greece alone. In 1837, the Foreign Committee of the Domestic and Foreign Missionary Society gave its overview of the "four great mission fields."[40] The leading one was Greece; the second was the Muslim world. They were followed by China and Africa, where Episcopal efforts were just beginning, both showing prominent influence from Virginia Seminary graduates. The energy given to Greece was conflated with designs on the Muslim world. Greece was envisioned as a staging area for evangelism in the Middle East. The attention paid to having a printing press signaled the intention of producing tracts and other literature to aid evangelism. Images of early Christianity and the influence of Greek intellectual life were not lost. The missionaries wondered if ancient history would repeat itself: would the Mediterranean turn decisively toward Christian faith?

Gradually the Episcopal Church tested the waters of mission to the Middle East. The pivotal figure was Horatio Southgate. Born a Congregationalist, he studied theology at Andover Seminary, becoming an Episcopalian by confirmation in 1834. Wasting no time, he impressed the Foreign and Domestic Committee, and late in 1835, he departed on an

---

39. Santelli, *Greek Fire*, 136.
40. Emery, *Century of Endeavor*, 87.

extended trip to assess the prospects for mission in Turkey and what was then Persia, now Iran. Julia Emery's history of Episcopal mission ascribes Southgate's initiative to the influence of his education at Andover and to the mission effort among Muslims already begun by the ABCFM.[41] Southgate, only twenty-three years when he left for the Muslim world, was energized by the idea of evangelism. In 1836 he arrived in Constantinople, now Istanbul. In a nearly three-year journey, he would cover an impressive expanse of lands and faiths, immersing himself especially in the ancient Eastern churches that were little known in the West. When he returned to the United States and reported to the Foreign Committee, he also noted that he had formed connections with the Church of England's mission agencies during a London stopover.

From Greece, J. J. Robertson urged that a bishop be appointed for mission in the Levant. The request was tabled for the time being. But in 1839, the Foreign Committee seemed to find fresh focus for its mission in Greece and Constantinople. An initial mission station at Syra in Greece was closed. As the Hills built their educational program at Athens, Robertson was assigned to work in Constantinople, and Southgate was sent to work with him. By that time Southgate had been ordained to the priesthood in the United States, and he had returned to work with Robertson in 1840. Soon he was sent to confer with church leaders in Mesopotamia, what is now known as Iraq. The mission work seemed to have reached a promising state.

The nature of Southgate's work was shifting perceptibly but with no loss of enthusiasm. He was increasingly drawn to the Nestorian and Syrian churches among whom he sensed an open door.[42] Emissaries of the Church of England had a similar experience and shared a similar intention with their American confreres. Imbued with evangelical fervor to convert, yet mindful that they were working amid fellow Christians, Episcopalians and their English counterparts imagined they could inspire fresh religious energy in historic, seemingly moribund churches. The conversion of Islam would be best approached through collaboration with a spiritually revived Eastern Christianity. Southgate seemed ready to accept this challenge but soon the wind went out of his sails. In 1843, J. J. Robertson resigned his appointment as a missionary and went home.

41. Emery, *Century of Endeavor*, 89.
42. Emery, *Century of Endeavor*, 91.

Soon the work at Constantinople was given up. In 1844, mission work on Crete, which had barely begun, was also abandoned, and funding for the Hills' work in Athens was reduced. Southgate received a new appointment to work among the Greek and Syrian churches. The idea of converting the Muslim world had evaporated. The reality was that the Foreign Committee was conflicted. As we shall describe, Episcopal mission work in Africa and China had begun and drew immediate interest. It became harder to sell Greece and the Middle East. Yet interest continued, especially when relations with the "Eastern Churches" was cited. Enough influential supporters surfaced to keep the idea alive. At the General Convention of 1844, Bishop George Washington Doane, an advocate of mission, called for the appointment of a missionary bishop "in the dominions and dependencies of the Sultan of Turkey."[43] Horatio Southgate, the obvious choice, was appointed bishop for Turkey. His tenure was brief, for he ignited disputes more than he built bridges with leaders of the ancient churches. In 1848, the Foreign Committee concluded that it could not sustain a bishop and a mission in Constantinople. In 1849, Southgate returned to the United States where he served in parish ministry for the remainder of his career.

Meanwhile, John and Frances Hill steadily built their educational program in Athens. The work was not unique. As Greece achieved its independence, the noted reformer Emma Willard became interested in the education of women there. She organized the "Troy Society" which was dedicated to education. Significantly, she negotiated with the ABCFM and persuaded some of her former American pupils to join in establishing a school in Greece. As one historian comments, for Willard "it was imperative to establish schools in Greece while it was still a new nation in order to establish the roots of a successful and free society where 'half of these are females.'" In Greece as in America, the new nation required educated, virtuous women if it was to fulfill its ideals. Her sentiment was not an isolated one. Support for the education of women in Greece was widespread throughout the American Northeast.[44]

Interest in Greek schools was also apparent in the career of Samuel Gridley Howe. Soon after his graduation from Harvard Medical School in 1824, Howe went to Greece to serve as a surgeon in the revolutionary army. He returned to the United States in 1827 to raise funds for

43. *Journal of the 21st General Convention*, 183–84.
44. Santelli, *Greek Fire*, 175.

famine relief in Greece. He also brought Greek children to America after awakening to the need for education. By the early 1830s, he began to exchange ideas on Greek education with Emma Willard and became a supporter of her work. Willard's sister, Almira Phelps, joined the effort and, assisted by the ABCFM, encouraged the training of women teachers to be sent to Greece to establish schools. Phelps linked the Troy Society's work to the Christian ideal of benevolence. A convergence of motivations unfolded; reformers and missionaries collaborated effectively. When "the Troy Society raised revenue to enlarge the building occupied by the Episcopalian Mission School at Athens, a Boston women's committee 'formed themselves into a society co-operative with the Society in Troy for the Advancement of Female Education in Greece.'"[45]

From its inception the Episcopal mission in Greece focused on education for women. In 1831, the Hills and Robertsons had started a school for young women in the basement of the home they shared. After two months the enrollment had grown to 167 students.[46] Few of those enrolled could read when they arrived. As they learned to read, they were led through passages from the New Testament. Rudimentary religious instruction grew naturally. Male students were organized separately and instructed in part by a Greek priest. As the educational program expanded, the Episcopal missionaries began providing basic instruction in a variety of subjects, creating a school curriculum. Concluding that Greece had a shortage of teachers, they imagined that their charges could help to address this need. It was apparent that the Hills and Robertsons were intent on making the school indispensable by addressing the roles of women.

The school grew steadily and soon was associated solely with John and Frances Hill. The Robertsons departed Athens for service elsewhere. A key benchmark was early recognition by the Greek government, which accorded the school status "for the instruction of female teachers." Such endorsement was made tangible when "twelve girls, selected from various parts of Greece, were sent to (the school) to be trained as teachers at public expense."[47] By 1834 there were five hundred students, of whom four hundred were girls. The school drew from various social classes and was already appealing to girls from wealthy and influential families. As the school's reputation grew, it added students from beyond Athens.

45. Santelli, *Greek Fire*, 175.

46. Saloutos, "American Missionaries in Greece," 165.

47. Saloutos, "American Missionaries in Greece," 166.

Mission staff grew as well. By 1839, there were nineteen Episcopal missionaries serving in Athens.[48]

The school's development in its early years can be readily tracked. In 1836, the Foreign Department of the Episcopal Church had begun publication of a monthly magazine, the *Spirit of Missions*. In time, its editions would often be as large as one hundred pages. Reports from the various sites of Episcopal mission work accompanied news of fundraising and accounts of the recruitment and training of new missionaries. As the work in Athens grew, John Hill began reporting regularly on it. One is struck not simply by illustrations of the school's growth but by Hill's clarity about the focus of the work and the dedication he and Frances gave to it. More than instruction, the Hills created an ethos, that is, a setting in which teaching, attention to personal development, and worship were incorporated. A letter from John Hill dated October 24, 1836, appeared in the *Spirit of Missions* early in 1837. The sense of the school's influence and of the relationships built is palpable. John Hill was especially energized because Frances recently had returned after being away for eight months.

> For several days our house was thronged with visitors, but the most affecting scene was meeting with the dear children, the nineteen beneficiaries under our own roof, and afterwards with our 500 pupils at the school. The interview with the latter took place on Sunday morning at usual hour for religious instruction and explanation of the Gospel; and it served to quicken our grateful sense of the kind dealings of our Heavenly Father towards us.[49]

Hill added that with its current enrollment, the school was overflowing. There was no room for more students despite "numerous applications to admit others." He and Frances had given up two rooms of their residence to allow for more instruction. He added, with evident enthusiasm, that they were adding students from families "who can afford to pay for the education of their children." He felt that when parents paid, they were more invested in their children's education. "At the same time it will induce parents to be more attentive to their children at home; they will be more willing to second our efforts at home, when they pay something for the children's education."[50] The school was succeeding. In 1839, Hill

48. Emery, *Century of Endeavor*, 99.

49. *Spirit of Missions* 2 (1837) 85.

50. *Spirit of Missions* 2 (1837) 85.

wrote a further update: "It is really cheering to see the spiritual improvement of so many fine young girls, daughters of the rich and influential, whose parents, although themselves ignorant of the truths of the Gospel, seem affectionately desirous that their daughters should know the truth." The parents, Hill added, had indulged their daughters with everything "but the one thing needful."[51]

The Hills stayed their course but not without challenges. As interest in Episcopal mission in the Middle East waned, so did support for the school. In 1846, John Hill tried to report in a realistic and encouraging way. Noting that his appeal for increased funding had been declined, he reflected on the course of the Athens ministry. "We have had our joys and our sorrows—our days of adversity and prosperity—but never for a moment have the tender loving kindnesses of our God failed, nor the hopes which we trusted Him to accomplish, been defeated." He added with evident pride that "we have had the satisfaction of observing the daily walk and conversation of those who have grown up under our nurture. In these active and intelligent young Christians, we find truly spiritual helpers, and their uniformly correct deportment strongly contrasts the principles in which they have been educated with those which unhappily prevail around us."[52] He noted the growth of the public worship offered by the mission, stressing that they had moved from simple worship for their charges to a sanctuary "where our pure and beautiful form of divine worship is exhibited before this people in a manner well calculated to call their attention to it."[53] The work of the school attained various avenues of public influence.

In no sense did the Hills or their supervisors at the Foreign Committee intend to attract children or their families away from the Greek Church. In its report for 1839, the Foreign Committee had made this stance plain. While the missionaries "have carefully avoided every attempt at proselytism to our own Church, or of offensive imputations on theirs, so on the other hand, both by bishops and by the political government of Greece, our efforts to enlighten and instruct their youth have been well received, and much good acknowledged to have been done."[54] It would not always be the case.

51. *Spirit of Missions* 4 (1839) 44.
52. *Spirit of Missions* 11 (1846) 145.
53. *Spirit of Missions* 11 (1846) 263.
54. *Spirit of Missions* 4 (1839) 259.

By 1846, "popular opposition against missionary establishments in Greece and neighboring countries increased noticeably."[55] The Orthodox Patriarch in Constantinople was the principal instigator. But an edict he issued gave unintended praise for work by various missionaries. While accusing them of heresies and efforts to "pollute our spotless faith, and to tear to pieces the flock of Christ," he acknowledged that missionaries performed works of philanthropy, healed the sick, and taught. But the "pretense of doing good" masked efforts to instill "blasphemies" in "the hearts of the Orthodox, and especially of their tender offspring." The patriarch emphasized that parents should not send their children to the mission schools and should not receive materials printed by the various mission presses. The furor calmed for the Hills when parents of students at their school "rallied to [their] support and a government investigation exonerated [them]. The evidence supported Hill's claim that he had always conformed to Greek standards."[56] As the patriarch accused the Hills and other missionaries of proselytism, some voices in the Episcopal Church accused Frances and John Hill of insufficient efforts to convert students and their families. In the eyes of some, the Hills had settled into Athens and were accommodationist in their work. Though funding from America diminished, the Hills adroitly maintained the mission, gaining endorsements in Greece and offering enthusiastic reports to the Foreign Committee. Avoiding the topic of conversion, they made plain the religious character of their work. This delicate balancing act ensured the longevity of the school.

Thus, the mission school became rooted and even honored in Athens and continued to draw students, especially young women, from across Greece and the region. As he grew older, John Hill became more reflective yet no less enthusiastic. On June 16, 1863, he wrote a lengthy letter that appeared several months later in the *Spirit of Missions*. "What may be our future course, time and circumstances will show us. . . . There can be little doubt, from what we see and know, that there is a religious Eastern question to be settled as well as a political one. Perhaps we may be called to take a part therein." Yet, he added, Frances Hill was about to enter her sixty-fifth year, and two months later, "I shall have closed my

55. Saloutos, "American Missionaries in Greece," 166.
56. Saloutos, "American Missionaries in Greece," 166–67.

seventy-first year. We can no longer make plans for the future. Day by day, we must do what our hands find to do."[57]

Continuing, Hill added something of a valedictory for his work:

> I have endeavored to trace out the remarkable way in which the principles of this mission have been brought out, and its importance as a link to the great chain which is, in due time, to bind in one bond the scattered flock of Christ's fold in these regions. This really noble mission seemed to be a mere educational scheme; and it was sometimes referred to as that school at Athens! But I hope I have succeeded in showing that it always had far nobler objects in view than ever such persons imagined. Some of those objects have been accomplished, and much still remains to be done.[58]

John Hill stepped back from the school in 1869. Both he and Frances spoke of retirement. But their later years were spent in the city they had made their home. They continued to participate in the work of the school, and their names appeared in discussions of mission in Greece. As late as 1872, there was a gathering of missionaries in Athens, and much attention was devoted to the school. Reports continued to be glowing and personal, with particular students cited and relations with their families warmly noted. A particular emphasis on Christian unity had taken root, one which didn't gloss over the reality of confessional differences. It was proudly noted that even some Greek clergy attended meetings at the school. Frances Hill wrote a letter detailing the exercises given to children and emphasized the reading of biblical passages and singing of hymns. This was no closing exercise for the Hills. In 1874, they reported the creation of an industrial school intended to convey practical skills to young women. Sewing, especially making lace, was highlighted. The school endeared itself to the Greek public by offering both basic and practical education.

John Hill died in 1882, Frances following him in 1884. Through steady leadership at the school, their imprint was plain. Eventually the school would be turned over to the government. As Episcopal mission grew in Africa, China, and then Japan, attention had shifted away from Athens. Yet the Hills—along with the Robertsons, Southgate, and others—were the first, and they blazed a path for others to follow. The Hills

---

57. *Spirit of Missions* 28 (1863) 183.
58. *Spirit of Missions* 28 (1863) 183.

epitomized a cosmopolitan sensibility and illustrated its necessity in mission. Further, they showed that missions could gain traction through an emphasis on education. In the process, they displayed a cultural sensitivity and a capacity to adapt—both of which were fundamental to the development of cosmopolitanism. Given the Hills's readiness to communicate and their sheer persistence, they became an important example. The growth of Episcopal mission would be characterized by unprecedented levels of cosmopolitanism.

4

Navigating Sociocultural Difference

PAYNE AND LIBERIA

A LEAD EDITORIAL IN the May 1868 edition of the *Spirit of Missions* was headlined, "What is the Protestant Episcopal Church Doing to Evangelize the World?" It was a well-timed rallying cry. Once the Civil War ended in 1865, Americans, including Episcopalians, were taking stock. The editorial writer in 1868 observed that the Episcopal Church "is no longer a mission church in this country." Mustering steam, the writer noted the "material wealth" of many Episcopalians, and the "hundreds of stately churches which adorn our cities and principal towns." Unrelenting, the author added that "in her stately and beautiful worship, in her noble history, and in her able and faithful ministry [the Episcopal Church] has many privileges and blessings." But "is it enough that we build churches for ourselves and schools for our children, and support the stated services of our Church in our midst?" Was it enough to build churches in destitute American neighborhoods or send missionaries to the West? No, the author declared. "What are we doing for the evangelization of these nations in proportion to our privileges and opportunities?"[1]

"Eighty millions of people are yet in heathen darkness in Africa," the editorial thundered. "Have we no obligation concerning them?" The obligation extended to "four hundred million in China" and then to Mexico and Haiti. But Africa and China loomed the largest, partly for their sheer numbers of people, partly for their cultural complexities.

1. *Spirit of Missions* 33 (1868) 366.

Yet there was scant Episcopal presence in either locale. "But little more than fifty labourers, including native teachers and helpers, constitute the representatives of the Protestant Episcopal Church of the United States in heathen lands."[2] There was no denial of previous mission work. But it had not been sufficient. "Instead of sixteen ordained missionaries in heathen lands, we ought to have at least a hundred with a proportionate number of native teachers and helpers. Instead of the seventy or eighty thousand dollars contributed annually for the evangelization of the heathen we ought to raise by this time at least a quarter of a million with a yearly increase of the sum."[3]

It could not be known at the time of the editorial that a new generation of Episcopal mission was about to begin. Over the next half century, there would be dramatic expansion of the church's mission in Liberia on Africa's West Coast, in China and in Japan, where the Church's presence was less than ten years old. The hoped-for numbers of active missionaries and money spent on their work would be met. It would seem amazing. But the editorial did not look beyond the quantity of mission work to consider its qualities. If the number of workers at mission sites were inadequate, and monies spent fell short, what was being learned in the actual conduct of the church's mission? How could monies available be more wisely spent? More questions arose and could not be avoided. They awaited substantive response. More workers and more money, and even more conversions to Christianity, would not simplify the sorts of issues that beset mission. Such questions first arose in the 1830s as mission efforts in Africa and China began. In both cases, Virginia Theological Seminary played prominent and ongoing roles. The imprint of the "seminary in Alexandria," as it was often named, would be prominent.

Writing in William Archer Rutherfoord Goodwin's centennial history of the seminary, Paul Due observed that the "real history of the African Mission . . . began in 1835, when three students of the Virginia Seminary, after much prayerful consultation, decided to devote their lives to this work. These men were Launcelot B. Minor, John Payne, afterwards first bishop of Liberia, and Thomas S. Savage, M.D., of the class of 1836."[4] If by "real history," Due meant continuing mission, there was considerable truth in his characterization. There had been false starts. In 1822,

---

2. *Spirit of Missions* 33 (1868) 367.

3. *Spirit of Missions* 33 (1868) 368.

4. Due, "Work of the Seminary in Liberia," 295–323.

Ephraim Bacon, formerly an agent of the American Colonization Society, wanted to return to Liberia as an Episcopal missionary. He raised the necessary funds but was denied transit by the society.

In the early 1830s, the Black colonists James and Elizabeth Thomson launched work intended to build an Episcopal congregation and a boarding school. This vision would be enacted by white missionaries, and the Thomsons would not be prominent in it. James Thomson was expelled from mission work by Thomas Savage within a year of the latter's arrival late in 1836. Thomson had been charged with adultery, and the case was dismissed. Savage was not persuaded and followed through on Thomson's dismissal. Nevertheless, based on Thomson's initial work, the site he favored, Cape Palmas, was chosen for the first mission station. Similarly, Thomson's instinct to blend education and evangelism proved an enduring strategy. Thomson and the inheritors of his vision foresaw the creation of a Christian ethos as the basis of evangelism. Mission entailed more than conversion and belief. The goal was to create an all-encompassing Christian way of life. When Minor and Payne joined Savage in 1837, this approach advanced.

In his study of the early years of the Episcopal Church in Liberia, James Yarsiah, himself Liberian, comments that Savage, Minor, and Payne, all fresh from Virginia Seminary, held decidedly different personal attributes.[5] Savage, the physician, was observant and recorded extensive notes on the people and culture of the area. During his eleven years in Liberia, Savage wrote prolifically. Of the three original Episcopal missionaries, Savage was the most critical of indigenous people, whom he distinguished from the settlers who arrived through the work of the American Colonization Society. Even in his dealings with tribal kings, Savage was critical. In 1839, he described one king as "a heathen, having no hope, and without God in the world, consequently under the influence of no moral principle." Terms such as "degradation" and "treachery" flowed from Savage's pen. The more one traveled from the coast to the inland, Savage concluded, the more "benighted" the people proved to be.[6]

Savage admitted that the mission school at Cape Palmas flourished with twenty-five male and twelve female students, most of them "natives" as opposed to "settlers." In 1840, Payne echoed Savage's optimistic perspective: "Much interest has for some time been manifested by the young

5. Yarsiah, *Early Missionary Work*.
6. *Spirit of Missions* 4 (1839) 180.

men of this place in education." When they met, he added that religious exercises were conducted in Grebo, the local tribal language. Worship included singing, prayer, and "comments upon some appropriate portion of Scripture. Those present appear to be interested; whether they really see remains to be proved." Payne could be critical of tribal mores, but he proved more willing to engage with local peoples and saw more inherent possibility for Christian faith in them than Savage usually allowed. Also in 1840, Payne wrote that a plan "of operating upon the natives" had arisen, and he hoped much good would come of it. The intention was to form a small village near the mission, excluding all practice of tribal religion and keeping Sunday free from work. "We propose limiting the number at first to ten families, and if the plan works well, to increase it gradually as our experience may suggest."[7]

Payne's vision extended to a unity of peoples and cultures achieved by Christian faith and sparked by Episcopal mission. He took scant notice of other Christian denominations in his focus on engaging tribal culture and melding it with the culture of the settlers. Several challenges confronted Payne as he grew more appreciative of the cultural complexities he faced. First, it seemed impossible to eradicate tribal culture. A familiar pattern of drum performance summoned people to the mission's Sunday worship, for example. Even worse for Payne was the fact that habitual patterns of superstitious practice, some proving deadly, persisted among people who had become Christian, or who had at least shown an affinity for the faith. Payne and other Episcopal missionaries faced the reality of syncretism, that is, the blending of religious ideas and practices as an accommodation to missionary influence.[8]

The persistence of some habitual practices could prove maddening. In 1845, Episcopal missionary E. W. Hening, a Virginia Seminary graduate, described the ordeal of a tribal king who felt compelled to drink a poisonous concoction. Hening explained that the king had been accused of causing the death of a child by sorcery. To disabuse his subjects of such suspicion, the king submitted to this ordeal. He told Hening that he liked the gospel but that he must act in accord with what was expected of him culturally. The outcome was that the king survived and seemed to be reinvented in his royal role.[9] By contrast, Hening also recorded the death of

7. *Spirit of Missions* 6 (1841) 13–19.

8. Yarsiah, *Early Missionary Work.*

9. *Spirit of Missions* 12 (1847) 81.

a young woman from drinking "gidu," also a poisonous concoction. The woman had been accused of attempted murder in her tribal community. As with the king, the ordeal reflected its own kind of moral logic. If the woman survived, she would have been adjudged punished, perhaps even vindicated. Unlike the king, however, she failed to survive.[10]

Navigating such entrenched practices, the Episcopal Church's mission grew. Even allowing for reports that may have been embellished, the trends in worship attendance and school enrollment pointed upward. On Easter, April 12, 1845, Hening reported that five persons had been baptized. "They were all pupils of the school . . . one of them as an adult, who had been for some time employed by me as a trade-man. The candidates had been publicly instructed in a course of lectures on the Creed, Ten Commandments, and Baptismal Service, and also by private conversation. It is gratifying to state, that since their admission into the Church of Christ, their walk and conversation have been such as to adorn their profession."[11] In other words, Hening didn't just seek conversion. Baptism, proceeding from "private conversation," suggested the building of personal ties, a sense of faith community. Reference to "their walk and conversation" implied the creation of a way of life that was more than a mere break with their personal pasts. A new social fabric was instilled. Baptism and education were the components of evangelism and the measures of its results. The intention was more than creation of the church. Evangelism intended to be the catalyst for the rise of a Christian civilization.

John Payne's initiatives to this end were notable. Even before becoming bishop, he had encouraged the raising up of "some natives to act as teachers and assistants." Scant numbers of missionaries required such sharing of leadership. The dawn of Christian civilization would be marked by a gradual transfer of responsibilities. The church in Liberia needed to raise up those who can "relieve the Missionaries, and by their example as well as their employments, give form and strength to the cause of Christianity and civilization."[12] The effort seemed to bear fruit. Even Thomas Savage, prone to cynical assessments, noted on the eve of his departure from Liberia that there had been "a perceptible gain as a Mission, upon the confidence of the native population at large, in our mode of dealing, and the sincerity of our profession of *a desire to do them good*. They have

10. *Spirit of Missions* 12 (1847) 87.

11. *Spirit of Missions* 12 (1847) 87.

12. *Spirit of Missions* 12 (1847) 229.

learned to distinguish between the Missionary and trader, and perceive a difference between their objects, principles, and practice." They know that "they can turn to the Missionary without fear," Savage proudly concluded.[13] He could swing from prejudicial criticism to undue optimism concerning the missionary's role among the peoples of nascent Liberia. Nevertheless, he developed appreciation for indigenous peoples and took care to distinguish the church from other forms of Western influence. For the growth of a cosmopolitan outlook among the missionaries, these were important first steps.

The numbers of churches and schools grew, the missionary force slowly expanded, more indigenous people were trained alongside the colonists, a few of them were even ordained, yet some problems remained intractable. An obvious issue was the health of the missionaries. Launcelot Minor died in 1843 at the shocking age of twenty-nine. Of the first three Episcopal missionaries, he had been the one who most readily engaged tribal culture. He even gave up his missionary accommodations to live in a local village. He was the most avidly evangelistic, while seemingly bringing a readiness to understand. Yet his life was cut short. He was not the only one. Before Savage left, his wife died. Payne's wife, Anna, herself energetically engaged with tribal life and especially with women's experience, also succumbed, as did other clerical and lay missionaries. The consistent problem was tropical fever. Missionary literature is filled with laments over the threats to health that could bring premature death.

The other problem that was apparent from the mission's inception was a tension between the freed slaves who arrived as colonists and the indigenous people who found these uninvited arrivals in their vicinity. For the freed slaves, the colonization program often proved life-saving. Though they landed in unfamiliar territory, where being Black did not mean they felt at home, they no longer were enslaved. In the novel, colonial setting, there were greater opportunities for self-government. Yet they also arrived with American cultural assumptions that did not accord well with indigenous people. In some cases, Black colonists felt culturally superior over the Grebo, and they tended to identify with the white missionaries, whose ways reflected their own. Christianity's spread on the whole, and the life of the Episcopal Church in particular, drew upon the initiative of the Black settlers as they became colonists. The church only

13. *Spirit of Missions* 12 (1847) 232.

grew slowly toward the Liberian interior, first building its base on the coastal area by rooting itself among the colonists.[14]

Especially after his consecration as bishop, Payne believed that the indigenous peoples required superintendence more than those who had settled in Liberia. "The natives do not yet rank with the colonists."[15] Yet he struggled with this reality because it challenged his goal of assimilating disparate people into one church and encouraging a comprehensive Christian civilization. That goal seemed remote as outbreaks of violence between the settlers and the Grebo occurred, notably in 1856 when a state of war existed for a time. Conflict worsened as the Grebo became a dynamic force from 1850 onward, including in the church. Payne's vision was stymied for this and other reasons.

His leadership style did not help. At best, he could be described as paternalistic; at worst, he proved autocratic. His appreciation for Grebo language and culture deepened, and he proved to be an able translator of the Prayer Book and portions of the Bible into Grebo. He even created a written form of the language. He also intended to topple superstition and to expand the church inland, meeting with modest success. Gradually Payne drew indigenous people and found a few young people whom he groomed for leadership roles. Along with his emphasis on education as the principal avenue of evangelism, Payne wanted the church to be a fertile ground for culture. But there his cosmopolitan instinct stopped.

Early in his episcopate, Payne faced challenges to his authority. In retrospect, these challenges heralded the rise of an indigenous Liberian church. At one of the periodic meetings of the church's missionary convocation which Payne had organized, he presented a proposal to modify his title, giving him a more expansive claim to authority. Perfunctory approval seemed assured. But Black clergy were opposed, especially Eli Stokes. The issue was less the title than Payne's presumption in wanting to grant himself a greater sphere of influence. Opposition to his intention was a sign of momentum for a Black-led Liberian church. At first this initiative centered on Stokes and Alexander Crummell. Following the lead of Edward Blyden, Stokes emphasized Liberian nationalism. Stokes formed his own Episcopal congregation at Monrovia and joined forces with Crummell throughout the 1860s. The alliance peaked in 1863 when Black Liberian clergy formed their own council apart from the

---

14. Ciment, *Another America*, 53–76.
15. Yarsiah, *Early Mission Work*; cf. *Spirit of Missions* 13 (1848) 233.

convocation identified with Payne. But in the waning years of Payne's episcopate, energy for a Black-led church dissipated. The intention was not gone, merely postponed.[16]

Payne left in 1869, returning to Westmoreland County, Virginia, where he died in 1874. His efforts to evangelize, to promote education, to launch indigenous leadership, and to understand Grebo culture cannot be dismissed. But they were compromised by his views and his style. He was not racially dismissive, but he thought in racially hierarchical terms. He assumed that a race or a class of people was better the more they appeared to be like white people from the Western world. Thus, he favored the Black colonists, seeing them as the means of evangelizing indigenous people. His paternalism and his flat-footed response to calls for Black autonomy obscured his vision. Over time, the Liberian church would approach what its Black leadership envisioned, though the issue of dependence upon America would not be readily resolved.

BOONE AND CHINA

Chance meetings set the stage for the beginning of the Episcopal Church's mission in China. For unknown reasons a young Episcopalian named Augustus Lyde became energized by the idea of mission to China in the early 1830s. His own health was weak, preventing him from missionary service. However, he happened to meet E. A. Newton and James Milner, who were traveling to a meeting of the Board of Directors of the Domestic and Foreign Missionary Society. Lyde persuaded them to advocate for mission in China, and they did just that, winning approval. Before his premature death, Lyde visited Virginia Theological Seminary with the intention of enlisting support.[17] William J. Boone was moved by Lyde's message. "I believe I will offer myself to the Episcopal Church to be sent to China," Boone told his roommate, Charles Pinckney.[18]

It was 1834, and Boone was a student. The Mission Board responded promptly but was not yet prepared to accept him. Instead, in 1835, the board sent Henry Lockwood, a recent General Theological Seminary graduate like Lyde, and Francis Hanson, a Virginia Seminary graduate serving as a parish priest in Maryland. After nearly five months at sea, Hanson

16. Yarsiah, *Early Missionary Work*, 91–94, 105.

17. *Historical Sketch*, 6.

18. Richmond, *American Episcopal Church in China*, 5.

and Lockwood arrived at Canton (now Guangzhou). Once ashore, they met the few Protestant missionaries there, including two from the American Board of Commissioners of Foreign Missions (ABCFM). They also learned that they were forbidden entry into the city and would remain within a narrow strip of land near it. They found the Chinese language equally impenetrable. There would be no missionary work without mastery of the language, which required extensive, dedicated study.[19]

Lockwood and Hanson adapted to the situation. On the advice of British missionaries, they resolved to go to Singapore. That decision proved temporary. Batavia (now Jakarta) in the Dutch East Indies (now Indonesia) offered more advantages. There was a substantial Chinese population among whom the language could be learned, and the cost of living was lower than in China or Singapore. Lockwood and Hanson settled there late in 1836. In October 1837, they were joined by William J. Boone, recently graduated from Virginia Seminary and accompanied by his new wife, Sally. The Boones joined the intensive language study. There was no minimizing the difficulty or the necessity of developing language skill. A person "with something more than an ordinary talent for acquiring languages . . . may be actively and usefully employed among the Chinese in two or three years."[20] Even then, Boone had realized, continuing improvement would be necessary.

He would have the time. It was nearly five years before he would be able to enter China. Neither Hanson nor Lockwood would make their destination. Shortly after the Boones reached Batavia, Hanson's health compelled him to return to the United States. In 1839, Lockwood's failing health also compelled his return. The Episcopal vision of mission in China lay solely with the Boones. But, for an extended period, they had to remain in Batavia. Nevertheless, they were not indolent. In 1838 they began a school for boys which grew to forty students by late that year. Meanwhile, in addition to studying Chinese, they learned Malay. Already a physician, Boone began offering medical care which, as one early history of the Chinese mission noted, aided him "in reaching all classes of people."[21] Evangelism was ever the priority.

The prospects for mission in China brightened in 1842 when five port cities opened to foreigners. The opening was not attributable to Chinese

19. *Historical Sketch*, 7.

20. Richmond, *American Episcopal Church in China*, 6.

21. Richmond, *American Episcopal Church in China*, 6–8.

largesse. Chinese military forces had been soundly defeated in the Opium Wars, concluding in that year. European pressure was producing openings for foreigners and their panoply of influences, religious mission among them. The question of accessibility was not fully resolved. Anti-foreign public sentiment was evident, especially as one moved inland. Even so, Boone went to Amoy (now Xiamen) on China's southeast coast, where he began to conduct worship. A congregation grew to fifty or so men and boys on each Sunday. But at this juncture, Boone's own health worsened. He planned a visit to the United States, ostensibly for recovery, but in fact to generate further support for mission in China. What he could not anticipate was the sudden death of Sally, his wife, in 1842.

Still, Boone persisted in his intention of promoting the fledgling Chinese church. At the time, Episcopal foreign mission interest centered on Greece and Liberia. Almost single-handedly, Boone raised the profile of the Episcopal presence in China. Living in America from 1842 to 1844, he proved indefatigable, devoting his gradually restored energies to what would now be termed "networking." His travels were both relentless and fruitful. Eight new missionaries were enlisted including two clergy and three unmarried women. Before his return to China, Boone won sufficient recognition to be consecrated as the first Episcopal bishop in China. He also married Phoebe Elliott, sister of Stephen Elliott, bishop of Georgia. His life and work reconstituted, Boone returned to China, settling in Shanghai by mid-1845.[22]

Even before the mission in China was conclusively launched, Boone's personal story bore the marks of heroism. It is tempting to be cautious about applying such a description; the literature of Christian mission in nineteenth- and early twentieth-century America could be effusive in its praise and superficial in its critique of personal shortcomings. The human dimension will be noted repeatedly, personal and institutional, not relenting on justifiable praise or criticism. Certainly, the beginnings of mission work relied on assertive, single-minded figures such as Hill, Payne, and Boone. How they applied ideals of faith to the realities of mission, and how they brought influences from their work back to Virginia Seminary, are the core themes of this narrative. At the outset of their work, each of these figures made formative decisions and endured painful sacrifices. Boone's selection of Shanghai as the prime location proves illustrative.

22. Richmond, *American Episcopal Church in China*, 13.

This choice was fortuitous. As the China mission expanded, and at times contracted, Shanghai remained its constant base. In her doctoral study of the early years of Episcopal mission in China, Mei-Mei Lin identifies three ongoing challenges: location, language, and evangelization.[23] Having found a base of operation, the mission emerged around basic worship, preaching, and distribution of tracts with religious messages. Translation of portions of the Bible and the Book of Common Prayer advanced. The factor of language, as Lin demarcates it, was a constant. New missionaries required instruction, and rudimentary evangelism relied upon facility in Mandarin Chinese. During 1846, Boone busied himself with translation, assisted by two new clerical missionaries, Edward W. Syle and Richardson Graham, both members of the class of 1844 at Virginia Seminary. Other missionaries, clergy and lay, were arriving. By 1860 their number would include Thomas Franklin, John Hubbard, Cleveland Keith, John Liggins, Robert Nelson, Henry Parker, Henry Reardon, Dudley Smith, Elliot Thomson, Channing Moore Williams, Henry Woods, and Thomas Yocum, all Virginia Seminary graduates.[24] Their number was supplemented by some graduates of General Theological Seminary, especially Samuel I. J. Schereschewsky. He would later be an Episcopal bishop in China and, even more notably, the consummate translator of the Bible and Prayer Book. Yet the numbers of Episcopal missionaries and their converts remained small when compared to the work of other confessions, especially the ABCFM and the Church of England.

In a letter dated September 30, 1854, then published early in 1855, Episcopal lay missionary John Points sounded a discouraging note. "The congregations in the city are at present very small, sometimes consisting of hardly any besides our old communicants and those who have been registered as candidates for baptism." There were "several very interesting and hopeful cases; and though the mass of the people of the city seem to have sunk into a state of apathy and almost total indifference to everything . . . those few whom we have gathered together seem to be more than ever alive to the importance of seeking Him who alone can protect them in this time of grievous distress."[25] The continuance of armed struggle near Shanghai stymied church growth and kept a high stress level upon the lives of the missionary community. Points added that the life of church

23. Lin, "Episcopal Missionaries in China," 95.

24. Richmond, *American Episcopal Church in China*, 17.

25. *Spirit of Missions* 20 (1855) 58–60.

schools continued, and the church had not been damaged by political violence. Points was hopeful for the renewal of evangelism.

Slowly, the Episcopal effort gained cultural momentum. The church's identity in China was beginning to center on education. As in Liberia, schools became a primary avenue of evangelism. The integration of basic, Western education with Bible study and devotional exercises became a template. By 1846, a school had been started for boys and soon after one began for girls. As enrollment grew, outpaced by interest, the Episcopal mission started both boarding and day schools. Boone created a multifaceted mission, one which was reflecting sufficient Chinese interest to allow for gradual expansion. However, tension arose within and without the mission. Two women missionaries, Eliza Gillette and Lydia Fay, showed resolution that created friction with Boone. For a time, he would not accept unmarried women missionaries after his encounters with Gillette and Fay. At the same time, issues of ecclesiastical jurisdiction plagued Episcopal relations with missionaries of the Church of England. Such tensions became fruitless distractions from the spirit and the intention of mission.

The American Civil War further strained mission work. Financial contributions dropped alarmingly and did not rebound when hostilities ended in 1865. Funds raised for mission were more likely to remain in the United States for use on domestic initiatives including programs to address the needs of freed slaves. Mei-Mei Lin concludes that as the second half of the nineteenth century began, the Episcopal Church's missionaries in China faced a striking gap between "their evangelical mission and missionary reality [which eroded] the missionaries' trust in Boone and shattered their own vision."[26] Boone's dogged determination was both an asset and a liability, a striking parallel to the experience of John Payne in Liberia. An autocratic leadership style accompanied their insistent visions.

More than half of the Episcopal mission staff served no more than five years during Boone's tenure. Another 18 percent served less than ten years in what had been presented as long-term service. Morale further diminished as most missionaries began to feel a psychological separation between themselves and the Chinese people they worked to convert; equally painful was their physical distance from their American homes. Nevertheless, the growth of church-run schools marked the creation of

26. Lin, "Episcopal Missionaries in China," 152.

a meeting ground between missionaries and Chinese students and their families. The longing for Western education was matched by the eagerness of missionaries to contact the Chinese. Although the missionaries worked in a religious bubble of their own creation, they engaged Chinese culture creatively. Boone's determination paid off.

Such determination was needed to face vexing issues. Translation remained focal. It was the key to all mission work. In January 1851, for example, the *Spirit of Missions* noted the debate over which Chinese term best conveyed the Christian meaning of God. Hard at work on translation, Boone preferred the word "shin." Yet linguists of the time differed, some opting for "Shang-te" or a variant of it. The case could be made that the Chinese themselves used this term for divinity, as it was understood to mean "supreme ruler." Boone opted for "shin" as being more colloquial and having been adopted by missionaries. Others insisted that "shin" could be taken to mean ghosts or spirits and was thus insufficient for God.[27]

The matter resisted resolution, and translation proved stubbornly difficult. In May 1861, Cleveland Keith, missionary and son of early Virginia Seminary faculty member Reuel Keith, reported that translation needed further attention. "So far, we have only the gospels, Acts, and Genesis, published by our own and the Church Missionary Society missionaries, and the Epistle to the Romans and that of St. James, published by a member of the American Board."[28]

The work was urgently needed. "It is true that our native ministries, as well as ourselves, can prepare any passage of Scripture for a special occasion. But neither they nor the people can gain familiarity with scriptural allusions and language, which is so desirable for their spiritual advancement and edification. Their numbers now are becoming sufficiently large to make their right training a matter of great responsibility."[29]

The numbers of schools and churches gradually increased, and the numbers of missionaries rose to meet the opportunity. By 1855, the Episcopal mission had sixteen on its staff, and eleven new missionaries had been added by 1859. A sense of personal wonder accompanied their arrival. An earlier missionary, Edward Syle, had noted in a letter dated December 1845 and published in 1847 how moved he felt at receiving Communion for the first time on Chinese soil: "It is administered by

27. *Spirit of Missions* 16 (1851) 23–24, 40–52.

28. *Spirit of Missions* 26 (1861) 147.

29. *Spirit of Missions* 26 (1861) 147.

the Bishop at his own house on the afternoon of each first Sunday of the month, some of the foreign residents joining with us. At our last Communion seventeen were present."[30] A decade later the sense of wonder had increased. China seemed to open. By the late 1850s, the Episcopal mission had two Chinese deacons, Wong Kong-Chai and Tong Chu-Kiung. Newly arrived missionaries John Liggins and Channing Moore Williams, both recent Virginia Seminary graduates, "having a desire to preach the Gospel where it had not been heard, set out . . . on a journey to the interior. They went from place to place, distributing tracts and books, and delivering their message; they were kindly treated and their tracts and books were kindly received."[31] They had advanced ninety miles beyond Shanghai and seemingly used their newly learned Chinese to good effect.

Yet multiple challenges continued to burden missionary work. The second Chinese person ordained deacon, Tong Chu-Kiung, resigned his ordination and left the church in 1861 after only five years of service. Apparently, he sought greater income in a different profession in order to support his family.[32] In addition to short tenures, the deaths of missionaries and their spouses occurred with dismaying frequency. Edward Syle's wife died in 1859, and he left the mission in 1861. Phineas Spalding was lost at sea in 1849 after only two years' service. Cleveland Keith's wife died suddenly in 1862. Then, returning to China from the United States, he died at sea when fire consumed his vessel. The combination of early resignations and tragic deaths required constant efforts to recruit and train new missionaries, lay and ordained, as well as increased Chinese leadership in the mission church.

Two departures from the China mission signaled hope for expanded Episcopal work in Asia. In 1859, John Liggins and Channing Moore Williams moved to Japan to launch the Episcopal Church, what would later be known as the Nippon Sei Ko Kai. Each had been in China for three years, and though Liggins had persistent health issues, they had been an effective evangelistic team. As Japan opened to Western influences, Liggins and Williams faced basic challenges of proclaiming the faith and building the church. In an early report published in 1861, Williams commented that they needed an additional missionary who could aid in the translation of Scripture and the preparation of mission literature in

---

30. *Spirit of Missions* 12 (1847) 181.

31. Richmond, *American Episcopal Church in China*, 32, 41.

32. *Spirit of Missions* 26 (1861) 265.

Japanese. Clearly, he and Liggins were compelled to add Japanese to their linguistic repertoire. They did so with impressive facility.[33]

By 1875, when Williams submitted a report on the Japan mission, there had been notable change in one respect. In 1866, Williams had become bishop for Japan. But following Boone's death in 1864, Williams inherited Episcopal leadership for the China mission as well.[34] It was an impossible task. The result was that Episcopal mission in China received inadequate attention until the consecration of Samuel I. J. Schereschewsky as bishop there in 1877. He had already served as a missionary priest and had sparked improved efforts at translation of the Bible and church materials. He would renew those efforts as bishop. Before Williams assumed office, in his report for 1875, he wrote in regard to Japan that though there was not "any great increase in our numbers, still we find this field far more encouraging than ever before." There were indications "of a wide-spread interest in Christianity—a desire to hear the Gospel, study the Bible, and seek information such as we have never yet known." The "Spirit of God is working on the hearts of the people."[35]

In China, there also were signs of grassroots initiative and collaboration that would build the church—and not merely as an institution. But the seeds of church life continued to be planted. In 1873, Episcopal missionaries Robert Nelson and Elliott Thomson reported that they were working with an early Chinese ordinand, Huang Chin-hsia, to pastor two congregations at Shanghai and had extended this work to two new mission stations. There was renewed energy for the emphasis on education that Boone had encouraged, and four boarding schools were established at Shanghai. One was a boys' school under the vigorous leadership of Lydia Fay. Two other schools were created by Elliott Thomson and his wife, Jeanette. Fay and the Thomsons became enduring forces in the China mission, at times to the dismay of bishops.[36]

Periods of absent or distracted Episcopal leadership meant that advances in mission work came from below and often involved informal personal ties between the missionaries and sympathetic Chinese persons. Building the church was a grassroots effort. A substantive Episcopal identity was emerging.

33. Tucker, *History of the Episcopal Church in Japan*, 73–93.

34. Richmond, *American Episcopal Church in China*, 53.

35. *Spirit of Missions* 40 (1875) 712.

36. Lin, "Episcopal Missionaries in China," 184.

In her study of the first decades of the Episcopal mission in China, Mei-Mei Lin depicts leadership by bishops as often disorganized. The interregnum between Bishops Boone and Schereschewsky, when Williams provided nominal superintendence, was such a period. The tenure of Samuel I. J. Schereschewsky as bishop, from 1877 to 1883, proved little better.[37] It was a paradoxical time when centralized direction did not emerge. But he had already begun to make his mark in translation and extended that beginning. We sense a broader dynamic than merely unfocused leadership. Schereschewsky was not the leader who could secure pragmatic guidance for church development. Not until the consecration of Frederick R. Graves as bishop in 1893 would such leadership be secured. But even if they did not fulfill the demands of Episcopal office, Schereschewsky's translation efforts and the team he built to extend them offered a key basis from which an indigenous church could emerge. The translation team included four American clerical missionaries and one Chinese priest, Yen Yung-ching, who was emerging as a leader of the "native clergy." Having studied in America, apparently at Kenyon College, Yen became a mediating figure between the emerging Chinese clergy, the Chinese public, and Western missionaries.[38] Together with his American counterparts, Yen Yung-chin produced histories and catechisms with the intent of broadening the scope of missionary literature in Chinese. He epitomized Schereschewsky's intention of producing a Chinese Christian elite through the educational system of the Episcopal Church mission. Yen's influence broadened from the late 1860s onward as a Chinese missionary society, led by Chinese clergy, began to meet monthly. During Schereschewsky's tenure as bishop, there were nine new Chinese clergy, and by the time of his resignation, mission staff overall had grown to fifty-six. By 1890, the number of ordained Chinese men had jumped to thirty. Increasingly they would be educated for ministry in the theological department of St. John's College, founded at Shanghai in 1879 during Schereschewsky's time in office. At virtually the same time, the church's medical work coalesced under the leadership of Henry W. Boone, MD, a son of Bishop Boone. The Episcopal Church was finding Chinese footing and creating infrastructure needed for growth.

Yet it continued to be handicapped by leadership issues. When Schereschewsky retired from the episcopate, he remained for a time as

37. Lin, "Episcopal Missionaries in China," 156.
38. Lin, "Episcopal Missionaries in China," 230.

a missionary. William J. Boone—son of the first Bishop Boone—was his replacement, serving from 1884 to 1891.[39] He had already served as a missionary priest in China, starting in 1870. His brief episcopate was characterized by an effort to revive evangelism. In a sense, he strove to continue Schereschewsky's priorities. Thus, he sought to reinforce Episcopal authority, to more thoroughly institutionalize the mission's operations, and, above all, to expand the sphere of operations by conversions and extensions of educational and medical services. He presumed the instinct of his father that all aspects of mission work led ultimately to evangelism. But even as he worked to enhance the missionary role, he ran into conflict with some of the missionaries. One priest, William S. Sayres, who had arrived in 1878, worked to discredit Boone but was pressured to leave the mission and did so in 1886. Boone enhanced the place of St. John's College in the mission and encouraged the creation of new mission stations. But anti-Christian riots at the beginning of the 1890s, including threats near Shanghai, proved unsettling to the bishop's health. Boone died late in 1891.

From 1835 to 1900, Lin concludes, the Episcopal Church and its missionaries in China ignored contextual social and cultural realities. The mission board and the successive bishops envisioned the creation of a Christian commonwealth, one that would follow the presumptions of American culture and religious life. Distinctions in Chinese life were taken as impediments that were to be overcome. At the same time, missionaries lived in isolated cultural bubbles while neglecting "the impact of the western powers and their imperialist actions on the Chinese people. All [the missionaries] focused on were religious matters relating to the problems of location, language, and evangelization." It was an Asian analogue of the realities of mission in Liberia. Yet in both cases, the Episcopal Church put in place the ingredients of cosmopolitanism. Lin concludes that the first phase of mission succeeded in laying the groundwork for cultural dialogue.[40] There were even glimmers of such dialogue in Virginia.

39. Richmond, *American Episcopal Church in China*, 83.
40. Lin, "Episcopal Missionaries in China," 336–37.

PREPARING FOR CULTURAL DIALOGUE
AT VIRGINIA THEOLOGICAL SEMINARY

After the hostilities of the Civil War ended in 1865, the Episcopal Church tried to put fresh emphasis on mission. The nation was different, and the wounds of war were far from healed. The Episcopal Church launched domestic initiatives designed to address the needs of freed slaves. At the same time, periodic editorials and articles in the *Spirit of Missions* made wistful references both to the extent of need for mission and the lack of adequate initiative both domestically and abroad. Thus, in March 1869, an editorial headline declared "The Spirit of the Church of Christ Essentially a Missionary Spirit." This spirit, the text explained, "is an element of its original constitution, essential, vitally important to the completion of the glorious work for which Christ came into the world—the enlightenment and salvation of mankind."[41] It is notable that salvation and enlightenment, however the latter might be understood, went together. What we term "cosmopolitanism" would not seem far removed. Certainly, it would begin with a kind of enlightenment or awakening to the reality of difference.

The narrative continued by arguing that the church had revived its apostolic commission. It was a turning point when the Episcopal General Convention of 1835 declared itself a missionary body. More than the creation of an organization, this meant that the Episcopal Church granted "formal recognition of the primitive truths that she, as the Church of Christ, is essentially a Missionary Church," that the church and its members should "rise to the solemn responsibilities of her trust, to her whole duty in respect to God and the world."[42] The issue was a recurring one. Already, in August 1867, the *Spirit of Missions* had asked pointedly, "What Are Our Theological Seminaries Doing for the Heathen?" The editorial's response was not very encouraging. "The commencement exercises of our theological seminaries have recently closed, and each one has sent out a certain number of men to preach the Gospel." But, the editorial writer lamented, among the recent graduates "not one has offered himself . . . to preaching the Gospel to the heathen." It could not be denied that there were pressing domestic needs. The Civil War remained vivid, and its destruction was apparent. But "shall we neglect the heathen until there is nothing more to do at home?" The writer laid responsibility at the feet of Episcopal seminaries. "Are our theological seminaries doing their duty

41. *Spirit of Missions* 34 (1869) 162.
42. *Spirit of Missions* 34 (1869) 163.

to the heathen in this day of great opportunity? Do they cultivate the missionary spirit in those committed to their training, as the state of the world and their obligation to Christ demand?" With thinly veiled mention of Virginia Seminary and General Seminary, the writer added that the "seminaries that have cultivated most the missionary spirit among their students by maintaining missionary meetings and habitual prayer for the success of mission, have always furnished the greatest number of foreign missionaries."[43]

The number of foreign missionaries entering service from Virginia Seminary had dropped precipitously with only three responding to the call between 1860 and 1870. The reason was obvious: war forced closure of the seminary. During the war years, it served as a hospital for Union soldiers.[44] The reality was painful. On the eve of war, in the 1860–61 academic year, the seminary enrolled seventy-one students, its largest enrollment yet. Already its graduates had assumed prominent leadership roles in mission and in the church domestically. Notably, the seminary's student body included Northern as well as Southern students who parted quietly, Joseph Packard notes. Faculty dispersed, Packard going to stay in Fauquier County, Virginia, west of Washington and Alexandria.[45] There was a brief effort to relocate the seminary to Staunton, Virginia, farther west, but little came of the effort. Virginia became one of the war's principal battlegrounds. Sheer movement, as Packard noted, could require passing through the lines of warring armies. The memories of those linked to the seminary spoke of war's horror. Their words reflect sorrow at the disruption of their lives and of the society they had known.

But that society, so readily praised by seminary faculty, had presumed the existence of slavery. Human beings could possess other human beings as chattel. There were enslaved persons on the Virginia Seminary campus, and faculty members William Sparrow and Joseph Packard relied upon their labors. It is also noteworthy that Bishop William Meade had spoken against slavery and been a founding member of the American Colonization Society with the romanticized and flawed idea of ameliorating slavery. Yet Meade was a segregationist who harbored a patronizing racism. Several historians note that Meade referred to Black people as

43. *Spirit of Missions* 32 (1867) 594.

44. Booty, *Mission and Ministry*, 109.

45. Packard, *Recollections*, 277.

"the most amiable race of savages which I believe exists on earth."[46] It is also worth commenting that Meade did not oppose the state of Virginia's secession to the Confederacy or the hostilities that resulted. The Confederacy argued that secession was the only means with which to defend a noble way of Southern life against the intrusions of the Northern states. However, this was a smokescreen obscuring moral truth.

There is no disputing the fact that a particular way of life linked the Southern states. The glaring reality was that slavery figured prominently in the patterns of Southern life, socially, economically, and religiously. Historian Jennifer Oast does not describe the situation at Virginia Seminary per se. However, she assesses the ways in which slavery functioned at several educational institutions in the state of Virginia up to the eve of the Civil War. From our contemporary perspective, it is remarkable just how unremarkable slavery seemed to white Southerners, even as hostilities loomed. Oast argues that the College of William and Mary created a paradigm that was widely replicated. Many slaves "spent their lives working for and belonging to William and Mary from its founding to the Civil War. They did many kinds of work at the college, from keeping the buildings clean and maintaining the grounds, to cooking and serving the students meals, to nursing sick students and running errands for them in town."[47] It was typical that an educational institution such as William and Mary, and other similar institutions in Virginia, would speak of themselves as "family," but this ideal was flawed. Some human beings were not willing participants, however "amiable" they may have appeared. It appears that such an outlook characterized the Virginia Seminary "family."

The writings of Joseph Packard and William Sparrow make scant reference to their social assumptions. Sparrow spoke briefly and in a patronizing tone: "We have dealt hardly with the poor Indian and Negro," he observed in 1855 in a letter to a former student.[48] Notably the letter's recipient was E. W. Syle, by then a missionary in China. Sparrow drew a telling comparison between Chinese people, with whom he had no contact, and Native Americans and African Americans. "I hope we shall not push the poor Chinese to the wall in the same way. Some restrictions on their political, if not their civil and social interests, may, for aught I know, be indispensable for a little time, but I hope nothing of that kind

46. Booty, *Mission and Ministry*, 89.

47. Oast, *Institutional Slavery*, 127.

48. Walker, *Life of William Sparrow*, 225.

will be permanent, or in the slightest degree interfere with the general progress and improvement of the race. A semi-civilized people ought to be so dealt with that they will soon become a wholly civilized people."[49]

Sparrow's perspective sheds important light not simply on racism but on widely held views about the purpose of mission, domestically and abroad. By the middle of the nineteenth century, mission meant more than evangelism for many American Christians. It entailed the cultural imperialism necessary to uplift various races and peoples. Implicit in Sparrow's words, and increasingly explicit in missionary literature until well into the twentieth century, was a presumed hierarchy of development. White, Western people presumed to be at the pinnacle of development. Asian people, especially in China and Japan, represented cultural advance but hardly completion. Missionary fascination with East Asia, including at Virginia Seminary, was wrapped up with the project of completing Asia's historic cultures by converting them to the Christian faith. It would not be uncommon to imagine how they would function as Christian nations. On the other hand, though missionary work in Africa intended to uplift cultures, the task was viewed as a steeper climb, and white religious leaders held out even less hope for the improvement of non-white people in America. Worse, Black people in particular had been used to create a social system that oppressed them and which most white people avidly defended.

The Civil War's conclusion, following on the heels of the Emancipation Proclamation, did not bring immediate change to life on the campus of Virginia Seminary. The centennial history includes reminiscences of several former students. For example, William Dame recalled his arrival in 1866, having traveled with another entering student, Charles Clifton Penick, who would subsequently become the third Episcopal bishop in Liberia. Dame recalled being fondly greeted by the seminary's matron, an unmarried, white woman who managed student housing. They also met "Uncle Nathan, the good old darky who cleaned the rooms and toted water to students for so many generations." Nathan, no family name given, also "fixed up our rooms with the simple furniture, proper to the time." By other accounts Nathan provided firewood as well as water and was expected to respond to all such needs. He was hardly emancipated.[50]

---

49. Walker, *Life of William Sparrow*, 226.
50. Dame, "Reminiscences," 452.

Even in an atmosphere of prejudice, a glimmer of future cosmopolitanism could be discerned. Another faculty member, James May, clearly differentiated himself from the mindset that justified slavery. Around 1850 and 1851, three Liberian students arrived at Virginia Seminary for studies, their presence facilitated by John Payne. May housed the students and served as their mentor. Scant details of their presence remain, apart from a few warm mentions by May. Their stay was singular. No other international students came until the second half of the nineteenth century. But May was a warm supporter of foreign missions, encouraging students to consider such a vocation and remaining in contact with some when they took missionary roles. He was the primary faculty advisor to the Missionary Society for several years.[51]

As war neared, May had no doubts about its cause or his course. While "colleagues at the Seminary, swept by the influences of the hour, were floating Southward," May moved north to Philadelphia. "In all his nineteen Seminary years, great as was sometimes the difficulty of obtaining 'help,' he would not *own*, nor, if he possibly could help it, *hire* a slave." The point is driven home. "The training of his childhood had made slavery distasteful to him. Long contact with it had left that distaste unremoved." May was "content to dwell amidst it quietly," but when war approached, "he could not find it in his heart to take its side." He loved the seminary and "was grateful for [its] kindness to him," but could not endorse slavery or secession to preserve it. Nor could he tolerate defense of slavery by religious leaders. May's last essay, written in 1863 just before his death, offered biting criticism of an Episcopal bishop who used the Bible to defend chattel slavery.[52] May's views were isolated for Virginia Seminary at the time. But further development in the ideals and outcomes of mission encouraged cosmopolitan sensibilities.

51. Shiras, *Life and Letters of James May*, 82.
52. Shiras, *Life and Letters of James May*, 84, 98.

5

Fostering Social Aspirations

THE CHURCH TAKING ROOT

THE CIVIL WAR HAD a devastating impact on American life. It also adversely affected the foreign missions of the Episcopal Church. Contributions to support mission shrank significantly, and recruitment of mission personnel largely stopped during the war years. As in any organizational crisis, there were also less obvious aspects that would become apparent in the second half of the nineteenth century. One was a broadly obsessive focus on developing the church as an institution by missionaries and those who trained and supported them. On the one hand, it could be argued that, like other denominations, the Episcopal Church resolved to heighten the effectiveness of its mission work. It could also be argued that the creation of institutional forms bespoke greater emphasis on Western control. We shall find evidence of both outcomes as missionaries renewed their efforts in Liberia, China, and Japan. More than before the Civil War, Virginia Seminary and its alumni assumed large roles as a new missionary ambitiousness took hold.

While missionaries resolved to secure their work in terms of institutions and their intended effectiveness, the new Christians nurtured by mission began to advance their own priorities. In the contexts where our attention is focused, mission would be measured less by institutional effectiveness and certainly not by heightened Western control. Rather, as one emerging leader after another articulated, the church in its new contexts must reflect a cultural imprint that was not obscured by Western influence. As we shall see, a fascinating consensus was emerging between missionaries and the young churches they were encouraging. Both Western and indigenous voices were intent upon building the church and proclaiming the Christian faith. From both perspectives, the Christian faith needed to shape rather than ignore the various aspects of social life. In other words, there was complete agreement on the urgency of building indigenous churches reflective of Episcopal mission and on the emphasis these young churches should give to the social aspirations of their flocks.

But missionaries and converts took decidedly different pathways toward the same goal. The nature and outcomes of this divergence will become clear in this chapter. We will show that, as mission churches grew, missionaries devoted their energies to critiques of new Christians and their young churches. In effect, such critiques reflected missionary efforts at control, even as missionary ambitions grew. The idea of creating Christian civilizations, not simply clusters of converts and congregations, flowered among missionaries in the nineteenth century. Conversely, the growth of mission churches prompted first-generation Christians to seek indigenous Christianity on their own terms. As indigenous voices surfaced, they sought to build self-directed forms of church life. Missionaries tried to direct such efforts, creating a dynamic that would characterize mission life until well into the twentieth century. Such debate over the shape of the indigenous church created a conversation that fostered cosmopolitan ties.

In the wake of civil war, Episcopal missionaries began to regroup by deepening their personal devotion and redoubling their focus on basic evangelism and Christian commitment. In 1877, Charles Clifton Penick was elected bishop of Liberia by the Episcopal Church and soon went to assume his duties there. Penick had not previously served in Liberia. Born in 1843 in Charlotte County, Virginia, Penick attended Hampden-Sydney College before joining the Confederate Army's quartermaster corps when civil war broke out. He resumed his education at war's end, graduating from Virginia Seminary in 1869. First ordained deacon shortly thereafter, he was ordained priest in 1870. Both ordinations were held in the seminary chapel. Only seven years later, he was consecrated as missionary bishop to Liberia, the liturgy being held at St. Paul's Church, Alexandria.[1] In other words, Penick was illustrative of Virginia Seminary's life as the church emerged from conflict.

1. White, "Two Bishops," 479.

Penick's diary from his years in Liberia is a moving, daily record of spiritual devotion. On January 1, 1879, for example, he recorded a solemn prayer, asking God to grant that the new year would "bring no more of strain and demand no more of me than any other year has done. . . . I pray for more purity of heart, holiness of life, joy of faith. May I care less for earth's opinion. I know that earth can neither give nor take away glory from me. True glory consists in the estimates God puts on me, only relation to him." His diary mingled devotion with reflections on his duties as bishop, including addressing human foibles. On February 1, 1879, Penick wrote that he had celebrated communion while another missionary had preached. He revealed that even amid a liturgy, he was "much exercised over Rogers. Poor fellow has committed adultery. What are we to do in such?" Penick devoted more ink to theological reflection than to possible responses. "God's church stands for a testimony of God's character. But alas how we often lack courage to Christian will, to openly shun this sin against Him."[2]

Penick even recorded bits of his dreams, consistently infused with sheepish feelings of personal failings that were bolstered by assurances of God's grace. His faith was earnestly, profoundly evangelical, and he approached his role in mission on this basis. Thus, he focused the Episcopal mission on evangelism and education. He presumed to be building the church from the ground up, continuing the missionary emphasis on directing affairs that began with the arrival of the first Episcopal missionaries four decades earlier. Unfortunately, Penick's health suffered in the Liberian climate. He returned to the United States in 1882 and resigned as bishop in 1883.

Fortunately, Penick recovered sufficiently to live three more decades, during which he had an active ministry. Tellingly, he worked for the evangelization and education of freed slaves and their children. In effect, Penick continued the philosophy of his work in Liberia and of the colonization movement, of which he was a supporter. Sadly, he retained the flawed logic of race relations that permeated the defeated Confederate states. On the one hand, he wanted to enhance the Episcopal Church's "colored work." On the other hand, he based such work in a justification of white racial superiority and a defense of segregation. His writings reveal racist stereotypes that were framed by patronizing calls for remedial

2. Penick, papers, box 3.

action. Penick held that African American people should have their own sphere, one that could require a new phase of removal to Africa.

Penick even offered paeans of praise for the Confederacy, especially for its principal military figure, Robert E. Lee. On the one hundredth anniversary of Lee's birth in 1907, Penick published an ode of pious admiration. He described Lee as sent by God "with a mighty mission." Lee was "a noble statue of glorified manhood," whose life was "so true to our loftiest ideals of greatness, grandness, gloriousness, and God." Penick lamented "the agonies of a dying civilization" and the "sorrows of his broken-hearted people, dying with the agonies of their crushed ideals." Yet "the manhood of this man revealed far beyond the Confederacy, and its power is laying stronger and stronger hold upon the lives of men everywhere as the struggle deepens." Penick proved to be a devotee of the "lost cause," the perpetuation of ideals derived from the defeated Confederacy—including that of racial discrimination. Penick signed this article not as a cleric, but as a member of "38 Va. Regt., Pickett's Division, Army of Northern Virginia."[3]

If Penick's convictions and his ministries were defined by the past and its mistaken social ideals, the ideals and pursuits of his successor as bishop of Liberia were decisively different. In 1885, Samuel David Ferguson was chosen by the Episcopal House of Bishops to succeed Penick. Although Penick advanced Ferguson to the role of business agent of the Cape Palmas Missionary District, and although Penick became president of Liberia's diocesan standing committee, he did not participate in Ferguson's consecration as bishop. Whatever the explanation for Penick's absence, Ferguson represented a decisive break from Penick's outlook and missionary strategy.[4]

Personally, Ferguson was a product of colonization. An African American man who had been born in South Carolina, he came to Liberia with his family at the age of six in 1848. Upon his elevation to the episcopate, Ferguson focused on developing indigenous clergy for the church in Liberia. He made fundraising trips to the United States and saw the link to America as crucial to Liberian development. Ferguson was successful in generating American support, but he channeled that support into creating a church that was simultaneously distant from the tenets of the Confederacy and unconstrained by white American views on racial relations. It

3. Penick, papers, box 3.
4. White, "Two Bishops," 481.

would be wrong to assume that Penick's Southern piety was widespread among Episcopalians. It was a white House of Bishops that had appointed Ferguson to the episcopacy. It also appears that Ferguson's impetus to create an indigenous Liberian leadership was received well in America.

Ferguson's intention had precedent. Like Eli Stokes and Alexander Crummell, he built upon the yearning for a nationalist identity.[5] Crummell had declared that the Episcopal Church could have special appeal and give distinctive response to the needs of ordinary Liberians. Ferguson's tenure of thirty-one years, and his timely emphasis upon an indigenous church, advanced Episcopal life. It is not simplistic to say that while Penick reverenced the past, Ferguson looked to the future. Donations from American Episcopalians financed school and church construction in eight Liberian locations. The crowning achievement was the founding of what is now Cuttington University College in 1889. Ferguson died in 1916.[6]

A key measure of becoming indigenous, woven through Ferguson's work, was the goal of "self-support." That is, the mission church aspired to achieve its own internal leadership and resources. The idea originated with Henry Venn, who served as secretary of the Church Missionary Society in England from 1841 to his death in 1873. By the time of his death, "self-support" had become widely acknowledged as the intention of mission and was echoed in the United States by Rufus Anderson, Venn's counterpart in the American Board of Commissioners for Foreign Missions. It is not surprising that Ferguson would envision "self-support" as the Liberian church's goal. Yet this intention did not entail suspension of relations with the Episcopal Church. Something similar played out in Japan. The urge to build an indigenous church emerged there as it unfolded in Liberia.

In the May 1887 issue of the *Spirit of Missions*, Henry D. Page noted the "Organization of the Church in Japan." A graduate of Virginia Seminary in the class of 1882, Page detailed the recent six-day conference in Osaka to discuss proposed constitution and canons. The Episcopal mission in Japan was transitioning into a Japanese church, albeit with a Western template and missionary direction. At the time, the major achievement appeared to be the surprising collaboration between missionaries of the Church of England and those from the Episcopal Church.

5. Yarsiah, *Early Missionary Work*, 91.
6. White, "Two Bishops," 484.

Tension, especially disputes over which mission controlled which jurisdiction, seemed eclipsed. A design process began and, though envisioned
carefully, revealed shortcomings. The committee which prepared drafts
of the constitution and canons sent copies to the various mission stations
for approval by missionaries who had not participated in the drafting.
Drafts also were sent to church authorities in America and England.[7]

"Still, the missionary body as a whole had not yet met to discuss
them," Page reported. Worse, "the Japanese had not considered them at
all." In other words, the American and English missionaries had failed
to consult the people for whom the church organization was ostensibly
being created. Fault lines began to appear among the missionaries:

> Certain brethren on the English side of the house . . . took a
> very pessimistic view of the whole matter, considering that
> the time was not yet ripe for such a movement, and at any rate
> the present temper of the Japanese was such that the proposed
> plan was sure to be materially modified, and perhaps so flatly
> rejected as not even to be taken by them into serious consider-
> ation. Most of us were hopeful, but with a hope dashed with a
> good deal of apprehension.[8]

An "us and them" outlook emerged, fueled by Western presumption.

When the conference met to consider the proposed organization of
a Japanese church, missionaries in attendance were struck by the readiness of the Japanese leaders present to gather separately. As Henry Page
noted, Japanese delegates at first met in prayer as the Western delegates
deliberated. Page was struck by the spiritual emphasis. "It is fine to see
how thoroughly these Japanese, who but a few years ago were without
God or hope in the world, realize that this God is their God, and how
very near at hand for all that they call upon Him for." He sensed that
the Japanese wanted "a truly national and comprehensive Church, which
shall include so far as possible all the baptized followers of Christ."[9] It
was possible to imagine a form of Christian unity in Japan that seemed
impossible in the West.

However, as drafts of the church's canons and constitution were
debated by Western individuals, the Japanese delegation unexpectedly
asked to raise questions about certain points. Prayer had been followed

7. Page, "Organization of the Church in Japan," 186.
8. Page, "Organization of the Church in Japan," 186.
9. Page, "Organization of the Church in Japan," 187.

by discussion among the Japanese persons present. One Japanese man posed the key question directly, albeit without hint of confrontation: "Were these canons, etc., prepared only for those churches and congregations which were dependent upon the missions?"[10] Apparently, the man posing this question belonged to a congregation that did not rely upon missionary resources. Page noted that three men from St. Paul's Church, Osaka, were present. They were clear that the proposed church structures did not appear to benefit them.

The point could not be ignored. It was a question that pointed to the intended indigenous character of the church and its capacity for "self-support." Seemingly, there was momentary surprise and awkwardness in the meeting. But missionary intentions and processes were only briefly delayed. Page records that most Japanese delegates felt a continued need for reliance upon missionary guidance and resources. This was a memorable point. The timing may not have been right, but the Japanese branch of the Episcopal Church was headed toward defining and directing its own identity. As in Liberia, missionaries were not in theoretical disagreement. But an indigenous, self-supporting church would advance in ways and toward intentions that defied missionary imagination or control. Over time, the conversation about the nature of an indigenous church would advance. With that conversation would come a welcome cosmopolitan sensibility. But such consensus, though hinted at, proved elusive at first. All concerned wanted the church to take root. What that meant and how that would happen required elucidation. Virginia Seminary would become central to this conversation.

ASIA'S APPEAL

In the spring of 1883, Elliott Thomson published an article on the "Extension of Mission Work in China." A graduate of Virginia Seminary in 1859, Thomson was considered the senior Episcopal priest in China at that time and capped his career as archdeacon there. His assessment was blunt. There had been much initial romance about mission in China for over four decades. Then, reality set in—China was "a field of hard work." Thomson noted the extent of idolatry as he saw it in historic Chinese religions. But groundbreaking Christian mission had occurred and there were reasons to be hopeful:

10. Page, "Organization of the Church in Japan," 187.

> It remains now to be seen whether the Church will press for-
> ward with zeal or let the work drag on, barely holding its own.
> In twenty-five years more, if she presses on with that zeal, ear-
> nestness and love which so great a work for so great a Saviour
> demands, she may expect to have by that time a native Church
> with a native Ministry largely, if not entirely, self-sustained. The
> present is not the time for a close-handed policy.[11]

Importantly, Thomson knew that the goal of a "native Church" required
an elaborate strategy, one that went beyond previous efforts.[12]

> What system shall we adopt in pressing forward? We have
> passed beyond the day of mere rudiments. We have most of
> the necessary institutions for advance—Day-schools, Training-
> schools, College, Theological School, Female Seminary, Medical
> schools, with Christian Hospitals; but above all a rapidly in-
> creasing native Ministry. Only one instrumentality needs yet to
> be added, and that is the organized training of women of mature
> age for work among women. This want is seen and felt, and that
> is enough to have it shortly supplied.[13]

Presciently, Thomson had identified not merely what was needed
but how the further development of mission would unfold. The basic
work of evangelism would continue. Gradually, the church's Chinese
clergy would continue to develop. Yet the church's principal public identity would be education as well as social service. These two efforts would
be construed as the arms of evangelism, but they were but the beginning
of a grander project. An ambitious goal was surfacing in China and in
Japan. Among the missionaries of various confessions, it seemed possible
to cultivate a Christian civilization in east Asia. An emphasis on basic
evangelism would never disappear. However, the appeal of mission in
Asia centered on this civilization-building vision. It was imagined that
through education especially a new generation of leaders, responsive
to Christian tenets and the church if not personally converted to them,
could be groomed. In business, the professions, and lay leadership in the
church, Christian influence could begin to permeate society.

By 1884, the numbers of those touched by mission institutions were
not great, but they were growing. St. John's College, Shanghai, enrolled
seventy-five boarding students, and St. Mary's Hall enrolled forty-two.

11. Thomson, "Extension of Mission Work in China," 290.

12. Thomson, "Extension of Mission Work in China," 290.

13. Thomson, "Extension of Mission Work in China," 290–91.

There were four theological students. Yet there were thirty-three day schools and forty-nine teachers, thirty-seven of whom were Chinese. There were also three Chinese priests and eight deacons, ten candidates for holy orders and six Chinese catechists.[14] The numbers trended upward, even as the numbers of converts fell below even modest expectations. The romance of mission had passed and may have been "an article of home manufacture" as one missionary put it. But a new vision was apparent, and as the end of the nineteenth century neared, that vision had been clarified.

"We bear three relations to the Chinese, political, commercial, and religious," Episcopal clerical missionary Sidney C. Partridge wrote in 1895. He did not believe the Chinese culture possessed comprehensive truth. Despite their Confucian ethics and Buddhist practice, they lived in darkness. Through the church and faith in Christ, China could find comprehensive truth. It seemed obvious to missionaries. China and Japan represented advanced, ancient civilizations. Christianity could complete them, uniting disparate systems into a whole. Partridge's mention of politics and commerce was no passing reference. Their unity could occur through mission schools where more than religion would be appropriated. Church schools, especially St. John's College, would equip Chinese teachers, including young women. Through the church, a new China would be created.[15]

Also in 1895, when St. John's College celebrated the opening of new buildings on campus, the address of Bishop Frederick Graves made plain the role of education in mission. The college and all church schools offered a meeting ground for the Chinese people and foreigners such as missionaries. Graves's declaration made cosmopolitanism a more apparent goal. The college had won public standing, he added. It should be plain that foreigners had come to benefit China.[16] His conviction was earnest. But it begged the question: what sorts of relations should characterize the missionary presence, and how long should that presence last? At what point would the mission church become sufficiently self-supporting in the estimation of indigenous people versus the scrutiny of the missionaries? The question was obsessively posed. It touched the heart of Episcopal

14. "Report of the Foreign Committee—China," 605–8.
15. Partridge, "Our Mission in China," 14.
16. *Spirit of Missions* 60 (1895) 144.

mission and, in fact, was evidence of both numerical growth and the rise of mission's social influence.

As Frederick Graves broached the question in China, Theodosius Tyng posed it for the Episcopal mission in Japan. In an article published in April 1895, Tyng addressed "The Kind of Workers Needed in the Mission." The matter of foreign control versus indigenous direction came into focus. "The foreign clergy count year by year for less and less, the Japanese for more and more," he concluded. "The Christian Church is even now the only part of the national life where foreigners have a controlling influence of any kind, and it is necessary that the foreign control which still remains should pass away as speedily as possible if the Church is to have the confidence of the nation."[17] The vision of Christian civilization required the surrender of control, a difficult realization for many missionaries. But no wholesale withdrawal was in the offing. In the short term, more, not fewer, foreign workers were needed. There were too few Japanese clergy, Tyng reasoned. There also were many places where basic evangelism was needed. Out of basic evangelism would come the sorts of social services that would solidify individual lives and the nation as a whole. Thus, in order to eliminate control of the indigenous church by foreigners, more foreigners were needed.

In 1896, discussions at the Second Conference of the Chinese Mission provided interesting glimpses of missionary strategy. A paper on medical work by E. M. Merrins, MD, linked the basic goals of mission to health care. The conference discussed not only evangelism, but the goal of a "native, self-supporting, self-propagating, self-governing Church."

> To accomplish this is the work of the clergy, but to assist them to reach the people, and as part of the work of the Church in caring for the physical and intellectual as well as the spiritual nature of man, we establish schools and hospitals. If, as the result of medical treatment, men and women are persuaded to listen favorably to the truths of Christianity, if later they forsake heathenism and enter the Church, then medical work is a complete success; if it does not accomplish this, no matter how effective it may be in other ways, considered simply as a part of Christian mission work, it does not reach the end desired.[18]

17. Tyng, "Kind of Workers Needed in Mission," 149–50.
18. "Second Conference of the Chinese Mission," 271.

Thus, the goal was apparent and consistent. As a subsequent commentary observed, "In the far East, stirred to its depths by the events of the past few years, we seek to show to China and Japan that the Faith of Christ is the secret of all that is true and beautiful and good in that modern Christian civilization which they so admire and in so many ways are trying to imitate."[19] The churches hoped to build on widespread fascination with all things Western. The point was made repeatedly but with a consistent note of missionary caution. No wholesale embrace of Western ways was intended. Especially in relation to church schools, there was discussion of discipline and of "the institution of bounds." Students could acquire greater privileges in school life as their deportment and academic achievement advanced. As the numbers of persons baptized and enrolled in schools increased, the theme of discipline gained prominence. Neither uncalculated church growth nor uninhibited immersion in Western culture was advisable.

This theme surfaced even on the most somber occasions. In 1903, James Addison Ingle, who had been bishop of Hankow in China for little more than a year, died of fever at the age of thirty-six. It was a tragic loss of an energetic leader. Educated at the University of Virginia and Virginia Theological Seminary, where he graduated in 1891, Ingle went almost immediately to China.[20] In eulogizing Ingle, F. L. Hawks Pott, president of St. John's College, reiterated the turn mission had taken: "From the first he grasped the idea that, if the Church were to grow in China, it must grow according to the laws which are laid down for us in the New Testament. It must be a self-propagating, self-discipling, and a self-maintaining Church."[21]

Pott emphasized that Ingle devoted much of his time to "educating and energizing and spiritualizing his native assistants." He "poured all his life's strength out upon them—upon molding their characters, and developing their minds. He soon showed them that he was their friend; treated them as his equals, brought them into his house and to his table and took counsel with them in every matter of importance."[22] Ingle, Pott added, was intent on training Chinese clergy and catechists. The missionary record was increasingly attentive not simply to numbers of people

---

19. "Second Conference of the Chinese Mission," 271.

20. Richmond, *American Episcopal Church in China*, 118.

21. Pott, "Bishop Ingle," 11.

22. Pott, "Bishop Ingle," 13.

converted or enrolled, to numbers of churches and schools built, but to actual encounters between missionaries and those they sought to convert. Moreover, Western ears were beginning to listen for the first time to what indigenous people were telling them. As early as 1897, the *Spirit of Missions* published an elaborate account of the life's journey of a Japanese deacon, Masakazu Tai. He recalled that, leading up to his baptism in 1876, he had devoted "three years" to "carefully and earnestly investigating Christianity." He went on to write: "In those three years my inward man was completely changed, and after I was baptized I could not keep the truth and way of salvation to myself."[23]

Tai spoke candidly and with vivid imagery about giving up his former life to become a Christian. "It is a hard thing for a man to give up his old home . . . Such is . . . the condition of mind of the people when thinking about becoming Christians and giving up the old belief." Many Japanese people saw Christianity as an evil sect, Tai continued. When he converted, his family and old friends abandoned him. "I was told afterwards that when I became a Christian my people held a family council and were going to imprison me in one of the rooms of the house. Such was not my case only; many a son was denounced by his parents and other relations; many a man lost his good position; many a wife was divorced."[24] Tai's account was notable not only for the personal pain he disclosed, but for the very fact that he disclosed it at all—and in a Western publication, at that. Indigenous people were beginning to speak, and missionaries in particular were beginning to listen.

We have described listening as the doorway to cosmopolitanism. Now we are able to illustrate how Episcopal missionaries began to listen, even as they were drawn overseas by the desire to make conversions. Evangelism, and the educational and social services that unfolded from it, focused on speaking in ways designed to captivate indigenous peoples. By the late nineteenth century, missionaries also had begun to listen in ways that extended the agenda with which they had arrived. The experience of Henry St. George Tucker offers a fascinating view of how a missionary was able to cultivate the ability to listen in another culture, even as the dynamics of conversion framed the encounter. Tucker was a graduate of Virginia Theological Seminary in the class of 1899, and it must be noted that his life was exceptional from his young adulthood onward. His

23. Tai, "Report," 318.
24. Tai, "Report," 318.

family produced various Episcopal clergy and even bishops, and his own life followed in this direction. Tucker received BA and MA degrees from the University of Virginia, giving him more prior education than most of his seminary classmates. It should be noted that his intention to serve in mission was not unique. The ship that carried him to Japan listed various missionaries as passengers, including five Virginia Seminary graduates.[25]

Eventually, Tucker would become bishop of Kyoto before resigning in 1922 to enable Japanese leadership of the Japanese church, a rare step at the time. He would join the Virginia Seminary faculty before serving as bishop of Virginia and, from 1938 to 1946, presiding bishop of the Episcopal Church.[26] But his more than twenty years of mission service in Japan prove notable in part because they were the predominant subject of his memoirs. He chose to highlight his maturation and tenure in Japan over his later achievements. Apparently, he regarded his time as a missionary as his most significant work. This emphasis makes the development of his capacity to listen all the more important.

Tucker began his tenure in Japan as all missionaries did—in language study. Once sufficiently grounded, he was sent to evangelistic duties. In January 1901, John McKim, bishop of the Episcopal mission, assigned Tucker to work under W. F. Madeley, who was in charge of the Episcopal presence in Sendai, 250 miles north of Tokyo.[27] On his arrival, Tucker learned that the ten Christian missions there totaled slightly over sixteen hundred people, despite Sendai having long been a site of mission activity. Tucker mused that the Greek mission drew more response than others because "through its educational institutions [this mission] was able to make contact with the element in the population which was most responsive to the Christian message." Making contact with Japanese people became Tucker's preoccupation.

In part, he made connections by deepening his ability to speak. On March 31, 1901, Tucker gave his first sermon in Japanese. He assessed his effort apologetically: "Of course it was translated, that is, I wrote it first in English and then with the help of my teacher translated it into Japanese. Although I do not know how much of what I read the congregation understood, it is at least encouraging to me to make a beginning of preaching to them in their own language." To preach in Japanese was one thing,

25. Tucker, *Exploring the Silent Shore of Memory*, 34.

26. Tucker, *Exploring the Silent Shore of Memory*, 170, 288.

27. Tucker, *Exploring the Silent Shore of Memory*, 61.

but he also needed to learn how to listen, usually in gatherings that were novel for him. Tucker spoke of attending prayer meetings which had the "atmosphere of a family gathering. The conversation is interspersed with prayers, very unliturgical in their form, sounding like remarks addressed to the head of a family group by its members, naturally and freely expressed but at the same time perfectly reverent."[28]

Evangelism defined all aspects of Tucker's work, from the small gatherings just described to occasional, mass "evangelistic meetings." He desired to cultivate more than momentary assent to the Christian faith. "If our work was to be of any real and lasting value, we had to domesticate Christianity so that it could become an integral part of their everyday life as Japanese."[29] His appreciation of Japanese people deepened over the next two years, the result of his extended contact with those "whose native characteristics were not obscured by a superficial layer of undigested westernism."[30] The emphasis was shifting from speaking to listening, then to learning and seeing in a more substantive way:

> From this experience I learned to some degree at least to understand their points of view, their reactions to various circumstances, the real meaning that lay behind their outward way of expressing themselves. When later it became my lot to work among students in Tokyo, this understanding assisted me greatly in presenting western and Christian ideas to them in such a way that they could be assimilated instead of being swallowed whole and retained in their Japanese system as an indigestible foreign element. In return for my understanding they gave me their confidence.[31]

Tucker cut through stereotypes about Japanese peoples as "mysterious orientals" and grasped "the real meaning that is intended to be conveyed to us."[32] The presentation of Christianity in Japanese culture entailed a mutual opening of eyes and even of missionaries gaining deeper insights on their own faith. The process of becoming faithful could even be seen as a mutual journey, one that crossed languages and cultures.

Further extension of his contacts among the Japanese people became Tucker's focus. He started an informal English language school and

28. Tucker, *Exploring the Silent Shore of Memory*, 65.
29. Tucker, *Exploring the Silent Shore of Memory*, 69.
30. Tucker, *Exploring the Silent Shore of Memory*, 69.
31. Tucker, *Exploring the Silent Shore of Memory*, 70.
32. Tucker, *Exploring the Silent Shore of Memory*, 70.

extended these classes to a nearby Japanese army base. He moved to a new Japanese-style house, persuading his landlord to allow glass for paper in the sliding doors. The landlord allowed the further concession of a wood stove in one of the rooms. Even so, the Japanese-style home allowed Tucker to entertain various Japanese guests more on their terms than on his own. "They would almost forget that I was a foreigner. The removal of this barrier was a great help in promoting mutual understanding and in enabling me to win their confidence."[33] Evangelism remained the goal, but mutual understanding framed the intention. He also extended his reading in older as well as more recent Japanese literature. "The real benefit that I derived was a greater understanding of the aims and methods of the men who played the chief part in directing the development of modern Japan."[34] His ability to build ties with those whom he met gained nuance.

His own theological framework shifted in the process. The Christian doctrine of the incarnation became the subject of intense study. As Japanese Christians matured in their faith, Tucker hoped that the idea of incarnation would become a guiding star, one which enabled converts to retain their culture while embracing newfound faith. His realization of this avenue to faith development "was a real turning point in my missionary career. While I never became a theological expert," the ever-apologetic Tucker added, "at least I was able, as a result of this study, to be of some help in removing the barriers to belief on the part of the educated Japanese with whom in later years I was brought into contact."[35] The art of mission centered on contact, prompting ongoing and mutual growth in faith. The term "cosmopolitan" does not appear in Tucker's lexicon, but the process of encountering, listening, understanding, sharpening, and revising bespoke an unfolding cosmopolitan sensibility.

The process Tucker described was not uniquely his own. Perhaps he considered his own development more closely and more insightfully than many of his missionary colleagues. But others gained similar sensibility. Even when he was no longer an actual guide, Tucker would prove to be something of an example as an evangelist, teacher, and bishop. His abilities in these efforts certainly reflected the learning that shaped him once he arrived in Japan. But in what sense did his earlier seminary years prepare him? Was his time overseas simply a break with his American

33. Tucker, *Exploring the Silent Shore of Memory*, 79.

34. Tucker, *Exploring the Silent Shore of Memory*, 82.

35. Tucker, *Exploring the Silent Shore of Memory*, 83.

education, or was he in some sense formed for mission during his years as a seminarian? What role did Virginia Seminary play for Tucker and for others in their preparation for mission, and even for the awakening of cosmopolitanism?

WHAT MANNER OF FORMATION

In the fall of 1877, Arthur Selden Lloyd entered Virginia Theological Seminary. He had graduated from what is now Virginia Tech in 1875, then studied briefly at the University of Virginia. His decision to enter the ministry was carefully considered even though he was raised in a deeply religious family. His mother ensured that Lloyd heard lessons from the Bible and recited prayers from the Book of Common Prayer. In other words, he was a product of Virginia's evangelical Episcopal identity, harkening back to the faith and practice of Bishop Meade and his peers. A Calvinist theological framework was balanced with an emphasis on Christ's sacrificial death. Those who believed in Christ's revelation of God's love found a pathway to salvation that was open to all. As Lloyd's biographer observes, "Salvation was due solely to the unspeakable mercy of God who saw fit to save . . . because of Christ's sacrifice [as] it was appropriated solely by faith; and faith must issue in a life of austere righteousness."[36]

But, Lloyd's biographer adds, the theology which defined Virginia Seminary at the time caused Lloyd and others to face "a hard struggle." It is an especially candid admission because Lloyd's biographer was Alexander C. Zabriskie. As he told Lloyd's story, Zabriskie was the dean of Virginia Seminary. He also was professor of church history and a proud alumnus, having graduated in the class of 1924. However, Zabriskie was unsparing in detailing Lloyd's struggle as a seminary student. On the one hand, Lloyd had anticipated a restrictive environment, a fear that was allayed when, on his arrival, he discovered that students could smoke on the seminary's grounds. Even so, there was a stifling classroom environment that caused Lloyd to wonder whether he should remain in the seminary or not.

The academic experience did not encourage him. Zabriskie wrote bluntly that "the Seminary was at a low ebb in Lloyd's day. The great Dr. Sparrow was dead and there were no creative theological thinkers left. All four professors were genuinely learned men; but two were very old and

36. Zabriskie, *Arthur Selden Lloyd*, 15.

declining and the other two were of the drill-master type who always insisted that the students must know precisely [what their textbooks] said."
Truth was viewed as a system, Zabriskie explained, and "the students'
business was to commit it to memory." Thus Lloyd "received no inspira-
tion to study; no clearly grounded philosophy of life; only a rigid system
of theology which he gravely doubted. Perhaps this was the reason why
some of the older professors had less hope for his usefulness in the ministry than for any other man in the Seminary."[37]

The experience of Henry St. George Tucker was little different from
that of Lloyd even though Tucker entered the seminary in 1897, twenty
years after Lloyd matriculated. "While the spiritual atmosphere of the
Seminary was very stimulating, its scholastic standards were at a low ebb,"
Tucker recalled. He added that the seminary "was strong on religion but
weak of theology and pastoral technique." Tucker quickly added that he
owed "a debt of gratitude to the Seminary which I can never adequately
repay. It gave me a conception of the spiritual character of the ministry
and imbued me with its evangelical purpose. Without these no amount of
learning would make one's ministry fruitful."[38] Tucker was not disparaging the academic dimension but seeking its rightful place in a balanced
process of vocational formation.

Lloyd's earlier experience pointed to a similar concern and a similar resolution. He found informal conversations with faculty members
benefitted him personally and intellectually. He sought faculty mentor-
ing beyond the classroom and was pleased to find it. There was a "deep
spirituality of the professors" which provided lasting examples of character and judgment. Lloyd also liked his fellow students; his room became "such a general gathering place that most of his studying had to
be done late at night." But what proved most memorable for Lloyd was
"his work on the country mission to which he was attached, and where
he conducted services, preached, taught Sunday School, and did pastoral visiting. One Sunday he . . . conducted Sunday School and services
at the two chapels, involving about ten miles' walking." Thus, Zabriskie
emphasized the "warm devotional life was to his liking. For it was a *praying* seminary."[39] Zabriskie took care to emphasize that Lloyd relished the
seminary's evangelical style, including its low church, simplified liturgical

37. Zabriskie, *Arthur Selden Lloyd*, 16.
38. Tucker, *Exploring the Silent Shore of Memory*, 37.
39. Zabriskie, *Arthur Selden Lloyd*, 18.

practice. Simple vesture with no adornments and no worship enhancements was the prevailing style.

Tucker's motivation for mission arose similarly though with an important distinction. Like Lloyd he was not enamored of the seminary's faculty, with the exception of Carl Grammer, who had arrived after Arthur Lloyd's graduation. Tucker described Grammer as a "real teacher with the gifts of arousing in his students' minds an interest which made them seekers after truth. The subject that I studied under him was the first four centuries of Church History, the formative period of Christian Theology."[40] Describing Grammer as a "liberal-evangelical," a term which gained recognition later thanks in part to Zabriskie's influence, Tucker noted that Grammer "was somewhat in advance of the prevailing theological attitude of that period in Virginia. This, combined with a rather provocative way of presenting his arguments, tended sometimes to drive his hearers to the opposite side."[41] Clearly Tucker was not alienated. He praised Grammer's "modernism," which was apparent in his handling of biblical criticism yet did not undermine such crucial theological doctrines as the trinity and the incarnation. Tucker regretted that, before he graduated, Grammer had left the seminary for parish ministry.[42]

Tucker's missionary vocation arose outside the classroom. "One of the most helpful features of the training given by the Seminary was the assignment of the students to work on one of what were known as the 'missions.'" Here his experience resonated with Lloyd's. "There were some ten or twelve of these missionary chapels, most of them within reasonable (for those days) walking distance from the Seminary." Three students served in each chapel. An important aspect of their work was learning how to preach. Recounting his initial pulpit awkwardness, Tucker mused that "it must have been pretty hard on the congregation to be used as a guinea pig for new students' oratorical experiments, but they endured it philosophically." Moved by the opportunity to serve in a local mission chapel, Tucker, like other seminary students, participated in military drills at the outbreak of the Spanish-American War. Oddly, perhaps, the war helped to excite his interest in foreign mission.[43]

---

40. Tucker, *Exploring the Silent Shore of Memory*, 37.

41. Tucker, *Exploring the Silent Shore of Memory*, 37.

42. Tucker, *Exploring the Silent Shore of Memory*, 40.

43. Tucker, *Exploring the Silent Shore of Memory*, 40.

In the winter of 1899, during his senior year, Tucker was selected as one of Virginia Seminary's representatives to an inter-seminary missionary convention, held that year in Cambridge, Massachusetts. He recalled that, as a result, "for the first time I became personally interested in the missionary work of the Church."[44] Shortly after, Tucker learned that Bishop John McKim in Tokyo urgently needed new personnel and had appealed to Virginia Seminary. With no further prompting, Tucker volunteered. "I knew nothing of the nature of the work, but when confronted with such an emergency call, there was nothing to do but respond."[45] Before his departure, Tucker was ordained first as deacon, then as priest. Then he sailed. On October 18, 1899, his ship entered Yokohama harbor.

By then, in a profound sense, Arthur Selden Lloyd was also entering the mission service of the Episcopal Church. Having graduated from the seminary in 1880, he was ordained to the priesthood in the seminary's chapel on June 24, 1881, having served as a deacon for a year. Already he had served several small Episcopal churches in southside Virginia. Then, from 1885 to 1899, he was rector of St. Luke's Church in Norfolk, Virginia. There Lloyd cultivated the sensibilities of a cosmopolitan worldview as he looked for opportunities to serve. He developed a "group of young society girls" in the parish for the purpose of visiting "the poor and shut-ins." Lloyd refused to let the young women "take things on each visit lest their calls be simply a series of handouts." The main things to be given, Lloyd emphasized, "was their friendship and personal service. For only thus could they learn about the life of the less fortunate; only so could they meet the deep need for human understanding."[46]

Zabriskie explained that "Lloyd's concern for people was by no means limited to his own parishioners. People of all communions, including Jews and Roman Catholics, came to consult him. Blacks as well as whites regarded him as 'our pastor.'" Lloyd magnetically drew people of all sorts and often conversed with individuals and groups until late in the evening. He looked to draw out latent possibilities in all people, and repeatedly voiced the need to respect every human being. As Zabriskie noted, "In every person he saw the latent image of a Christ-like personality." Mission and pastoral concern flowed together.[47]

44. Tucker, *Exploring the Silent Shore of Memory*, 41.
45. Tucker, *Exploring the Silent Shore of Memory*, 41.
46. Zabriskie, *Arthur Selden Lloyd*, 31.
47. Zabriskie, *Arthur Selden Lloyd*, 34.

This commitment extended to his work with African American churches as well as persons. Even though he had not traveled or served in mission abroad, he was well-equipped by his outlook, experience, magnetism and pastoral breadth. In 1899, as Henry St. George Tucker began his service as a missionary in Japan, Arthur Selden Lloyd was appointed as the general secretary of the Domestic and Foreign Missionary Society. In effect, Lloyd assumed control of the Episcopal Church's mission. He would serve in this role for most of the next twenty years.

John Hill, Missionary to Greece

John Payne, Missionary to Liberia

William Boone, Missionary to China

Launcelot Minor, Missionary to Liberia

Channing Moore Williams, Missionary to Japan

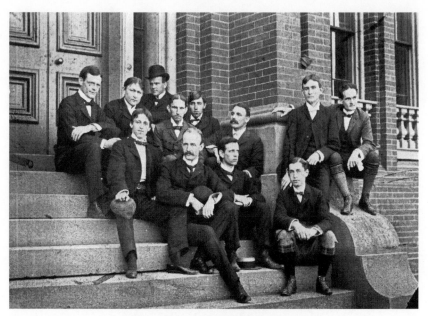

Class of 1899 and 1900 Missionaries

Carl Grammer, Seminary Faculty

Japan Clergy Gathering

Henry St. George Tucker, Missionary, Educator, Bishop

Lloyd Craighill, Missionary to China

Alexander Zabriskie, Seminary Dean

Kenneth Heim, Seminary Faculty and Missionary

Albert T. Mollegen, Seminary Faculty

Class of 1961

Charles Price, Seminary Faculty

Robert Prichard, Seminary Faculty

Richard Jones, Seminary Faculty

Martha Horne with Bishop Peter James Lee and Archbishop George Carey

Martha Horne, Seminary Dean

African Anglican Clergy at Virginia Theological Seminary, 1995

Class of 2012

Sandra McCann, Missionary

William L. Sachs, Wanjiru Gitau, Robert Heaney, Canon Sarah Snyder,
and Joanildo Burity at Washington National Cathedral

Archbishop Justin Welby with Center for Anglican Communion Studies team, Courtney Henderson-Adams, Hartley Hobson Wensing, A. Katherine Grieb, and Garrett Ayers at Virginia Theological Seminary

Albert T. Mollegen Forum panelists at Virginia Theological Seminary, Patricia Kisare, Archbishop Justin Welby, A. Katherine Grieb, Bishop Ketlen A. Solak, and Ragan Sutterfield

6

Into All the World

BRAZIL AND THE CONSOLIDATION OF MISSION

ON JULY 13, 1889, the *Richmond Dispatch* newspaper reported the arrival in Virginia's capitol city of James W. Morris and Lucien L. Kinsolving. Recent graduates of Virginia Theological Seminary and more recently ordained as deacons, the young men had chosen to go as missionaries to Brazil.[1] It was a controversial calling. The Episcopal Church's foreign mission board refused to endorse this step because Brazil was a predominantly Roman Catholic country. Similar hesitation would greet the mission that founded the Episcopal Church in Cuba. High-church Episcopalians in particular did not want to give offense. Thus, the beginnings of the Episcopal Church in Brazil and Cuba lay with the American Church Missionary Society (ACMS). An American version of England's Church Missionary Society, the ACMS was grounded in evangelical convictions and held a strong base of support at Virginia Seminary. Eventually the ACMS would merge with the Domestic and Foreign Missionary Society.

There was no hesitation about mission in Brazil as Morris and Kinsolving arrived in Richmond. They were there to prepare for their ordinations as priests in the see city of the Diocese of Virginia. Richmond's newspaper noted that they had preached and spoken at several local churches. Building on a culture of mission that had become prominent across Virginia as well as at its seminary, Morris and Kinsolving easily rallied support for their intended work. Already, in the seminary's

---

1. Quoted in the *Southern Churchman* 56 (July 18, 1889) 2.

vicinity, the Fairfax Brazilian Missionary Society was organizing and would become a major artery of support. Commitment to the Brazil initiative was firm and broad.

The ordination of Morris and Kinsolving received detailed newspaper coverage. On Sunday morning, August 4, 1889, Bishop Francis M. Whittle of Virginia conducted the rites, and Carl Grammer of Virginia Seminary preached, choosing Matthew 28:19–20 as his text. The service was held at Richmond's Grace Church, but later in the same day, a farewell service for the missionaries was held at St. James' Church. Various clergy participated, with Bishop Whittle giving "a brief address on the importance of the mission work, and with his usual clearness told how the present work was inaugurated." In turn, it was reported that the new missionaries gave "earnest and interesting addresses."[2] At least in Virginia, mission had become a matter of public import.

By mid-October Morris and Kinsolving were in Brazil, pouring forth a steady stream of letters which appeared in the *Southern Churchman*, the Episcopal magazine based in Alexandria. Travel and communication were becoming speedier and more reliable in the second half of the nineteenth century, allowing frequent descriptions of the birth of the Episcopal Church in Brazil. There were obvious parallels to the founding of other missionary branches of the church. The new missionaries had to learn the language, in this case Portuguese. The letters also revealed their vivid and at times astonished impressions of Brazil. A democratic revolution had recently inaugurated a government more open to wider worlds, thereby making way for the arrival of Episcopal missionaries. Morris and Kinsolving reveled in the sense of opportunity this political openness afforded.

Some of their first contacts were the easiest to make. Their letter of October 10, 1889, described meeting Presbyterian missionaries and admiring the extent of their work and resources. The apparent spiritual energy of the Presbyterians gave the Episcopal newcomers hope. They did not come to Brazil to convert as much as they came to promote spiritual awakening. Thus, on December 10, 1889, celebrating Brazil's new government, Kinsolving and Morris wrote that "it seems a foregone conclusion that the superior privileges that have been given heretofore to the Roman Church and that have fostered its corruptions and fed its arrogancy, must soon be swept away. Brazil is from this time open to

2. *Southern Churchman* 56 (August 8, 1889) 2.

the preaching of God's truth fairly and freely, without let or hindrance; every church will be compelled to stand not on privilege but on merit."[3] Perhaps without recalling the precedent, they were echoing sentiments reminiscent of the American Revolution. As democracy grew and the reality of religious establishment, whether formal or *de facto*, faded, mission to secure the growth of confessional community became necessary. Episcopal missionaries took advantage of this reality as religious pluralism grew in the wake of democratic revolution. Given their focus on spiritual vitality, Episcopal missionaries were certain that Brazil could be won for evangelical Christianity in the absence of a state church.

By July 1890, seven months after the Episcopal missionaries reached Brazil, Kinsolving wrote a glowing letter to the Sunday school children of Christ Church, Alexandria, Virginia, a letter that was sent to them by way of Henderson Suter, the rector. Thanking the children for their support of the Brazil mission, Kinsolving could not resist commenting that "some good and wise men [hardly thought it] worth while to have a mission in Brazil." Sunday school children knew better, he added with a flourish. He proceeded to describe several cities in Brazil, including Porto Alegre in the south, where the Episcopal Church was building its base.[4]

A little more than a month later, another Kinsolving letter spoke enthusiastically of the growth of the Episcopal Church in that southern city. Several "preaching points" were active, and "independent services," i.e., worship, had begun. Printed cards distributed widely invited people. At one of the first worship services, "our 72 seats were all taken, and the hall and entry were crowded to overflowing, standing room and all." Many had to be turned away. Several people asked if this was a "Catholic church . . . that was not Romanist" and received affirmative answers. Even more exciting to Kinsolving, "every class seems to be represented, high and low, rich and poor, Brazilian and German, white and some few blacks."[5] He knew that not all would return to future services. But enough did to sustain growth and his enthusiasm.

The *Southern Churchman* continued to report regularly and enthusiastically on the growth of the mission in Brazil. Early in 1891 the *Churchman* wrote a detailed assessment of the work, apparently in response to vaguely noted criticisms. On the one hand, entry into a largely

3. *Southern Churchman* 57 (January 30, 1890) 2.
4. *Southern Churchman* 57 (July 24, 1890) 4.
5. *Southern Churchman* 57 (August 7, 1890) 2.

Roman Catholic setting sparked unfocused fears of slippage from low church origins into the clutches of ritualism. On the other hand, the mission had been sponsored by the American Church Missionary Society, enough on the institutional fringes of Episcopal mission to elicit concern of low church Episcopalians taking unwarranted initiative. The *Churchman* directly made its own estimation of the work in Brazil: "To those who are unacquainted with the teaching of the Theological Seminary of Virginia, and with the objects of the American Church Missionary Society, it may be well to say that there is little danger that the graduates of the one, or the emissaries of the other, will carry the advanced ritualism to Brazil that our critic has depicted. Our missionaries carry to that land neither our controversies, nor our architecture. . . . These are the gloomy companions of a disturbed imagination."[6]

Tirelessly, Morris and Kinsolving extended their work to other cities, notably Rio de Janeiro. But Porto Alegre remained the base, and their growth justified additional staffing. August 1891 saw the arrival of the Rev. William Cabell Brown; his wife, Ida Dorsey; the Rev. J. G. Meem; and Miss Mary Packard, daughter of sometime dean and longtime faculty member of Virginia Seminary, Joseph Packard.[7] It was a doubly significant link. Mary Packard extended the seminary tie. Brown would expand the work in Rio de Janeiro, founding the first congregation in that region. In 1914 he was elected bishop in Virginia and would later head the seminary's board, giving mission—and the Brazilian mission in particular—added prominence.

Mission to Brazil from the Episcopal Church drew wide interest. In November 1906, Edward Francis Every, English bishop for the Falkland Islands, reported on the extensive visit he had recently paid. He spared no praise when he wrote of his impressions. "The American Church in Southern Brazil," as he termed it, "appears to be a model mission of its kind, i.e., just what a Church mission ought to be in a Latin American, nominally Roman Catholic, land."[8] In part the mission's character could be attributed to its solid support at home, misgivings about being in a nominally Catholic country having diminished. Then, Every continued, the combination of lively worship, schools, and the training of Brazilian clergy had prepared the way for the infrastructure of a Brazilian church.

---

6. *Southern Churchman* 58 (February 26, 1891) 2.

7. *Southern Churchman* 58 (August 27, 1891) 1.

8. Every, "Some Impressions of the Brazilian Episcopal Church," 922.

Flexibility sufficient to allow for formal as well as informal worship and Bible study struck Every forcefully. "The Brazilian church will have no formal converts," Every further emphasized. Rather, "it aims at making them whole-hearted in their faith, enthusiastic and instructed."[9] The Falklands bishop grasped the intent and tracked the development of a dynamic mission. He expended little ink on hierarchy or authority. The mission in Brazil focused on grassroots spiritual vitality, the result being the emergence of an indigenous church.[10]

The unfolding of the Episcopal Church in Brazil followed the lines of development that preceded it in such sites as Liberia, China, and Japan. Thus, in March 1908, a priest of the church in Brazil, C. H. C. Sergel, reported on the organization of Sunday schools. The church's nearly two decades of experience offered a valuable perspective. Sergel observed that in Brazil's Episcopal churches nearly all of the organists "are the young people we have trained, and everywhere we have teachers in the Sunday-schools and serving-classes, and quite a number of the students in the theological seminary who are the direct results of the Sunday-school work."[11] In other words, more than creating congregations and a church structure, the Brazilian church was creating a religiously inspired culture all its own.

Sergel, one of the fourteen Brazilian clergy by 1908, focused on the rise of a new generation of Episcopalians: "We have now another generation and they are the offspring of those who were brought up in our Sunday-schools and married in our church."[12] A logical next step would be the creation of Episcopal parochial schools. More would be accomplished than attracting the parents of enrolled students, as important as that would be. The schools would be "developing Christian character with a solid basis of intellectual and mental training [in order to] produce an even higher class of Christians and that type of men which will mould a nation for the glory of God, like those we boast of in the Republic of the United States of America."[13]

Even more than Sergel, James W. Morris saw 1908 as a propitious moment to assess the state of the Brazilian church. He was well-positioned

9. Every, "Some Impressions of the Brazilian Episcopal Church," 923.

10. Every, "Some Impressions of the Brazilian Episcopal Church," 922–24.

11. Sergel, "From One Generation to Another," 180.

12. Sergel, "From One Generation to Another," 181.

13. Sergel, "From One Generation to Another," 180–81.

to offer such an assessment, having founded the church in Brazil with Lucien Kinsolving. In the *Spirit of Missions*, Morris wrote an extensive assessment. Growth unfolded at once. Four years into the mission, George Peterkin of West Virginia became the first Episcopal bishop to make a visit, during which he ordained four deacons and confirmed 140 persons. Peterkin also encouraged the church's organization, for which Morris praised him. The Brazilian mission created an annual council in which laity and clergy, Brazilian and foreign, sat together. "Local canons for the government of the Church were adopted," and both education and spirituality were emphasized. The focus lay on "preaching and expounding the Word of God."[14] From this core affirmation, an indigenous church was emerging.

Soon this church had its own bishop. Early in 1899, in New York City, Lucien Lee Kinsolving was consecrated as Bishop of Southern Brazil. Nearly a decade later, Morris reported that there were over a thousand communicants, fifteen hundred children in Sunday schools, and eight young men studying for the ministry. There were six church buildings and one self-supporting parish with two others nearing that goal. Morris emphasized that "the Brazilian work had differed from that in the Far East," given its origin in the American Church Missionary Society. But that body had merged into the Episcopal Church in 1907. Organizationally the church showed clear advance. Even more important, Morris concluded, the Brazilian church "draws from all sorts and conditions of men. But she appeals more especially to the artisans and the smaller merchants, the people that constitute the hope and the heart of the community."[15] The church's advance was measured by its appeal to diverse people and appreciation of them. In other words, the advance of mission was the advance of cosmopolitanism.

This was no isolated, rhetorical sentiment. A doorway leading to appreciation of indigenous people was opening. One of the most fruitful ways across its threshold was to engage with children. In Brazil and in other sites of Episcopal mission, many seized on this opportunity. Various articles in church publications were making this strategy plain. As a result, the annual council of the Brazilian diocese featured a children's service in 1908, a hint of Sunday school growth. The Episcopal Sunday school "has not only grown in numbers and more faithful attendance,

14. Morris, "Church's Message and Mission in Brazil," 433.
15. Morris, "Church's Message and Mission in Brazil," 437.

but [it] has succeeded in imbuing God's little ones with the spirit of service and self-sacrifice, so that they make weekly offerings for missions
of something gained by each one for work done or by self-denial."[16] The
diocesan council also broached the idea of mission to the Indian population of the southern part of the country. The church was recognizing
Brazil's diversity and finding ways to embrace it.

Such diversity could be glimpsed personally given the church's
grassroots focus. The growth of the Episcopal mission entailed building
appreciation for the personal and not simply the institutional dimension.
In addition, it had become a priority to depict the personal side of mission to American readers. W. M. M. Thomas, priest in the Brazil mission,
played a key role in building its Sunday schools. He offered a vivid sense
of Brazil's children in a lengthy essay. To be sure, Thomas offered romanticized images: "Under the pure light of the Gospel that she embraced for
herself and her children, the little girl has now grown up to be a Christian
woman instead of an idolater."[17] Thomas referred to the story of a young
woman who had been an early participant in a Sunday school. Granting
his idealism, Thomas presented several portraits of young people that
pointed toward cosmopolitan sensibility.

He also pondered the general characteristics of childhood, then
considered "certain distinctive marks that will characterize [the child]
as a Brazilian."[18] He showed sensitivity to cultural patterns of dress and
speech, of behaviors encouraged, and relations in families. He noted how
patterns he observed applied to all races of people. The observations were
anecdotal. Surely exceptions could be found, and conclusions could acquire nuance, as Thomas hinted. But, for our purposes, the methodologi-
cal approach matters less than the instinct that compelled him to write. He
had grasped that mission entailed encounters between people in which
no gospel could be proclaimed nor church built without recognition
of difference and respect for both similarities and distinctions between
people. Unity before God could not mean uniformity. The church was
enhanced by its embrace of diversity. It was a mark of cosmopolitanism.

This sentiment was not only emerging in Brazil. Church schools
in China, Japan, and Liberia already had contributed similar accounts.
The rise of indigenous clergy, especially personal stories of those who

16. Kinsolving, "Brazilian Church in Council," 19.
17. Thomas, "Some Children of Brazil," 125.
18. *Spirit of Missions* 74 (February 1909) 125.

were ordained, transformed Episcopal assumptions about mission. In missionary reports, the focus shifted from broad religious and cultural generalizations to localized and personalized accounts. Clearly, these were often idealized. Even harsh dimensions of human struggle could be framed heroically. Yet the accounts of mission life were not superficial. A new perspective on mission had opened. More than the priority of missionary goals and strategies had to be considered. The human face of mission had become apparent. Increasingly missionaries had begun to learn and to listen, as well as to teach and to speak.

SOBERING APPRECIATION

In January 1906, the foreign mission board of the Episcopal Church asked its general secretary, Arthur S. Lloyd, to make an extended visit to mission work in East Asia. As Lloyd's biographer, Alexander C. Zabriskie, depicted it, Lloyd accepted the request "with alacrity." He recognized the need for firsthand knowledge. His wife, Elizabeth, joined him, as did Dr. and Mrs. Reese Alsop. The couples were friends, and Dr. Alsop was a member of the board. They sailed late in August 1906 from New York aboard RMS *Carmania*. The year-old vessel could hold over 2,500 passengers, a marvel at the time.[19]

The party made visits in England before heading eastward to India. There they marveled at the extent of the Church of England's presence. According to Zabriskie, Lloyd was struck by Indian religious and philosophical systems but glossed over irreconcilable differences among them and with Christianity. Zabriskie dismissed Lloyd's apparent perception that a Christian ethic could be grafted onto a Hindu foundation. Whatever the limitations of Lloyd's assessment, it would not be his last consideration of Christianity's relation to other world religions. By posing Christianity as an ethic, he seemed to be searching for a point of unity that would transcend cultural differences. Lloyd's outlook did presume that Christianity could be the catalyst for all that impeded social and commercial advance. Beyond the shortcomings in his perspective, there was refreshing readiness to listen.

From India, Lloyd's party made stops at Penang, Singapore, and Hong Kong before arriving at Manila in January 1907. Their six weeks in the Philippines gave them the opportunity to consider the dynamic ministry

19. Zabriskie, *Arthur Selden Lloyd*, 109.

of Charles Brent, Episcopal bishop there since 1902. It could be argued
that Brent was the most dynamic of the Episcopal Church's missionary
bishops. He had an energetic ministry grounded in a social vision of the
church that encompassed creation of services to people in need. Brent's
engagement with tribal peoples and Muslims across the Philippines fasci-
nated Lloyd. Such ministry offered both evangelism and a "social gospel."
Such creative approach to religious and cultural difference poured out of
Brent's numerous publications. Lloyd was further struck by the dedication
service at Manila's new cathedral. He wrote, "To it came people of five different races, the Governor-General and his staff as well as poverty-stricken
Chinese coolies, and the congregations of the Presbyterian and Methodist
churches which had suspended their own services that morning."[20] Brent
enacted the vision of Episcopal mission as a gathering place for all people
and a redemptive response to social needs.

The impression would deepen as the Lloyds and Alsops went to China and then to Japan. In both nations, the focus of their visits lay on grassroots mission work. The Lloyd party visited congregations, clinics, and
especially schools where they met for conversations with students. The
development of lay leaders in society and ordained leaders in the church
became central. Lloyd saw two mission churches envisioning the goal of
self-direction. He also saw the social obstacles which mission faced. The
most deleterious conditions arose from Western influence, Lloyd concluded. As Zabriskie comments, Lloyd returned from Asia "convinced
now that the influence of Western culture on the Orient would be thoroughly bad—though not quite *unrelievedly* bad because its medicine and
scientific agriculture were boons—unless the one redemptive factor in the
West also became influential."[21] That was the Christian revelation. Western influence brought materialism and immorality. Western influence also
confronted traditional religious and ethical norms. Lloyd adopted a stance
that was both critical and pastoral. Included in his awakened sensibilities
were the missionaries themselves who served on the front lines of this
religious and cultural confluence. The practice of mission acquired human
faces, and listening became its most valuable art.

The scale of Episcopal mission increased rapidly from the outset
of Lloyd's tenure as general secretary to 1909. The number of missionaries more than doubled to more than 2,300, and the budget more than

20. Zabriskie, *Arthur Selden Lloyd*, 115.
21. Zabriskie, *Arthur Selden Lloyd*, 127.

doubled to more than one million dollars.[22] Thus, the issues which Lloyd pondered grew in significance. His experience of difference, of mission, and of Western influence from the trip in 1906 combined with his growing responsibilities to inform a major project. In the summer of 1908, he delivered a series of lectures on mission at the Harvard Summer School. The lectures were soon published as *Christianity and the Religions*.[23] The work attempted to locate Christian mission in the midst of diverse human experience of the divine. Lloyd did not dilute his own faith. In his formulation, Christ exemplified what human beings can become. As Zabriskie assesses, the book defines religion as the human search for God. Whereas such a search is inherent in human nature, religions fall short. Christianity, however, is not a religion, for it does not rely upon human initiative. It is the revelation of God to make plain what human beings cannot secure by themselves. Through the Christian revelation, human relation to God can be established and become lasting. Becoming cocreators with God, people can become cocreators with each other. The basis for mission-building community appeared. It linked faith to human encounter.

The idea that Christianity was not a religion whereas the world religions were circumscribed in their intentions was a flaw in Lloyd's argument. It allowed Christians an unfair distinction that did not do justice to the convictions of other faithful people. His case for mission was stronger and drew on his firsthand experience. Lloyd grounded mission in gratitude and responsibility. God's initiative invited such human responses. In part, he depicted gratitude tendentiously. Coming from the West, missionaries should bear gratitude for "the spirit of cooperation and friendliness, of truth and purity, that makes life in Christian communities so much better than in pagan ones."[24] However, missionaries and, even more, Western culture have failed to embody the gifts they have been given. The ills within Western culture, and the ill effects of Western influence abroad, compromised the intention of conveying God's love. Christian mission needed to claim responsibility for recovering faithful intention.

Lloyd's recognition of the West's impact, of Christianity's responsibility, and of the gospel's potential were sobering realizations. He had come to an impressive recognition of the nature of mission's task in the early twentieth century. He was not alone in reaching such conclusions.

22. Zabriskie, *Arthur Selden Lloyd*, 76.

23. Zabriskie, *Arthur Selden Lloyd*, 78; Lloyd, *Christianity and the Religions*.

24. Zabriskie, *Arthur Selden Lloyd*, 81.

The scores of missionaries under his guidance were wrestling with similar perceptions and similar conclusions. They had gone forth from the United States and the Episcopal Church to proclaim the gospel, convert, develop leadership, and build the church. They had also begun to address the church's social role. In doing so, missionaries had confronted the reality of difference. Peoples and cultures could not be dismissed simply as "pagan" or "heathen." Mission entailed learning languages and contextual particularities just in order to communicate, to say nothing of bringing about conversions. In the process, a further startling realization occurred—missionaries were face-to-face with human beings. Generalizations, even theological ones, faced revision in the midst of encounter. The defining reality of mission was difference.

Decades later in the twentieth century, French philosopher Emmanuel Levinas would frame the encounter with another person as the basis of ethics. Levinas evaded theological categories yet spoke of transcendence and emphasized that the self is incomplete. One must go beyond oneself, for the completion each of us seeks lies beyond our individual lives. Transcendence requires what may be called "exteriority."[25] More than philosophical or psychological motivation, or times of one's choosing, the encounter with the other represents existential reality. Its recognition represents the beginning of ethics and the possibility of one's completion. The self cannot remain at the level of how things should be. Each human self must confront things as they are without presuming to ignore or change. Levinas maintained that responsibility to the other precedes responsibility to the self. But the reality of self and other can never be overcome. Difference is unassailable reality. It cannot be merged or subsumed. Even notions of being comparable must be resisted. The recognition of difference cannot presume its elimination. Difference is reality, and difference is necessity. Through it, ethical responsibility awakens.

The transcendence of which Levinas speaks is not easily equated with God, and it is far removed from religious life or confessional affirmations. Humanistic reviewers of Levinas have taken pains to make this point, perhaps extending the dismissal of religion much farther than Levinas ever intended.[26] The focus of his philosophy rested on the reality of difference and on his resistance to what he viewed as inadequate ways of dismissing or overcoming difference. Given his Jewish upbringing and

25. Bergo, "Emmanuel Levinas."
26. Nooteboom, *Beyond Humanism*.

his horror at the Holocaust, the stark reality of difference and its ethical implications guided his thought. Levinas emphasized, and we add our own emphasis, that "self and other can never merge, be subsumed in each other, become equal or even comparable." Further, the feeling of responsibility for the other "is not a rational choice but something that happens to you. . . . There is an ethical call to surrender to the other, and to suffer from his or her suffering, an imperative that precedes all other consideration."[27] Without drawing facile comparisons or conclusions, it is this sensibility that we speak of as cosmopolitan. Levinas's view makes it plain that missionaries did not choose to draw close to "the other" in the midst of their mission work. Missionaries were drawn into awareness and care, as Levinas theorized.

Arthur Selden Lloyd came to similar conclusions about the ethical dynamics of human encounter, and he guided Episcopal mission in light of these realizations. There was a brief and awkward hiatus. In the summer of 1909, Lloyd was elected bishop coadjutor of Virginia, a position which designated him as eventual successor to Bishop Robert Atkinson Gibson. There had been other overtures about elections in other dioceses. But Virginia appealed as no other diocese could. Nevertheless, only fourteen months after being elected, Lloyd resigned to return to the Board of Missions as its president.[28] The opportunity for continued contribution to mission proved even more attractive than Virginia. In his stead, Virginia would elect William Cabell Brown, who had served in Brazil. Lloyd would remain as mission president until the organization was revamped and his position eliminated in 1919. After brief service in parish ministry, Lloyd was elected suffragan, or assisting, bishop in New York. He died at his home in Darien, Connecticut in 1936.

Arthur Selden Lloyd glimpsed that the future of the church's mission was laden with cosmopolitan possibility because of the necessity of its grassroots focus. But his career hit its stride at the peak of Western Christianity's *ancien regime* prior to World War I. Though various church leaders, including Lloyd, were critical of Western culture, they could presume the church's institutional place in it. The task of mission was not to distinguish the church from culture but to use the church's spiritual influence to reshape culture. The task was even more important in the

27. Bergo, "Emmanuel Levinas."
28. Zabriskie, *Arthur Selden Lloyd*, 155.

context of mission, where appropriations of some aspects of the life of the West could betray religious intentions.

As a result, especially in China and Japan, attention given to Episcopal mission focused obsessively on the prospects for redeemed societies and the paths missionaries might take to encourage this outcome. Prior to the impact felt from world war, it was possible to believe that Christian mission could achieve more than extension of the church. Given the Episcopal Church's ties to economic and political influence, there was no conceivable reason why social gain could not be achieved. In a word, "progress" became the goal of mission for a time. It was not conceived naively. The realities of cultural nuance and missionary struggle were apparent. By 1912, it had been nearly seventy-five years since the first missionaries began working to enter China. But the growth of mission, and the extension of American influence generally, made progress seem possible. The progress that was envisioned centered on redeeming societies as well as their peoples.

Events in 1912 encouraged such a hope. In 1912, China's Manchu dynasty was overthrown, and a republican form of government launched under the presidency of Sun Yat-Sen.[29] Sun had been baptized as a Christian by a Congregationalist missionary of the ABCFM several decades earlier. His baptism and the appearance of republican government enlivened missionary discussion. The vision would not endure long as China fell into disunity, suffered the destruction caused by the Japanese, and witnessed the rise of Communism over the next few decades. For a brief time, however, the missionary vision of national as well as religious advance seemed near to fruition. Episcopalians drew on their missionary experience to join the chorus of optimism.

In the fateful year of 1912, Episcopal medical missionary Edward M. Merrins, MD, wrote both effusively and insightfully. In an article about the future of China, Merrins saw the hand of God in political events. He reasoned that God uses political movements and even governments to advance divine designs. Movements toward reform and democracy bespoke redemptive intention. A basic dynamic at work was expansion of the original scope of mission. The entry of missionaries into a context new to them began with individual conversions and creation of the

---

29. Spence, *Search for Modern China*; Wasserstrom, *Oxford History of Modern China*.

church. But the movement toward salvation must encompass "the whole man." This brought the salvation of the nation into focus.[30]

Here Merrins's account took an interesting turn. If missionaries were to have an influence upon the future of the nation, it would be largely through the education of youth. Future national leaders were being educated in schools and colleges run by the Christian churches. Here the Episcopal mission had unusual influence given the quality and extent of its educational programs. Merrins went further still in explaining the mechanism by which education proved salvific. Nations such as China and Japan had understandably relied upon ancient custom. The welding of a nation into a "homogeneous, orderly community by the force of imposed custom is necessary if they are to survive in the merciless struggle for existence."[31] Merrins took an emphatic view of national progress animated by a sense of evolutionary drive. Without progress, there would be no survival.

The role of Christianity was to be the arm of progress. Through its schools and the education of youth, Christian mission would break the shackles of outdated, imposed cultural and political customs. Christianity would show in practical ways the futility of clinging to ancient ways. The path would not be a straight one. The Chinese people would sort out vices from virtues, what would help their advance from what would hinder them. Mere overturn of the past was insufficient. Mere embrace of Western ways would be misleading. The church must hold its own in such a struggle. It could do so by remaining true to its confessions and expressing its faith through education. Thus, in a fascinating way, mingled with his progressive cosmology, Merrins sharpened the focus of mission on "the other," in this case, Chinese youth. He had elaborated the process of conversion into education for the dawn of a new day of nationhood.

Over the next several years, before the horror of World War I became apparent and the ideal of progress shrank, a flurry of figures echoed Merrins's thoughts and shared his belief in the Episcopal Church's role in God's providential intentions. Charles S. Reifsnider, who succeeded Henry St. George Tucker as president of St. Paul's College (now Rikkyo University) in Tokyo, argued in an essay published in 1913 that he saw Christian colleges exerting moral leadership in an age of social

---

30. Merrins, "Christian Education and National Progress," 355.

31. Merrins, "Christian Education and National Progress," 356.

possibility.[32] In the same year, the writer Hamilton W. Mabie, an Episcopalian, spoke of missionaries as "statesmen" above all else.[33] But the
summation of these sentiments came eloquently and passionately from
Tucker, by then bishop of Kyoto, in an address before the Episcopal
Church's General Convention of 1916.[34]

Tucker endorsed the idea of progress. But he drew back from linking God's intentions to political events. Instead, he chose two themes
which would recur in his ministry and writing. First, he emphasized that
mission entails practical work. Without daring to predict specific, social
outcomes, Tucker took a more measured and pastoral approach. The
church's medical and educational missions would improve the lives of
people who would then spread word of the gospel. The church also would
educate future leaders. The second of Tucker's intentions would be realized through education: missionaries would hand over responsibility to
those to whom it belonged, namely, the people of the host society. Tucker
foresaw what would later be termed the "euthanasia of mission."[35] That
is, the purpose of mission was not to enshrine itself, but to prepare for its
own demise; missionaries would withdraw as people in mission contexts
assumed rightful control of their own church and destiny.

He would follow through on this conviction. In 1922, Tucker resigned as bishop of Kyoto and returned to the United States where,
initially, he taught mission as a faculty member at Virginia Theological
Seminary. He felt strongly that the time had come for the Japanese people
to lead the Japanese church. It was not a rare sentiment, but it was rare
to see that sentiment put into practice. Even so, a missionary focus on
human needs and bridging difference was not subsumed by larger events.
The church's role, but especially that of its seminaries, was to encourage
mission focused on shaping human opportunity. Cosmopolitanism was
inherent in such an outlook.

THE WORLD COMES TO ALEXANDRIA

By the time Tucker delivered his address, it was possible to assess the
development of foreign mission by the Episcopal Church and to consider

32. Reifsnider, "Christian College and Moral Leadership."
33. Mabie, "Missionary as Statesman."
34. Tucker, "What This Church Is Trying to Do."
35. See Hanciles, *Euthanasia of Mission*.

Virginia Seminary's role in it. It had been a generation since 1890, when Virginia Seminary alumnus and leading China missionary Elliott Thomson had given a stirring speech at his alma mater. Hoping to recruit a new crop of missionaries, Thomson ended his address with the question: "Must I return alone?"[36] His message enlisted James Addison Ingle, later bishop of Hankow before his untimely death, and Robert K. Massie, who returned from China to become professor of missions at the seminary.[37] In the years between Thomson's challenge and Tucker's analysis, commitment to mission increased and Virginia Seminary's role was prominent. Though most of each year's graduating class went into parish ministry domestically, a steady number of the new clergy went into service abroad. In the second half of the nineteenth century, it was apparent that Virginia Theological Seminary graduates were going outward in mission.

Between 1870 and the late 1930s, on the eve of another world war, ninety-two graduates entered mission work. The majority of them went to Asia, twenty-eight to China and twenty-one to Japan. Eleven went to Brazil, including Kinsolving and Morris of the class of 1889 who founded the Episcopal Church there. Ten went to Liberia, illustrative of a continuing sense of linkage even as the church there became indigenous. Of further interest, eight graduates went to the Philippines apparently drawn by the strength of church life there under the leadership of Bishop Charles Brent. Of further interest, eight went to Alaska, an area which was seen as a frontier. Six went to Cuba, where Alexander Hugo Blankingship of the class of 1924 would be bishop at the time of the Cuban Revolution and would be forced to flee. Five graduates went to disparate sites including Hawaii, Panama, and the Virgin Islands. Yet during this period, mission in Asia was the jewel of the Episcopal Church's crown and Virginia Seminary played a prominent role. The missionary reputation of Virginia Seminary would continue well into the twentieth century.

There were four notable graduating classes in which five or more graduates entered international mission. The outstanding year was 1899 when seven entered such service. Three, including Henry St. George Tucker, went to Japan, and two of that class went to China. One went to Brazil and one to Puerto Rico. In the classes of 1921, 1924, and 1927, five of the graduates became missionaries. From these three classes, a total of fifteen entered mission work, seven going to China, two to Japan and

36. Goodwin, *History of the Theological Seminary*, 2:366.
37. Grammer, "Virginia Seminary," 366.

two to Alaska. One each went to Brazil, Cuba, Hawaii, and the Virgin Islands. Five members of the class of 1910 also went into mission, four of them going to China. The clustering of greater numbers of commitments in the 1920s invites comment. Despite notable numbers in other decades, the 1920s represented the pinnacle of Western, and particularly Episcopal, assurance about the necessity and direction of mission. It is also worth commenting that vocations to mission were not limited to these years. There was a steady annual commitment of the seminary's graduates during the years following the American Civil War into the late 1930s, the preponderance of such commitment centering on Asia. That pattern would shift after World War II, given the change in political conditions in China. The Japan connection would change in character but would continue to be important.[38]

Of the ninety-two graduates during this period, ten were missionaries of a different sort. They were international students, from China and Japan, intent on gaining academic credentials so that they could enter ordained ministry in their homelands. They ranged from Isaac Yokohama of the class of 1877 to Leighton T. Y. Yang of the class of 1938. The research of Troy Mendez in 2008 helps us to see these international students in greater detail. For example, Yokoyama returned to Japan and was ordained but soon left ordained ministry. Another student from Japan, Jacob Kobayashi, returned to his country in 1894; he became rector of a church and later professor of apologetics in the theological faculty. He was known as a skillful communicator of Christianity to Japanese culture. Mendez also cites the presence of students from China, Brazil, and Cuba in the years prior to the outbreak of World War II. The number and diversity of international students would multiply in the last quarter of the twentieth century.[39]

The presence of international students was but one indication that the world came to Alexandria by varied routes. In the late nineteenth century, the academic energies of the seminary increased dramatically. New faculty were emblematic. The most energetic was Carl Grammer, who served from 1887 to 1898, when he returned to parish ministry. He had graduated from the seminary in 1884 and pursued additional work in biblical languages at Yale. Grammer was a grandson of William Sparrow, but he set a different intellectual course than his ancestor. Grammer

---

38. Booty, *Mission and Ministry*, 380–85.
39. Mendez, "History of Mission."

taught biblical languages and church history with an outspoken and energetic style. There was a pedagogical turn from the old style of recitation and memorization toward a lecture style punctuated by moments of Socratic challenges to students. By William Archer Rutherfoord Goodwin's assessment, Grammer, an unabashed Protestant in his theology, flirted with the boundary of orthodox belief in his demonstrative style.[40]

It should not have been surprising. Grammer had been tutored at Yale by William Rainey Harper, a prodigy and visionary known for his own dynamism. Just a few years later, Harper would become the founding president of the University of Chicago where, among his varied accomplishments, there would be initiatives in teaching biblical theology and languages to diverse audiences. Harper's influence on Virginia Seminary could be seen in another member of the faculty. In the same year that Grammer arrived, Angus Crawford joined the faculty to teach Bible and biblical languages. He had been recommended by Harper, still at Yale then. Crawford's personality was more genial than what was seen as Grammer's dramatic, even confrontational, approach. Yet both brought more than the influence of Harper. They introduced the intellectual currents of critical biblical study then gaining momentum, especially in such centers as Yale and Chicago. The new academic rigor that would reshape theological education was arriving in Alexandria.

Academic standards advanced on a broad front in the late nineteenth century. During the academic year of 1898–99, the seminary gained approval to grant the degree of bachelor in divinity to its graduates. A more diverse faculty and a higher standard of teaching was presumed to be crucial for the quality of the seminary's degree. Thus, Robert K. Massie was appointed to the faculty in 1898 to teach mission and served in that capacity until 1913, when he became dean of Christ Church Cathedral in Lexington, Kentucky. Massie would give rise to a distinguished family lineage of journalists and historians, including a son, grandson, and great grandson bearing his name. He had served as a missionary in China for four years following his Virginia Seminary graduation in 1891. Massie inaugurated the teaching of mission, which would prove nearly continuous though not always offered by a dedicated faculty member.

At times the teaching of mission would be combined with the teaching of church history. That was the case when Wallace Rollins joined the faculty from Sweet Briar College in 1913. The academic approach to

40. Goodwin, *History of the Theological Seminary*, 1:660–63.

mission had been primarily historical and Rollins deepened it. He had received his seminary education at Yale Divinity School making him a rare addition. Yet he was not a complete stranger. He was ordained and had served Episcopal churches across Virginia. At Sweet Briar, he had served as chaplain as well as taught. Rollins would become dean of the seminary in 1931 and held the position until 1940. His insights on mission would be extended when Thomas K. Nelson joined the faculty in 1920. Nelson had been a missionary in China for several years. While teaching Old Testament, he enhanced understanding of mission on campus.[41]

When Angus Crawford—now dean of the seminary—gave a report on the curriculum in 1912, it was easy to sense the winds of decisive change. As John Booty explains, Crawford noted the addition of courses in mission, church music, ethics, and sociology. He added that such changes helped Virginia Seminary to keep in step with the leading theological institutions in America. However, the addition of courses in disparate academic fields was evidence of deeper developments. Booty cites the growth of professionalism among the faculty. For students, this meant both greater rigor and the advent of choices in course selection. Required coursework now offered a foundation for elective courses as students tested vocational options, including service as missionaries.[42]

One of the decisive academic changes arose from a revised approach to a familiar subject. In 1911, W. Cosby Bell joined the faculty to teach theology. He had graduated from the seminary in 1905 and served as a parish priest prior to his return to Alexandria. Bell embodied the new breadth and unflagging optimism of his age. He also brought an instinct to publish that had not seized many previous faculty. Bell's outlook was apparent as he built coursework in the philosophy of religion. Until his untimely death in 1933, Bell approached the Christian faith in terms of its relation to other religions and philosophies. From the perspective of a century later, there was a refreshing cosmopolitanism in his work. He argued for the truth of Christianity in terms of its relation to other faiths and viewed religion both historically and psychologically.[43] Such perspective encouraged an appreciative awareness of peoples and beliefs that was novel on Alexandria's Holy Hill. Bell was a major influence. Framed

41. Booty, *Mission and Ministry*, 377–78.
42. Booty, *Mission and Ministry*, 193–95.
43. Bell, *Making of Man*.

by optimistic assurance, Virginia Seminary deepened its sense of relation beyond its own locality and confession.

The world not only came to Alexandria in the person of international students or fresh approaches in the classroom. The Missionary Society extended its work as the nineteenth century transitioned into the twentieth. Its historic purpose of promoting "the cause of Foreign and Domestic Mission, by acquiring intelligence, and encouraging a missionary spirit among its members" now focused on bringing noted speakers to campus.[44] For the 1913–14 academic year, such guests included J. Hubard Lloyd, missionary in Japan, and Henry St. George Tucker, by then bishop of Kyoto. Similarly, William Cabell Brown, still a missionary in Brazil, joined his bishop, Lucien Lee Kinsolving, in addresses organized by the society. Missionaries from China, Alaska, and North Dakota also visited Alexandria. Cosmopolitanism features patterns of exchange, and these speakers became agents of promoting the ties represented in mission. Some ties arose from looking outward in new ways. Representatives from the seminary had begun to attend conferences on mission and church life. In 1915, Lloyd Craighill, a member of the senior class and later bishop in China, participated in an inter-seminary conference in Madison, New Jersey. Already such groups as the Evangelical Alliance and the Church Students' Missionary Association had met on the Alexandria campus. The scale of Virginia Seminary's role in such events was not as great as that of other institutions and leaders. There was no Virginia Seminary participation as such in the Pan-Anglican Congress of 1908 or the World Missionary Conference in Edinburgh in 1910. Yet the commitment to mission was no less substantial. As the seminary's catalogue declared for the 1927–28 year:

> Its Alumni have served in every department of the Church's work and in every missionary field. They founded the Church's mission in Liberia, China, Japan, and Brazil, and as Domestic Missionaries they have been at the front in most of our Missionary Districts. . . . Since it was founded, this institution has always stood for loyalty to this Church in its doctrine, discipline and worship, for a prophetic ministry, for the supreme value of the personal religious life and for missionary zeal. These last ten years have been marked by a zealous adherence to and a strengthening of these ideals. In that time twenty-nine of its

44. *Bulletin of the Theological Seminary* (1914) 8.

graduates have gone to the foreign field, a greater number than in any other decade of the Seminary's history.[45]

The catalogue also announced that Bishop Henry St. George Tucker, now bishop of Virginia, would also serve as president of the seminary's board of trustees. Mission had become a guiding theme of seminary life.

45. *Bulletin of the Theological Seminary* (1927–1928) 3.

7

Mission amid Social Upheaval

THE EROSION OF ASSURANCE

Lloyd Craighill and Marian Gardner met on their way to service in China as missionaries of the Episcopal Church. Only weeks before he departed in July 1915, Craighill had graduated from Virginia Theological Seminary. There he had been immersed in an educational culture that prized mission. In her memoir, Marian recalled the seminary that she later discovered and that shaped Lloyd's ministry. It appeared primitive. Small stoves heated student rooms with wood that had to be retrieved from the ground floor. The bath house was "detached from the dormitory," as she put it. Yet the seminary "was one of the greatest seed beds for the Overseas Missions of the Church." Marian's use of capital letters reflected the extent of her conviction. "In Prayer Hall in [Lloyd's] day the walls were hung with photographs of every man who had gone from the Seminary to mission overseas, and they were prayed for by name in succession."[1] It was in Lloyd Craighill's final year at seminary that he first thought of service in China. Edmund Lee, a missionary, visited Alexandria to summon volunteers. Craighill felt that he was called. There had been some preparation. He had written a seminary paper about Virginia graduates who had founded the Episcopal mission in China. Oddly, he never submitted the paper while receiving credit for it. Craighill would send the paper to the seminary from China in 1918.

---

1. Craighill, *Craighills of China*, 6.

Marian Gardner Craighill's description of meeting her future husband and of their entry into mission service opens a bygone era to later readers. Her description simply of transit and entry into China recalls a former world in which mission was both an elaborate organization and a culture all its own. The China mission was the Episcopal Church's most extensive. By 1915, there were three Episcopal missionary districts there: Shanghai, the original one; Anking, westward, where Craighill served; and Hankow, five hundred miles further westward. English and Canadian missionaries were active in much of the rest of China. Support for mission work required significant numbers of workers. Of the 130 passengers on the vessel that transported Lloyd Craighill and Marian Gardner, the majority were new missionaries.[2] There was no doubt about the further path to service. Once they landed, Lloyd and Marian promptly entered language school. The organization of mission had become formalized.

The sights and sounds of China, and of its missionary life, were vivid. There were shops and crowds and homes festooned with colorful banners and signs displaying large Chinese characters. But there were only brief moments to study the new environment. Lloyd Craighill soon was escorted to an American family with whom he would stay, and Marian likewise. There were introductions to other missionaries, especially Bishop Daniel Huntington. The pace accelerated over the next year. Language study was supplemented by travel to glimpse China's people and sights. Craighill may have paused in wonder at the elaboration of mission work since its beginnings. Given his study of its origins, he must have been struck not merely by the mission's extent but by its confident tone. By the time of Craighill's arrival in China, the Episcopal mission had peaked. There was unquestioning assurance about why they were there and what imprint they would leave. But the conditions making their work possible were eroding.

Lloyd and Marian's missionary prospects were not entirely encouraging at first. He was assigned to a boys' school where he served as principal. Marian acknowledged that this was not the best setting for Lloyd's gifts.[3] But in 1918 their fortunes improved decidedly. Lloyd and Marian were married in China and reassigned to a parish in Nanchang, inland from Shanghai. Now a hub for China's railways and a city of over five million residents, Nanchang had begun its growth as the Craighills arrived.

2. Craighill, *Craighills of China*, 13.

3. Craighill, *Craighills of China*, 18.

Lloyd became the priest at the new parish of one hundred members linked to boys' and girls' schools. He was assisted by a Chinese deacon but soon sought a Chinese priest. He found Kimber Den, who became both friend and colleague. Den would become bishop of Chekiang, then imprisoned by the communist government that seized power. By 1952, when Den was detained, the world had changed decisively.

It was difficult to foresee this outcome as the Craighills made Nanchang their home. There had been outbursts of violence in China, and they could sense ripples from war in Europe. But the Craighills, like other missionaries of the time, focused on their lives and their callings. As Lloyd ministered and Marian taught, they built a network of friends, especially among Western business representatives. The staff of British American Tobacco Company fondly remembered the couple's hospitality. The church was moving toward its own version of Chinese identity, yet missionary supervision was intact. Marian recalled nervously that Lloyd was the only American Episcopal priest and one of the few Western clergy in Nanchang. There were friendly if rather distant relations with local Chinese persons. Those whom the Craighills saw most often, apart from the church, were the servants who maintained their residence. As hints of change surfaced, the Craighills maintained both a lifestyle of presumed social advantage and a devotion to their religious cause.

There were obvious adaptations Marian and Lloyd had to make and not merely to each other. Apart from the regular commitments of missionaries, such as preaching and teaching, Marian declared that "life in China had little of the routine about it," as Americans would think of routine. "Callers would arrive at any hour of the day, and must be welcomed and served a cup of tea, with the accompaniment of peanuts and watermelon seeds."[4] The calls mostly were friendly, but some concerned the business of the mission and other groups. At one time Lloyd was treasurer for five organizations, including the American school which served missionary children. In the process, the Craighills learned Chinese customs and functioned culturally as they had never envisioned. They became cosmopolitan in a manner that reflected their circumstances.

Though the Craighills were diligent, a furlough in 1920 brought them a welcome respite to visit the United States. Marian was pleased to meet Lloyd's family and to make her first visit to the South. The time in North America also gave them a chance to benefit from the latest

4. Craighill, *Craighills of China*, 38.

thinking about mission in the Episcopal Church. World War I had ended, and there was a period of time, roughly a decade, during which Episcopalians were awash in optimism. As David Hein and Gardner Shattuck describe, the war "had provided an unprecedented stimulus to piety, and church leaders were determined to maintain that trend in the 1920s." Further, the war effort "had demonstrated the value of organization and centralization."[5] At war's end, the Episcopal Church, like other Protestant denominations, intensified its efforts to enhance church life and mission.

During the decade of the 1920s, the church would revise its Book of Common Prayer and create a Standing Liturgical Commission to consider later revisions. The church had reason for hopeful planning. Between 1880 and 1920, the number of Episcopal parishes doubled to 8,365, and the church's membership tripled to over one million. Episcopalians marked the end of World War I with changes enacted by the General Convention of 1919. Previously, the church's senior bishop served as presiding bishop. That changed to a system of election by the House of Bishops to renewable six-year terms. Later this would be modified to a single, nine-year term. A National Council was established consisting of bishops, priests, and laity. To consolidate organizational changes and the church's mission, the convention of 1919 announced the "Nation-Wide Campaign" to "identify the needs of their denomination and to increase its financial support."[6] The effort would unite the church's spiritual and material resources to enhance its mission.

The Nation-Wide Campaign elicited fresh energies across the Episcopal Church. Dioceses organized their own committees to conduct fresh initiative in the wake of war. As one diocesan newsletter described, "the world's greatest purpose now should be—the establishment of the Kingdom of the Lord Jesus Christ. Never before was there a time when the application of the teachings of Christ was so needed in the world. Statesmen, philosophers and seers of all nations and races have failed to solve the problems of the world's future. The great war has left the world bleeding and stunned. No scheme of lasting readjustment seems possible unless it measures with the plans of Jesus Christ."[7] Diocesan leaders invited local mission efforts as they sought financial donations for wider plans. The

---

5. Hein and Shattuck, *Episcopalians*, 111.

6. Hein and Shattuck, *Episcopalians*, 112.

7. *Hawaiian Church Chronicle* 12 (January 1920) 4.

church's organization would become efficient while its ends would be more distinct. The church would be in the world but not of the world.

When the Nation-Wide Campaign began, the Craighills were on furlough in the United States. They were gratified by it. Marian Craighill wrote that "our needs in Nanchang were included in the list of objectives, which made our efforts at fund-raising much easier. During the following year both Lloyd and I became acquainted with the process of 'Speaking about China'—trying in some way . . . to leap the chasm of distance, widely differing cultures, and abysmal ignorance of what our Overseas Mission really was trying to accomplish and make a positive impression."[8] In effect, they became missionaries to their homeland. Marian was encouraged, believing that "we made many friends." In the wake of world war, it was possible to believe that the church had a mission that was more urgently needed than ever. That mission was pursued by increased organizational efficiency. "Efficiency" became a key reference point for church life.

But the ripples of conflict soon reached China. Civil war broke out in 1926 between the forces of the Kuomintang, the ruling party of the Republic of China, and the forces of the Chinese Communist Party. The war was fought intermittently but without resolution until 1937, when Japan's invasion brought about a superficial unity among China's warring parties. Different parts of China were controlled by different forces. The Japanese installed a puppet government in portions they controlled, matching the puppet state they created with their conquest of Manchuria in 1931. Even with a common threat, and the outbreak of a second world war, Kuomintang and Communist armies continued their skirmishes at times. They were positioning themselves for the eventual defeat of Japan that would allow control of China. With Japan's defeat in 1945, full-scale conflict resumed, and the Communist Party gained control in 1949. Remaining elements of the Kuomintang were forced to carry their republican ideal to Taiwan.

There was bitter irony for Marian and Lloyd Craighill. They had made a home in China where they began to raise a family and to advance in their missionary work. There was much to mark their success. They not only built the Episcopal Church in Nanchang; they helped to link it with other denominations and wider Christian initiatives. In April 1922, for example, Marian wrote in her diary of the visit of a delegation from

8. Craighill, *Craighills of China*, 55.

the World Student Christian Federation. A little later she wrote with equal satisfaction of work with the Methodist mission in Nanchang. The Craighills' efforts centered on bringing China to faith in Jesus Christ and on building the church. Bridges over denominational differences and united student groups were viewed as stages in the steady advance of mission. For a while, progress remained a viable reference. The most tangible evidence was institutional expansion. Until military conflict and political upheaval shattered their work, it was possible to believe in the means as well as the ends of their callings.

But their world was steadily interrupted until it was overturned. There had been talk of unrest in 1926; a young Chinese general named Chiang Kai Shek had set his sights on completing unification of the country under the Nationalist Party, or Kuomintang.[9] When war broke out, Nanchang was a point of contention, conflicting forces moving back and forth across the region. Dozens of refugees sought shelter with the Craighills, who managed to welcome them. The sounds of gunfire became frequent, and bullets could be heard whistling by the house. No end could be glimpsed as China slipped into factionalism. As Marian Craighill recorded, Chinese forces were bitterly divided over the presence of missionaries and their institutions. Chiang Kai Shek's faction wanted missionary schools to continue, though under government control. Left-wing groups, including communists, wanted to abolish religion, shutter religious institutions, and expel missionaries. As hostilities spread, reports of anti-religious attacks, including murders of foreigners, multiplied. The Craighills' lives were upended. The parish school was commandeered for military officers' quarters. A few months later, in April 1927, word of assaults on foreigners prompted Lloyd and Marian and their family to flee.[10] A group of Chinese friends tearfully saw them off, a gesture which affected the Craighills deeply. They had deeper ties to China than they had realized.

Yet departure was necessary, even if they anticipated an eventual return. By late 1927, they were in Japan, sharing a rural cottage with American friends. But Lloyd Craighill had more work to do. He traveled back and forth between his family in Japan and his duties in China. He was even able to visit Nanchang and to participate in a regional church synod. He was the only foreign clergyperson in attendance, and one of

9. Taylor, *Generalissimo.*
10. Craighill, *Craighills of China,* 121.

only seven foreigners among nearly seventy delegates. Hasty work on modifications of canon law legitimized transfer of the church to greater Chinese control, at least in Western eyes. Still the work was not finished. The Craighill family returned to Nanchang in 1932 to participate in the work of rebuilding. Hostilities had abated for a time and again it was possible to hope. The Craighills' faith was irrepressible.

However new rounds of church meetings and conferences could not blunt the force of conflict. At first, the Craighills again became refugees in China, fleeing to Shanghai to seek a semblance of stability. Their children entered the American School there even as war neared. It was ironic that in 1939 Lloyd Craighill was chosen to succeed Daniel Huntington as bishop of Anking. He was consecrated in 1940 in a liturgy that also elevated Robin Chen to the episcopate.[11] Chen would be the last presiding bishop of the Anglican Church in China and would die during house arrest under communist rule. Lloyd Craighill's life would be similarly threatened sooner under Japanese occupation. But he would be repatriated to the United States in 1943. In March 1971, he died suddenly in Lexington, Virginia, where he and Marian had retired.

As war followed war in the first half of the twentieth century, every missionary could tell some version of the Craighills' story. All began their service with some degree of the assurance Lloyd and Marian embodied. All found that assurance challenged, and for some, it was simply shattered by pervasive upheaval. In every culture and context, the premises of mission as Western churches envisioned them eroded. China offered the most extreme confrontation with mission, but no setting could avoid the strain of conflict. An era of upheaval marked the end of colonialism. The churches had inadvertently relied upon their alignment with Western influence. They were forced to adapt to new circumstances and did so by returning to their theological foundations.

SEEKING THEOLOGICAL FOUNDATIONS

The development of Christian mission by American churches had relied upon a symbiotic relationship between religious institutions and cultural intentions. The religious motivation and what resulted from it cannot be dismissed. But the religious dimension of mission extended the alliance of faith and culture that characterized the American religious mainstream

---

11. Craighill, *Craighills of China*, 246.

into the twentieth century. Such terms as "progress" and "efficiency" flowed easily from the lips of leaders because they shared in the vibrant optimism that defined American public life. The dramatic recovery of American institutions after the Civil War did not address the question of racial justice, which had provoked the conflict in the first place. Yet American entry onto the world stage as a colonizing power meant that the question of justice would have to be confronted on a global scale, especially as tensions came to a breaking point by the mid-twentieth century. So long as the idea of "progress" inspired unquestioned belief, all else receded from the priorities of decision-makers. American influence, including that of missionaries, took precedent. However, the time would come when disillusion with progress would compel an examination of conscience. In their own ways, the churches came to grips with the reality of conflict and the deeper question of how faith best interacted with culture. The result would be a rethinking of the meaning of mission.

The refocusing of Christian identity and the church's mission in the twentieth century began with the Swiss pastor and theologian Karl Barth. He was horrified when a prominent group of German church leaders gave outright endorsement of their country's aims in World War I. Barth, like a growing swath of European and American religious figures, was further horrified by the devastation caused by extensive, prolonged conflict. He rejected the ready accommodation of church and state, or *Kulturprotestantismus*. Dismissing such accommodation as idolatry, Barth considered how the relation between God and the world must be construed. He formulated a challenge to the doctrinal and exegetical premises of his age, spurred by an idea from his friend, Eduard Thurneysen, that God must be seen as "wholly other." Guided by the conviction of God's transcendence, Barth wrote a commentary on Paul's epistle to the Romans. When the book appeared, it created a sensation and immediately became a classic. Barth's critique was biting. Religion is not on the side of God, he concluded, but of the world. "Church and mission, personally strong convictions and morality, pacifism and social democracy do not represent the Kingdom of God, but rather in new forms the old kingdom of humanity."[12]

For Barth, there was a different kingdom that had quietly begun. It was distinct from worldly pretensions of grandeur. The fact of Jesus Christ is the decisive statement of God's grace. Through Christ,

12. Tietz, *Karl Barth*, 89.

humankind hears the divine call to redeemed life. This is the step taken by the believing person, neither rejecting the world nor uncritically embracing it. Life is pursued in a new way, by new criteria: the Christian life is lived amid yet distinguished from the world. Such an electrifying stance revamped Protestant theology. The movement resulting from it was named "neo-orthodoxy," though Barth disliked the term. It gained momentum with the deepening of social crisis—world war was followed by economic depression, then another world war. Barth's ideas left a stark imprint, especially his central emphasis on God's transcendence. Yet different theologians took Barth's conviction in somewhat different directions. In part, the result would be a decisive reorientation of the theology taught at Virginia Seminary.

Reinhold Niebuhr of Union Theological Seminary in New York was the most obviously pastoral and ethical voice of the new theological turn in the United States. He built a powerful public voice for ethical reflection on policy, becoming a notable influence outside the churches and the academy. Niebuhr shared neo-orthodoxy's emphasis on God's transcendence, using this pillar of the movement to craft his public stance. A prophetic figure capable of thunderous jeremiads, Niebuhr defended democracy while critiquing society's moral failures. He elevated the moral role of the individual in an immoral world. Paul Tillich, a German émigré, spent much of his career at Union Seminary, then taught at Harvard and the University of Chicago. Tillich gave dazzling philosophical reflections on the human search for meaning, reflecting in his own way Niebuhr's emphasis on the individual's moral search. For Tillich, the fulcrum of life lay in the individual finding meaning through connection to larger, transcendent reality. Both Niebuhr and Tillich left powerful imprints upon two students doing advanced study at Union. Albert T. Mollegen, a graduate of Virginia Seminary and one of Tillich's first American students, would return to Alexandria to teach from 1936 to 1974.[13] Clifford Stanley, also a Virginia alumnus, would interrupt his teaching career in Alexandria to earn a doctorate at Union and to serve in parish ministry, returning to Virginia Seminary where he taught from 1946 until 1970.

Stanley and Mollegen brought both theological content and hortatory style from their studies in New York. They inspired significant

13. Mollegen, "Christology and Biblical Criticism in Tillich."

changes in teaching at Virginia Seminary.[14] As a result, mission also would be understood in a new way. Stanley's teaching and example to students drew on the seminary's legacy. He was appreciative of the optimistic liberalism of Walter Russell Bowie, who was a faculty colleague for a time in the 1950s. He represented the "liberal evangelicalism" encouraged by Alexander C. Zabriskie and others, including Henry St. George Tucker. In 1943, Zabriskie edited a volume which elaborated on the nature of Anglican evangelicalism. Tucker, by then presiding bishop of the Episcopal Church, wrote the book's foreword and joined Zabriskie to write a chapter on mission.

Not surprisingly, Tucker and Zabriskie declared that the "Church's task is to make the Gospel known by deed and word."[15] Christ's action and teaching embodied a duty that has become incumbent upon all believers. But this chapter reflected an older view of the church's relation to culture. Tucker and Zabriskie wrote of influencing "the structure and policies of governments," promoting policies "that can live harmoniously together . . . upon a fairly general agreement of the worth and function of the individual."[16] Cautious about the church's role in public life, they nevertheless were presumptuous about the church's public place. The critical sensibility that arose with the neo-orthodox movement was absent. Tucker, Zabriskie, and the evangelicalism that thrived at Virginia Seminary well into the twentieth century left a legacy of extraordinary conviction and commitment. In speaking of mission, Tucker and Zabriskie emphasized the goal of creating autonomous branches of the church, a theme Tucker emphasized repeatedly.[17] Yet, amid an impressive synthesis of faith, church, and mission there was a blind spot. That hole was filled by neo-orthodox influences, especially that of H. Richard Niebuhr.

Brother of Reinhold Niebuhr, H. Richard Niebuhr was cast in a different theological mold. Reinhold focused on the nature of the church's public role and cast it paradoxically, while H. Richard considered the nature of the church itself. Thus, he focused on the most critical theme of all in regard to mission: the church's relation to culture. His book *Christ and Culture* became a theological classic, and the issues it raised surfaced in his other writings. Five patterns of relation appeared: Christ against

14. Stevenson, *Theology and Culture.*

15. Tucker and Zabriskie, "Evangelicals and Missions," 191.

16. Tucker and Zabriskie, "Evangelicals and Missions," 193.

17. Tucker and Zabriskie, "Evangelicals and Missions," 195.

culture, Christ of culture, Christ above culture, Christ and culture in paradox, and Christ the transformer of culture.

For our purposes here, D. A. Carson's analysis of the issue of Christ and culture helps to delineate how the typology applies to mission history.[18] Carson describes the pattern of Christ above culture as a synthetic stance embodying an effort to marry the best of culture to the intention of the church. This attempt at synthesis depicts the goal of mission up to the era of the First and Second World Wars. The result was uncritical assumption that the church's mission proudly embodied Western culture. Following this era, neo-orthodoxy represented a shift toward the fifth category, Christ the transformer of culture—the category to which H. Richard was most attracted. Carson speaks of this pattern as "conversionist" in a genuine sense. His example of this approach is Augustine, for whom the integrity of the church's faith and practice as well as the necessity of its public role both mattered. The church must be in the world but not of the world. H. Richard Niebuhr gave this conviction modern theological grounding.

Fueled by the Niebuhr brothers and Tillich, Albert T. Mollegen forcefully embodied the ideal of Christ transforming culture. Like Reinhold Niebuhr, Mollegen spoke, wrote, and taught about the relation of the New Testament to modern moral challenges. However, more like H. Richard Niebuhr, Mollegen drew his conviction from the biblical ideal of the kingdom of God. Accordingly, in the volume edited by Zabriskie, Mollegen wrote a chapter on "Evangelicalism and Christian Social Ethics." It posed a different point of view, arguing that Christian life is framed by the kingdom of God, not by any earthly kingdom. The kingdom of God represents "God's Sway, not Man's."[19] The kingdom of God engages history, but it stands apart from human forms of achievement other than to transform them, encountering opposition in the process. It was not an isolated theme for Mollegen. He would utter it forcefully, often, and to diverse audiences.

One of Albert Mollegen's most influential efforts was a yearly series of presentations on the broad theme of "Christianity and Modern Man." Each Wednesday evening, for nine months of each year, starting in 1947, various Virginia Seminary faculty joined with Mollegen for lectures given at the Washington National Cathedral. Carefully preserved in spiral

18. Carson, *Christ and Culture Revisited.*

19. Mollegen, "Evangelicalism and Social Ethics," 232.

binders, the series was never formally published, but it was distributed nevertheless. Despite an academic format, the series drew audiences sufficient to sustain it until 1965. Mollegen believed not only in a theological response to modern life. He also believed that such discussion should not be confined to the seminary's campus. The church was defined not hierarchically, but in its pews, at its grassroots, he seemed to say. The crisis of church and culture was an experience lived widely by all people. In his own way, Mollegen encouraged reconsideration of the church's mission.

Such broad questions were the staple of "Christianity and Modern Man." Of course, Mollegen himself held clearly defined views and offered them in an energetically personal style. But he held the door open for views that resonated without echoing his own positions. Thus, on February 23, 1949, when a new series of Wednesday evening lectures began, the first eight were given by Kenneth Heim of the Virginia Seminary faculty. Heim was assistant professor of church history with a strong interest in mission. He assumed his teaching role at the end of World War II, having served as a Navy chaplain. He would not serve solely as a seminary faculty member for long. In 1952, Heim became the Episcopal Church's liaison to the Japanese church, the Nippon Sei Ko Kai. As such, he also became a prominent figure in guiding missionary strategy and rebuilding the church and its role after the destruction of war. For some years he would return to Alexandria each summer to teach an intensive course on mission. But the focus of his ministry became Japan, where he served until 1972.

In early 1949 at the Washington Cathedral, Heim devoted his presentations to the problem of Christianity and culture.[20] Framing his thoughts as a review of Christian history, he took a balanced view. It wasn't as if the modern world had suddenly awakened to the fact that culture and faith stood in uneasy relationship to one another. From Christianity's earliest years, the issue had been apparent. It was more than a matter of the church versus the world. At times, notably in the Middle Ages, the church had created its own elaborate culture and proposed to define social life broadly. That culture with its noble expressions had exploded. Within Roman Catholicism there had been creative response. But the Roman Church could not presume to be a straightforward continuation of the medieval arrangement. Upheaval around it proved inevitable.

20. Heim and Mollegen, "Christianity and History."

With apparent implications for the mid-twentieth century, Heim asked why the old order fragmented. It did not simply dissolve: the Roman Catholic church still existed after the Protestant Reformation. However, Heim argued, a situation arose that "I think perhaps explains our plight today," namely, that "we stand in the midst of cultural structures whose meaning is not (and cannot be) self-explanatory—and even whose inner meaning is a perversion of a religious insight which has been lost." He cited "political democracy" and communism as illustrative. The churches, which once provided a center of meaning "from which the whole life of a culture can flow," had become "simply weak rivals with rival organizations, bidding for time and energy with the state, with art, with technology, with philosophy, or with any of the other forms of life, including education." There was a crisis of meaning for the church as well as for the world.[21]

Over their sixteen lectures in early 1949, both Heim and Mollegen balanced their critiques of the church and culture with points of emphasis that might guide faithful response. Heim drew on Paul Tillich's assessment of culture to criticize the autonomous instinct of modern life, for individuals and societies, yet his reliance on Tillich also led him to allow that a "theonomous" view of culture gave both a superior, hence, divine law and invited human participation in it. The modern desire for freedom can only be fulfilled by means of the unity that finds its source in revelation. In other words, culture is not the answer for Christianity; Christianity is the answer for culture. Through culture the human longing for God appears. Such longing must begin personally, then move outwardly. Its aim is a joining of what has been isolated. As Protestantism had intuited, unity with one another and with God arises in ongoing search, not in reverence for social and institutional forms.

Mollegen began his lectures in this series with a summary of the classic Protestant view, emphasizing the possibility of grace amid the reality of sin.[22] The basis for redemption begins personally with individuals drawn toward right relationship with God and one another. But Christianity cannot remain at a private, individual level. The paradigm for finding God remains individual, but it extends socially. God put human beings on earth for fellowship, he stressed. Thus, Mollegen continued, the church's focus is on local expression and not on its alignment with

---

21. Heim and Mollegen, "Christianity and History," 5.
22. Heim and Mollegen, "Christianity and History," 73.

the state. The church makes its greatest contribution through education. In turn, education must involve the cultivation of a critical spirit. Mollegen affirmed the role of faith in a democratic state, but he shifted the emphasis from that of the previous generation. In his view, the church must support democracy and culture by honest, thorough critique. Mere endorsement no longer sufficed.

The opinions of Heim and Mollegen gave early signs of a change in thinking that would characterize theological education. Reflecting a new emphasis on religious integrity, the churches widely embraced the idea of a critical spirit. They absorbed the intention of becoming a distinctive fellowship with a role to play in education. Such emphasis grew as the local intention of church life suggested by Mollegen gained momentum. While the immediate locus of mission seemed to be in suburban America, the shape of mission was reconstrued at home and abroad.

SHIFTING THE FOCUS OF MISSION

By the mid-twentieth century, the world that facilitated extensive mission programs had changed forever. The presumptions and pretensions of the old Western way of life had eroded and would continue to erode. The most dramatic case was China. An obvious instance there concerned St. John's University in Shanghai. Founded in 1879 by Episcopal missionaries, it was esteemed as one of the finest educational institutions in Asia. It became a model of the sort of education that expressed the intention of mission. Even by the 1930s, speakers at university events such as commencements included American and British diplomatic, business, and military leaders. War's destruction followed by communist takeover led to closure in 1952. Like the entire apparatus of mission in China, it was gone. The reality was less stark elsewhere. But the need to reframe and regroup was apparent. Even where the flames of war had not intruded, the old ways of mission could not continue. The era of Western pretension was ending.

In the corridors of American theological education, the shifting focus of mission was not immediately considered. However, the need for theological restatement had been driven home by war. Kenneth Heim and Albert Mollegen brought insight to the classroom and to wider publics. In these settings, Heim challenged his audiences to recognize that changes were needed in mission. His eventual turn to work in Japan illustrated the readiness of mission leaders to engage on fresh terms. Rebuilding mission required theological guidance. For example, both Heim and Mollegen spoke of a local focus. Mollegen also emphasized "right relations" with God and among people as the intention of theology.[23] Mission would shift its focus in such directions. There was much more to be said, of course, and applying the insights of various disciplines as well as lessons from contextual experiences would become a lengthy process that has never concluded. The "Christianity and Modern Man" series made it plain that the church's mission and the role of theological education in it were changing. The prospects for a cosmopolitan approach to mission brightened.

Though not apparently related to mission, the teaching and writing of Reuel L. Howe held important implications. The immediate intention of his work was pastoral. During the twentieth century, but especially in the wake of World War II, pastoral care grew as a discipline and as a principal component of a seminary's curriculum. Howe was a pioneer in the theory and practice of pastoral care. Something of a summation of his work came in 1963 with publication of *The Miracle of Dialogue*. It was a masterful treatise on the meaning of reconciliation. It also signaled a cosmopolitan turn, that is, an in-depth treatment of what Mollegen had called "right relations." Early in this work, Howe took an unequivocal stance: "There is only one qualification to these claims for dialogue: it must be nurtured and proceed from both sides, and the parties to it must persist relentlessly. The word of dialogue may be spoken by one side but evaded or ignored by the other, in which case the promise may not be fulfilled."[24]

Howe saw dialogue as the main highway in the search for truth. "Religious people, for example, sometimes speak the truth they profess monologically, that is, they hold it exclusively and inwardly as if there was no possible relation between what they believe and what others believe, in spite of every indication that separately held truths are often complementary."[25] He warned of the ways that religiously narrow people could slide into the dangers of intolerance and bigotry. But he did not pose dialogue as dilution of deeply held truth for the sake of superficial agreement. "The dialogical thinker, on the other hand, is willing to speak out of his convictions to the holders of other convictions with genuine

---

23. Heim and Mollegen, "Christianity and History," 92.

24. Howe, *Miracle of Dialogue*, 3.

25. Howe, *Miracle of Dialogue*, 9.

interest in them and a sense of the possibilities between them."[26] Nor was there any diminishing of the character of the church's tradition or the importance of its ministry. Indeed, Howe called for a revitalized approach to education by the churches. The "transmission" of knowledge was not enough; "induction" of truth was also needed.

Informed by the Jewish mystical philosopher Martin Buber, Howe saw dialogue less as formulaic process and more as encounter. "It is that interaction between persons in which one of them seeks to give himself as he is to the other, and seeks to know the other as he is. This means that he will not attempt to impose his own truth and view on the other." Howe added that when "we talk to others with the sole purpose of getting them to do what we want, we are exploiting them." Such a posture of mutuality not only had the potential to reject exploitation; it could revitalize the church. By revitalization, Howe meant "to bring back the forms of life into relation to the vitality which originally produced them."[27] There must be generative tension between vitality and form, framed as dialogue, for the church and all institutions to thrive. He specified that one of the core tasks of ministry is to keep worship and teaching in tension with the meanings of daily life. This premise applied to theological education as well. The nature of theological education should shift "from that of transmitting knowledge about the faith to training men for action in the faith."[28]

"Tension" was not an abstract category for Reuel Howe and reference to theological education no less abstract. By 1963, when *The Miracle of Dialogue* appeared, he had been gone from Virginia Seminary for six years. He founded the Institute for Advanced Pastoral Studies in a Detroit suburb, but the departure from Alexandria represented more than the appeal of a new opportunity. In his history of the seminary, John Booty outlined the tension. In 1954, Alexander Zabriskie, who had returned to teaching church history after his tenure as dean, completed a manuscript he never published. Zabriskie described the tradition of Virginia Seminary, intending for that tradition to be embraced by later generations.[29] He took a broad view of Anglicanism while underscoring the "Protestant aspect of Anglicanism" manifest at the seminary. He spoke

26. Howe, *Miracle of Dialogue*, 37.
27. Howe, *Miracle of Dialogue*, 64.
28. Howe, *Miracle of Dialogue*, 149.
29. Booty, *Mission and Ministry*, 240.

proudly of the missionary legacy, noting that "two-hundred and eleven Virginia Seminary men have served overseas. . . . This is over 10% of all the alumni in our entire history, who total 2,238."[30] It was a touching miscalculation, softened by his insight into their motivations. Those who went into mission intended to "extend Christ's dominion everywhere, . . . to share the benefits of Christian discipleship with others," and he saw in these missionaries a conviction that "a stable and constructive world civilization could be reared only on the basis of Christian faith and moral principles."[31] Perceptively, Booty wondered if Zabriskie was "aware of the change of attitude at Virginia Seminary toward missions, change already occurring generally."[32]

Zabriskie was aware of the new approach to pastoral care fostered by Reuel Howe though he could not foresee its impact on mission. In his manuscript, Zabriskie seemingly praised Howe for "the new type of training" that tapped "the most recently developed knowledge and skills."[33] But he questioned whether the new training would produce pastors in the mold of William Meade, who was for Zabriskie an ideal which harkened back to the seminary's founding. Rather than the psychological approach which he identified with Howe, Zabriskie argued for the theological approach he traced to Meade, hence, to what appeared traditional. There was a larger debate, Booty noted, between theory and practice.[34] It was also a debate around faithful innovation in education and in ministry. Howe foresaw an emerging approach which married theory and practice in innovative ways. It was too much of a leap for the likes of Zabriskie, though its wisdom would prevail. Later, debate along such lines would touch issues of social justice, church and culture, spiritual renewal, liturgy, and sexuality. The tension that prompted Reuel Howe to leave Virginia and that moved Alexander Zabriskie to consider the place of tradition bespoke an emerging crisis over the nature of the church and its mission. For the time being, mission meant what it had long meant, at least to the church's leadership circles. On closer examination, change could be discerned.

30. Zabriskie, "No Mean Inheritance," 23; quoted in Booty, *Mission and Ministry*, 239.

31. Zabriskie, "No Mean Inheritance," 2; quoted in Booty, *Mission and Ministry*, 239.

32. Booty, *Mission and Ministry*, 239.

33. Booty, *Mission and Ministry*, 240.

34. Booty, *Mission and Ministry*, 240.

Such marks were most apparent in Japan in the 1950s. At one level, the tension appearing in American seminary life had an overseas version. In its Winter 1956 edition, *Japan Missions*, a publication of the Episcopal mission to Japan, bemoaned cuts in giving to mission work in a lead editorial. The Episcopal Church's recent General Convention had made seemingly drastic reductions, meaning that fewer missionaries and atrophied programs would result. Such cuts would subvert the Episcopal Church's announced goal for its mission in Japan. This goal had a familiar ring. "The only thing that matters is that Japan shall become a Christian nation. The future of the whole Church in the Far East may depend largely upon the future of the Church in Japan."[35] The editorial lamented that the Episcopal Church was not pouring people and material into the mission. It was an epitaph for a goal from fifty years before.

By contrast, the same issue of *Japan Missions* included an article by Timothy S. Iwai, a priest and chaplain at St. Paul's University who had studied at the University of Chicago. Iwai made no reference to the idea of Japan becoming a Christian nation. But in "Christianity and Japanese Culture," he foresaw the future task of mission. Japan had already absorbed aspects of Western material culture. Next, it should absorb the best of Western spiritual culture. There was ample historical precedent. Japan had incorporated other cultures and faiths, notably Buddhism. The time had come to absorb Christianity. The task, Iwai implied, was not to make Japan a Christian nation, but to make Christianity genuinely Japanese.[36] He captured the turn in mission intention that was beginning globally. It was a stark departure from prior American assumptions.

Outside the purview of Western church bureaucrats, Episcopal missionaries who were graduates of Virginia Seminary were moving in a similar direction. On April 29, 1954, William D. Eddy, missionary and Virginia Seminary alumnus, wrote to Miss Mary Dillon.[37] She was a potential donor who could supply the funding necessary to create a student center for Episcopal Church mission at Hokkaido University in Sapporo, Japan. Such a center would place the church adjacent to a major educational institution. There would be dormitory space, a chapel, and meeting space sufficient to attract significant gatherings. Later, Eddy reported that while funds from the Episcopal Church were insufficient, a Japanese

35. *Japan Missions* 6 (1956) 1.
36. Iwai, "Christianity and Japanese Culture," 16.
37. Eddy to Mary Dillon, April 29, 1954.

construction company pledged the needed amount. Encompassing over seven thousand square feet, the center would be a place where the church could influence education and contribute its moral voice.[38] By 1955, the center had begun a series of events. A dialogue with Japanese culture began. A new door to cosmopolitanism opened.

The emphasis on dialogue lasted. On May 28, 1959, another Virginia Seminary alumnus, Beverley Tucker, cousin to the late presiding bishop, wrote a lengthy letter to family and friends. Tucker described events surrounding the centennial observances of the founding of the Nippon Sei Ko Kai by missionaries John Liggins and Channing Moore Williams. Tucker noted fondly that "our Church was the first to send missionaries to Japan after it was opened by Commodore Perry, himself an Episcopalian, as was also the first envoy, Townsend Harris, who used to read the service of Morning Prayer in a loud voice even when it was forbidden." By contrast, "the Church today is fully independent under the leadership of the Japanese bishops of the ten dioceses and we missionaries serve under them with our fellow Japanese workers."[39]

For the centennial, Geoffrey Fisher, archbishop of Canterbury, and Arthur Lichtenberger, presiding bishop, were present. The first evening, organized by Kenneth Heim, featured talks by the missionaries themselves. Instead of a speech by the presiding bishop, he listened as others spoke. Presentations were followed by dialogue as a forum on mission began. Amid formalities and worship, more dialogue arose. "One of the best meetings," Tucker emphasized, "was a panel discussion in which questions and opinions were heard from the floor. This gave laymen a chance to make their views heard, and some of them were very good." Tucker regretted only that there was no time for small group discussions, for "freer exchange of ideas, spontaneous prayer and more general participation."[40] The church in Japan was grounded as never before.

Dialogue became a means to a new beginning. The necessary regrouping of the church's mission would deepen as intractable problems within and without the church tested its faith and its ability to adapt. Hints of cosmopolitan possibility, such as dialogue, would blossom into a new mission sensibility.

38. Eddy to Mary Dillon, July 20, 1954.
39. Tucker to family and friends, May 28, 1959.
40. Tucker to Mary Dillon, July 20, 1954.

8

Renewing the Church's Mission

NEW VENUES, FRESH APPROACHES

WITH THE DEPARTURE OF Kenneth Heim, Virginia Seminary's commitment to the teaching of mission seemingly waned. To be sure, Heim had focused much of his teaching on church history. Yet he devoted the bulk of his career to mission. Meanwhile, in Alexandria, students continued to show interest in mission, sometimes in striking ways. Eleven of the forty-three members of the class of 1950 entered mission service in various locales including five who went to Japan. Two members of the class of 1952 would increase the total of alumni serving there.[1] The Missionary Society functioned in notable continuity with its origins. In the spring of 1953, the society made financial gifts to ten mission sites totaling $4,500. The largest single gift was $1,000 sent to the church in Korea for relief efforts in the wake of war. A total of $900 went to four projects of the church in Japan, the largest being $500 to a scholarship fund at Central Theological College. Other recipients of donations included branches of the church in Brazil, Cuba, Alaska, and Hawaii. In other years, such as 1951, financial gifts were made to the church in Liberia, Costa Rica, and Mexico as well. Yet gifts to Japan often surpassed those to other branches of the church. Continued ties to Kenneth Heim may explain the discrepancy.[2]

The Missionary Society also continued to attract noted speakers. In the spring of 1954, for instance, theologian Paul Lehman of Princeton

1. Booty, *Mission and Ministry*, 380–85.
2. Missionary Society, "Proposed Appropriations," 1953.

Theological Seminary spoke at Virginia Seminary. The letter of invitation was sent in the summer of 1953 by J. Seymour Flinn, seminary student and president of the society, and it emphasized Virginia's legacy of commitment to mission. Flinn believed that Lehman would help to pull his listeners out of "an Episcopal rut." Seeing a need for a revised theology of mission, Flinn also hoped that Lehman could "spare an evening to come down and tell us something of the thinking that is going on in other churches as well as share with us some of your insights on the Christian motives for mission."[3]

Flinn's invitation and Lehman's ready response illustrate that interest in mission on the Virginia Seminary campus was not in abeyance. The departure of Kenneth Heim did not mean retrenchment on an historic commitment. As the invitation to Paul Lehman suggested, mission was being rethought. The interest was no longer in forming missionaries who would display an unquestioning loyalty to institutions and who would automatically accept the means and ends of a given project. Mission was being rethought, but not mission alone. Hints of tension between Reuel Howe and Alexander Zabriskie pointed to a trend in many theological institutions. In the wake of wars and in the face of intellectual challenges from those influenced by Marx and Freud, there was a broad impulse to rearticulate theological foundations. Albert Mollegen's work was an example. He devoted lectures and writings to the challenge of secularism epitomized by Freud and Marx. There was consensus that the churches should reinforce their basis of faith.

Accordingly, the Virginia Seminary faculty grew significantly. In the 1950s most of the additions came in the fields of Bible and theology. There also was new emphasis on church history and pastoral care. In 1945, there had been a faculty of six. In 1955, the faculty would number fifteen. By 1974, there would be twenty-five faculty and administrators.[4] Pastoral care was a striking aspect of this growth. Reuel Howe may not have had a long tenure in Alexandria, but questions about his deference to psychology did not obscure a need for courses in pastoral care. The rationale for this work and for wider attention to theological foundations was obvious. After World War II there was a new and obvious mission field just beyond the seminary campus: the suburb. In many American

3. Missionary Society, Correspondence, 1953 and 1954.
4. Booty, *Mission and Ministry*, 253, 319.

metropolitan areas, there was rapid population growth outward from the center city. Americans began to speak of suburbs and suburban lifestyles.

In the emerging suburbs, young Americans envisioned starting families in areas filled with families like their own. Formerly barren acreage erupted in development. There were new homes and shopping centers, followed by freeways linking residential areas to employment in the city. In the new areas, new churches had to be planted. Clergy had to be equipped with fresh skills to face novel issues brought on by unprecedented mobility and rapid settlement. Social upheaval after war added to a widespread feeling of dislocation, as welcome as new homes and opportunities could be. The promise of suburban living was not always fulfilled. New social realities inspired fears, doubts, instability, and even infidelity. The church needed to reaffirm its faith in ways that both challenged and comforted. Rearticulation of the foundations of faith, a new emphasis on pastoral care, creative local leadership—these features defined mission to suburban America.

The educational turn at Virginia Theological Seminary—and the growth of suburban Washington, DC, which necessitated this turn in the first place—were not unique. One study has persuasively linked changes in theological education and the growth of suburban America to the surge of military veterans returning home.[5] There was a search for the essence of faith coupled with impatience over what were deemed nonessential matters of religious identity. A new style of local faith community arose. Suburban church buildings included space for education and for social gatherings, such as coffee hours and church dinners. Denominational identity mattered, but one did not presume to remain in the religious confession to which one may have been born. There was new fluidity in religious identity, not unlike the fluidity of one's residence. Yet membership in a religious group was valued. As one historian has noted, "Millions of Americans in the same stage of family life cycle now lived in close proximity to one another."[6] Religious membership became an extension of local community. But such community had to be built and rooted in a secure, local identity.

The results of the rush for affiliation were not entirely surprising: in the 1950s the churches grew, and institutional religion in its local forms set the tone. What did prove surprising, at least in the case of the Episcopal

5. Walters, "Beyond the Battle."
6. Miller, "Growing Suburbs, Relocating Churches," 359.

Church, was that one-quarter of all persons baptized in 1950 were adults.[7] The reason for the popularity of Albert Mollegen's "Christianity and Modern Man" series becomes plain. There was a pervasive searching for faith and community by adults. As returning military veterans attempted to physically relocate, they were also trying to locate themselves spiritually, considering and testing the different outlooks available in the American religious landscape. Their building and rooting defined suburban America as the mission field in the 1950s and was one factor that distracted mainstream Protestant denominations from overseas mission.

Grant Wacker cites another factor that diminished overseas mission commitment in some denominations. After World War II, "pressure toward decolonization led the historic Protestant churches to question the legitimacy of foreign mission."[8] Some invoked reference to cultural imperialism, encouraging the erosion of support. This was less the case at Virginia Seminary, where interest in overseas mission never fully receded. There the energy expended was more about discovery of new forms of faith community and less on disparaging mission practice. Mission was being adapted, not dismissed.

In May 1961, it was plainly spelled out that interest in mission at Virginia Seminary had become diffuse. A survey of members of the junior and middler classes made it difficult to set clear priorities for the Missionary Society, which conducted the poll. The results were somewhat misleading because each student taking the survey could check multiple boxes to indicate multiple interests. That fact in itself underscores the range of mission interests. The largest category to be affirmed was "racial problems & the church," a barometer of what America's dominant social issue was becoming. "Urban work & work with juveniles" was next, followed by a tie (twenty-nine votes for each) between "industrial mission" and "overseas mission." Far down the list were themes that reflected church hierarchies or inter-seminary efforts. However, the categories of "rural missions" and "mission theology and strategy" had notable followings.[9]

The conclusion to be drawn is that mission must entail hands-on efforts in particular contexts. It involves facing conflicted situations on the basis of revised mission approaches, and it emphasizes locally sustained religious community, rather than affiliation with distant religious

7. Lippy, *Faith in America*, 1:8.
8. Wacker, "Pearl S. Buck and the Waning of Interest."
9. Stamper, "Results of Survey of Missionary Interest."

hierarchies. A search for a new, holistic approach to mission began, focusing on community and resolution of conflict. New goals of mission could be glimpsed. These included building understanding and promoting bridge-building. In the background, newly envisioned attributes of faith community could be glimpsed. Informed by wider discussion of the theology of mission, there was emphasis on "God's mission," the *missio Dei*, rather than the church's mission. The intention was to bridge differences as people of faith responded to the sovereignty of God, and the concern was no longer about institutions minimizing cultural differences by imposing Western priorities. The issue of mission began to move toward patterns of practice shaped by the realities of given contexts. The achievement of such an outlook seemed to occur in 1963 at an Anglican congress in Toronto.

That gathering produced a document long deemed pivotal to Anglican mission. It was entitled "Mutual Responsibility and Interdependence in the Body of Christ," or MRI. As William Danaher comments, MRI articulated a "basis for the structures and ethos of contemporary Anglicanism."[10] Specifically, there was a threefold vision:

1. The church's mission is a "response to the living God who in his love creates, reveals, judges, redeems, fulfils";

2. the "unity in Christ expressed in our full communion is the most profound bond among us, in all our political and racial and cultural diversity"; and,

3. this "unity and interdependence must find a completely new level of expression and corporate obedience."[11]

In part, the goals included the creation of diocesan networks for the empowerment of local leadership, the recruitment and training of lay and clergy leaders, and the creation of structures for regular inter-Anglican consultation. What was articulated could be seen as the launch of a new Anglican Communion and certainly the ideals advanced pointed in that direction. Later statements have treated MRI as emblematic of a paradigm shift in mission. But Danaher makes a telling criticism, referencing a presentation given by Max Warren prior to the congress which produced MRI. Then director of the Church Missionary Society, Warren previewed MRI's vision. It was one of "empathic vision," seeing people of "other"

10. Danaher, "Beyond Imagination," 219.
11. Danaher, "Beyond Imagination," 219.

cultures and contexts through their own experiences to seek mutual understanding.[12] The vision was refreshing and remains a vibrant ideal.

The problem was, Danaher urges, that Warren and the process that created MRI retained old assumptions while casting fresh vision. Warren relied on Western presumption and privilege, and "confidence in an enlarged Western perspective." Specifically, what legitimated MRI were continuing expectations of Western role in mission and Western institutional process. Yet, Danaher adds, "What *was* new in this emergent social imaginary was that it assumed contested social space."[13] That is, missionaries had long since understood that there must be indigenous leadership in mission churches. But the missionaries still could not fully grant that having indigenous leadership meant having indigenous control. The way in which leadership would be formed would follow Western norms. The new vision of Anglicanism, replete with suggestions of reformed and locally focused faith community, depended on old realities. Worse, it was unclear how Anglicans might actually function as a communion. Nevertheless, MRI posed a new ideal and granted the reality of contested social space. MRI offered a new basis for discussion, not its conclusion.

Writing in Virginia Seminary's *Journal* in the summer of 1963, Jesse Trotter, dean from 1956 to 1969, described at length the seminary's mission work in Uganda. The plan for this work advanced several purposes. Trotter sought "to educate a strong native leadership against the day when our common Christian cause will be solely in the hands of Africans." The seminary also proposed to bring seminary personnel from Africa to Alexandria for further education, and likewise, the seminary envisioned sending "missionary-teachers" to Africa in order to enhance theological education there. In the seminary's class of 1961, three new graduates left for Uganda to launch the project.[14]

Trotter seemed to grasp the vision of MRI, which was about to be published. He also anticipated something of Danaher's later objection, perhaps more than MRI's framers. Citing Max Warren, Trotter affirmed that "all Africa is now in rebellion" against colonialism. "Until my visit to Africa in February and March of this year, I had little realization of the handicaps to our American missionaries posed by their western and white skins." He spoke bluntly but with understanding. Alongside their

12. Danaher, "Beyond Imagination," 228.
13. Danaher, "Beyond Imagination," 228.
14. Trotter, "Virginia Seminary in Uganda," 1.

assertions of political and cultural autonomy, "African Christians are seeking to wrest control of the African Church from Europeans in high ecclesiastical office and from missionary agencies and societies overseas. These signs of vitality are welcome and their import cannot be ignored."[15]

Trotter would not have been surprised if Christians in Africa insisted on "going it alone," given the legacy of "our arrogant conduct over past generations and centuries. Now we must make our plans within the limits imposed upon us, or more honestly which we have imposed upon ourselves." Although the die was cast, Trotter considered ways in which Virginia Seminary could be of cooperative assistance. In passing, he noted the idea of bringing "African seminary teachers and other key personnel to Alexandria for further education."[16] He added that the seminary would offer scholarships for such persons from Africa in the coming academic year.

As Trotter wrote, three graduates in the class of 1961 were completing the second of their three-year commitments to teach at Bishop Alfred Tucker Theological College in Uganda. The rationale was that the theological college was understaffed and financial aid from Virginia could provide not only additional staff but enhanced facilities. Trotter proudly commented that over $280,000 had been raised from 1,050 parishes and over six hundred individuals. The effort was named the Henry St. George Tucker Memorial Mission to honor the late missionary and bishop. He had no relation to Bishop Alfred Tucker, who had been an English missionary.

Charles W. Tait, Todd H. Trefts, and Philip Turner were the three members of the class of 1961 who had made the commitment to teach in Uganda. But Trotter marveled that the idea's actual inception had been in the fall of 1958 when the class of 1961 enrolled. Twenty-six of the men in the class began discussions of mission, comparing the different settings in which it could be pursued. The class as a whole showed a striking amount of interest in the topic. In the end, six members of the class entered mission service, though one died in India early in his tenure. With consultations that included the Episcopal Church's Overseas Department, a link to Uganda was formed. The three men, all married and with children, went to Uganda soon after graduation. Tait taught Bible, Turner taught New Testament and ethics, and Trefts taught theology.

15. Trotter, "Virginia Seminary in Uganda," 1.

16. Trotter, "Virginia Seminary in Uganda," 1.

Outside the classroom, the theme of community took pride of place, which was somewhat novel in comparison with early twentieth-century mission practice. The American families lived on campus and readily interacted with students, their families, and residents of the vicinity. Ordinands in the student body lived in a "model village" on campus with which there was a particular connection. Interaction happened without restraint. Unabashedly, Trotter noted that, during his visit to the theological college, he met informally with some students: "I was impressed by their openness, their frankness and by the keenness of their intellectual curiosity. But they gave me no peace on race relations in the United States."[17] Obviously global awareness had heightened by 1963.

As a seminary dean, Trotter wrote in detail about the theological college's facilities, its funding and the costs they covered, and the profile of the faculty and student body. He wrote that there were eighty-five students from fifteen African tribes, a hint of increased cultural awareness. It was an extensive and upbeat article enhanced by pictures and revealing Trotter's energy for this work and sensitivity to its nuances. Thus, it seems surprising that the project was not renewed after its three-year commitment expired in 1964. Perhaps the lack of enthusiasm in Alexandria mirrored a similar feeling in Uganda. Issues of Western resources and institutional assumptions undoubtedly arose. Nevertheless, Virginia Seminary's attention to Africa, especially east Africa, was not concluded and would be reframed in the coming years.

REFRAMING FAITH COMMUNITY

There was precedent for Jesse Trotter's visit to Uganda. In 1935, before Trotter became dean, Alexander C. Zabriskie and his wife, Mary, paid an extended visit to the Episcopal Church in Brazil. Mary Zabriskie described the trip in warm detail in an article for the *Spirit of Missions* early in 1936. Her knowledge and respect for people, parishes, and church programs were impressive. There was a fulsome tone capped off by admiring reference to the statue of Christ overlooking Rio de Janeiro. She lauded the warm ties between Brazil and Virginia. One could readily feel her conviction that the work which founded the Episcopal Church in Brazil

17. Trotter, "Virginia Seminary in Uganda," 12.

had been done faithfully and skillfully. Virginians of all sorts could take pride in such a legacy. She looked back with a reassuring nostalgia.[18]

Mary Zabriskie did not diminish the challenges faced by the church nor the need for its continued ministry. There was more to be built. But a generation later, after Jesse Trotter's return from Uganda, the direction of mission and of Virginia Seminary's role in it, had shifted. Those at the seminary were asking how to relate cross-culturally in ways that united. Keeping aloof was not an option. They wanted to speak of the church less as an institution defined along the lines of Western presumption and more as a community capable of appreciating multiple faith experiences and perspectives. Indeed, references to the church as "community" and even to a search for community would proliferate in the second half of the twentieth century. In an article written for the seminary's *Journal* in 1985, Robert Prichard, a recent addition to the faculty, would speak of "The Search for Community" on campus.[19] His reference bespoke more than the dynamics of one seminary or the issues arising from shifts in theological education. There was a widespread search for new forms of community in American life.

In the second half of the twentieth century, the way people sought to define "community" reflected Christianity's opportunity and its challenge in the United States and beyond. The most obvious fact about the immediate postwar years were challenges brought by the church's striking growth across the new suburban areas. In turn, seminaries like Virginia expanded what they offered. But mere expansion was not the answer. The issues arising were more about qualities than quantities. The deep challenge before the churches and the seminaries concerned speaking of community in ways that actually aligned with lived, social experiences of diverse peoples. From this perspective, the issues arising in mission internationally epitomized the sorts of social issues arising in the United States at the same time. It will become clear that racial discrimination and the resulting estrangement between people of different races and cultures challenged casual notions of "community" and necessitated revision of what mission must mean. Community could not be achieved without comparable attention to the meaning of mission.

By the late 1950s, Virginia Seminary's legacy of mission was revisited regularly. At one level this occurred from afar. The March 1959 issue

18. Zabriskie, "Brazil Mission Shows Forth the Christ."
19. Prichard, "Virginia Seminary since World War II," 42.

of the *Seminary Journal* included an article recounting basic details of the church's development in Japan, noting the extent of Virginia's participation back to the founding. The next article in the same edition praised Castro's revolution in Cuba and urged Christians to resist instinctive moral condemnation.[20] Such views reflected an emerging diversity of outlooks as well as renewed attention to the church's role in international affairs. Shortly thereafter, the Missionary Society stepped up its historic task of information gathering from contexts where mission was active. There was, however, a decided difference. In the seminary's early years, correspondence had been exchanged with missionaries who described their settings often with disparaging commentary. By the early 1960s, the letters were being exchanged with indigenous church leaders, often younger, emerging ones.

Community, a building block of cosmopolitan sensibility, was encouraged by networking from one context to another. The matter was not taken casually. The Missionary Society went so far as to publish a set of correspondence from 1963. Admittedly it was an unusual effort that was endorsed by the dean's office. That fact legitimated publishing such letters in a booklet: the publication was sent to various of bishops of the Episcopal Church in order to solicit financial gifts for one or more of the ministries depicted in the letters. The varieties of programs and sites was intended to elicit interest among readers. Even a cursory glance at "Letters from Young Churches," as it was titled, revealed needs for church facilities, clergy support, transport for leaders, schools, hospitals, and even drilling equipment for water wells. The requests came from Japan, Iran, and Jerusalem and, noticeably, from multiple dioceses in east Africa, particularly in Uganda and Tanganyika.[21] Already an independent nation, Tanganyika would merge with Zanzibar in 1964 to create the nation of Tanzania. It would become of greater interest to Virginia Seminary as more than letters were exchanged in coming years.

During the 1960s, the seminary's commitment to mission was being reframed. There were difficult lessons to be learned, but periodic discussions and occasional visiting speakers signaled continuing interest, or so it would seem. To at least one set of eyes, however, there was little sign of fresh energy and vision, certainly not of the sort that C. FitzSimons Allison wanted to see. By January 1971, he was professor of church history

20. Cleaveland, "VTS Graduates," 26–31; LeRoy, "Cuba in Revolution," 33–34.

21. Missionary Society, "Letters from Young Churches."

and an unmistakable voice for the church's historic faith and priorities as he read them. He poured out his convictions and his laments in "Go Ye into All the World and Preach the Gospel," an article in the seminary's *Journal* titled after the biblical passage emblazoned above the chapel altar. It was intended as a rallying cry.[22]

Allison did not single out Virginia Seminary. The church at large could be faulted for having retrenched on what should be its primary commitment. He gave reasons for this perceived decline without pulling punches. Allison saw a failure of nerve in the Western world. He also saw a parochial focus on the church domestically coupled with "culture shock" resulting from waves of American social upheavals. Americans had become insular and resistant to engage cultural difference. Yet the very spiritual revitalization which many American Christians sought would only be found by going outward faithfully. He included words from Kenneth Cragg, Anglican bishop and scholar of Islam. Cragg declared "*that the Gospel is never known except as it is being encountered as we attempt to communicate our understanding of the Gospel across some frontier.*"[23] Allison reiterated, "It is the mission field experience that resets our priorities, re-discovers our Gospel." Such new perception only "occurs on the frontiers."[24]

Allison's insistence on the gospel did not point to older, Western assumptions about evangelism laden with prerogative. He emphasized that "some say . . . they do not want us now." He avoided specific citations but used recognizable references. Rather than authoritarian, colonial bosses, he held, "they want us as brothers, as servants; as servants of the Word and ministers of the Gospel. We would not have it said of us that we only went when we could go on our own terms when we were in control." The true way to go would be in the way of the gospel. On what Allison deemed to be "*radical* frontiers" one would be "stretched to see the difference between the doctrine and the Christ, between the broken vessels and the treasure."[25]

Allison's lack of concrete references and his otherwise dismaying tone were belied by the articles that accompanied his critique. In eight other essays, alumni and friends of the seminary described their

22. Allison, "Go Ye into All the World," 6–9.
23. Allison, "Go Ye into All the World," 8, emphasis original.
24. Allison, "Go Ye into All the World," 8.
25. Allison, "Go Ye into All the World," 9.

ministries in such disparate sites as the Fiji Islands, Colombia, Uganda, Japan, Pakistan, the Philippines, and Latin America. This was more than a travelogue, though details from varied situations proved illuminating and echoed the emergence of shared leadership and a community emphasis. There were also reflections on shared forms of leadership and on the expectation of fully indigenous churches emerging where they had not already done so. William Eddy, by then having accumulated two decades of experience in Japan, wondered if there was a future role for US missionaries. Eddy rejected the alternative roles of kindly benefactor and paternalistic controller of mission affairs. Instead, he argued for the missionary as a kind of spiritual guide and consultant, assisting but neither simply funding nor controlling church work. The focus must be on building the local church as faith community. The gospel must emerge at the grassroots and move outward, he implied. "We should go to be as much of a help and as little a burden on the new churches as we can be, remain deeply committed to our colleagues, and do what can be done for the cause of Christ that is theirs and ours."[26]

Eddy and the other authors in this issue of the *Journal*, including Allison, echoed an ideal that was unfolding in the Episcopal Church: a vision of the church, especially locally, as community. Terms such as "brothers" and "colleagues" bespoke a new intended relationship, moving toward cosmopolitan forms of mutuality and respect. The move in this direction was partly the result of mission discussion which encouraged the turn of direction. It also was clear that by the 1970s, more listening to diverse cultural voice had begun, at least at the seminary. In the pages of the *Journal*, one could read of church leaders and theologians from abroad who had spoken on campus. Visits to and from Africa began to figure prominently. In March 1972, then student and Missionary Society president Richard Jones described what he learned when he listened to Bishop Alphaeus Zulu of Zululand. In June 1973, Samuel Busulwa, a student from Uganda, argued that the cessation of mission work by Western churches would betray their nature. It was a matter of how to conduct mission, not whether it should be done. Busulwa's words were echoed by John Henry Okullu in his sermon at the annual Missionary Service. Okullu would become one of Kenya's prominent bishops. Such illustrations could be multiplied from the 1970s onward. There was a new

26. Eddy, "Is There a Continuing Role," 24.

emphasis on listening as a critical aspect of the church as community. In turn, the creation of community became basic to mission.

Reframing the church as faith community also gained impetus from the widespread Anglican movement toward liturgical revision that would reshape the Episcopal Church's Book of Common Prayer in the 1970s. In *A History of the Episcopal Church*, Robert Prichard called liturgical change the "most visible sign of the redirection of the church."[27] He traced the lengthy process by which church bodies and Episcopalians generally considered proposed changes, often embodied in trial liturgies. The most obvious innovation was adoption of alternative rites using Elizabethan or contemporary English. Advocates of revision cited a need for baptismal and eucharistic emphasis as the church's basic marks of identity, and they also desired greater liturgical roles for laity. One commentator, cited by Prichard, emphasized that the church must declare its distinctiveness. There was acute need for a "more independent basis for its life and mission."[28] He meant that the church must distance itself from Western social values which increasingly were secular. The adoption of a new American Prayer Book in 1979 paralleled similar processes of liturgical revision in much of the Anglican world and reflected extensive, new intra-Anglican discussion.

Though references to the church's mission were frequent in discussions of liturgical revision, it was not clear what such references meant or how they would be pursued. In *Liturgy for Living*, published in 1979, Charles Price of Virginia Seminary and Louis Weil of Nashotah House gave important clues as they explained the anatomy of the revised Prayer Book. The theme of community was prominent. Declaring their enthusiasm for the new book, Price and Weil avowed that "its long-range effect will be to revitalize and enormously deepen our common life in Christ. It will enrich the worship of all Episcopalians and unite us across a broad spectrum of churchmanship around a single flexible and beautiful Book of Common Prayer."[29]

Citing the history of Christian worship and lingering over the Protestant Reformation, Price and Weil noted the emphasis on recovering the spirit of early Christian life. They saw that impetus in the revised book. Previously, however, Protestant reformers had the right idea but

27. Prichard, *History of the Episcopal Church*, 322.

28. Prichard, *History of the Episcopal Church*, 324.

29. Price and Weil, *Liturgy for Living*, xiii.

succumbed to late medieval tendencies toward conformity and rigidity. In the late twentieth century, by contrast, there was a restive "hunger for meaning" and fresh contact with "the mystery of life."[30] As their narrative continued, the emphasis on community was featured. A new insistence on the "active participation of as many people in the congregation as possible" had a clear origin.[31] People "are learning to think of the church, as in New Testament times, not as a building, not as clergy, but as the entire people of God, all with significant parts to play both in worship and in the life of the church in the world."[32]

In the wake of social upheavals across the globe, it was apparent that the church must be a "body of many members where they who are greatest are servants of all."[33] Before describing in detail the new Prayer Book's various liturgies, Price and Weil added that worship as response to God has implications for the whole of life. In particular, worship must not be viewed as individual, private experience. "Worship is also a community affair, and the role of the community is at least as important as the role of the individual person."[34] The values expressed in worship must gather up the values of community. Worship intends "an unfolding life" that builds and then broadens community, overcoming divides. The authors urged that liturgy must point toward reconciliation and mission.[35] These themes would gain higher profile even as American spiritual energies rose.

Revision of the Book of Common Prayer had been an extended process that began in the 1950s. But it gained energies from varied sources including, from the 1960s onward, the eruption of what was known as the "charismatic" movement. Typically called "charismatic" to distinguish it from specifically Pentecostal denominations, the Episcopal version of this movement surfaced in parish life in Van Nuys, California, and Houston, Texas, when rectors of churches Dennis Bennett and Graham Pulkingham spoke in tongues. That is, Bennett, Pulkingham, and others spoke ecstatically and spontaneously in what was deemed the guidance of the Holy Spirit. The power of this movement for worship and parish life, as well as personal faith, was clear. Robert Prichard sees the implication

---

30. Price and Weil, *Liturgy for Living*, 7.

31. Price and Weil, *Liturgy for Living*, 8.

32. Price and Weil, *Liturgy for Living*, 8.

33. Price and Weil, *Liturgy for Living*, 8.

34. Price and Weil, *Liturgy for Living*, 20.

35. Price and Weil, *Liturgy for Living*, 54–57.

of such an experience as "an assurance of God's personal presence in a decade in which many of their coreligionists preferred to speak of faith in social terms."[36] He notes an implicit tension in the charismatic movement, even as there was extensive energizing of faith community. There were as many questions surfacing as there were answers revealed. For example, what about people and parishes where no such charismatic moments had arisen? What sort of identity and authority did the charismatic movement bestow in relation to other Christians and to church structures? In the long run, there would be evidence both of broad, positive influences and deep divisions.

In *Gifts of God*, published in 1985, Charles Price and Eugene V. N. Goetchius argued that too broad a distinction could be made between "ordinary and extraordinary gifts from God."[37] Citing this work, Prichard observes that charismata, or gifts, are given to all Christians and must be used for the good of all. As much as there was evidence of enlivened life, with the capacity to interact creatively with Prayer Book revision and to foster a lively sense of local faith community, there also was apparent tension and division over differing criteria of church life that begged the question of mission. It was yet another reality that impinged upon Virginia Seminary as it reconsidered its role in the church and its mission to the world.

A MATTER OF JUSTICE

As historian Charles Marsh has described, Martin Luther King Jr. glimpsed a lofty goal in his early advocacy for civil rights. In organizing the Montgomery, Alabama, bus boycott, he declared that "the end is reconciliation, the end is redemption, . . . the end is the creation of the beloved community."[38] The reference to the beloved community proved so compelling that Marsh adopted it as the title of his book analyzing the role of religion in the Civil Rights Movement. More specifically, Marsh argued that the sources of the movement lay in African American religious experience and the churches that embodied that faith. It meant more than the churches serving as staging grounds. The core of the Christian faith

36. Prichard, *History of the Episcopal Church*, 447.

37. Goetchius and Price, *Gifts of God*, 30; quoted in Prichard, *History of the Episcopal Church*, 448.

38. Marsh, *Beloved Community*, 1.

shaped the movement just as it already had shaped African American identity. The pursuit of social justice, as the direction in which the movement would evolve, was deemed pivotal for the Black church's mission. The movement for justice also would reshape the way predominantly white denominations like the Episcopal Church considered their own vision and mission, with both enthusiasm and dismay summoned by such debates. The vision of "beloved community" touches the identity and mission of all Christian bodies, and their seminaries as well.

King received avid opposition. In April 1963, after being arrested in the midst of demonstrations for civil rights in Birmingham, Alabama, King was the object of a public "Call for Unity" by eight Birmingham religious leaders. They opposed the public action and the man who was its leader. Instead, the eight religious leaders urged Black people to end the demonstrations and rely on the courts to secure justice. The role of "outsiders"—a reference to King—was held suspect. Two of the eight religious leaders were Charles C. J. Carpenter, Episcopal bishop of Alabama, and his bishop co-adjutor, George M. Murray. Carpenter was a graduate of Virginia Seminary in the class of 1926, and Murray was an alumnus in the class of 1948. In a subsequent diocesan realignment, Murray would serve as bishop of the Central Gulf Coast, based in Mobile, Alabama.[39]

King's response to the eight, his "Letter from Birmingham Jail," has become one of the Civil Rights Movement's enshrined documents. He insisted to the eight leaders, and to the broad public that would read his words, that there was a moral responsibility to break unjust laws, that injustice required direct action rather than waiting for the courts to act. The "Letter" clarified both the aims and the urgency of the movement.[40] Later that year, on August 28, 1963, Martin Luther King Jr.'s famous speech, "I Have a Dream," became the keynote address of the March on Washington. Again, King's words reinforced his vision and made plain its biblical roots. It was a vision of beloved community grounded in recognition of the hope of unity and respect for the particularity of diverse identities. It was for that vision that King worked and for that vision he was murdered on April 4, 1968. Among his many achievements, Martin Luther King Jr. made a call for revised and renewed mission by the churches at home and abroad.

---

39. Bass, *Blessed Are the Peacemakers*, 21–26.
40. Bass, *Blessed Are the Peacemakers*, 24.

In its own way, Virginia Seminary had begun to take tangible steps by this time. In 1951, John Walker became the first African American student to enroll at Virginia Seminary. He graduated in 1954 and would eventually serve as bishop of Washington. In 1953, Bishop Payne Divinity School, founded to educate African American people for service in the Episcopal Church, merged with Virginia Seminary. Later the seminary's library would be named the Bishop Payne Library.[41] The name recalled the first bishop in Liberia. Even more, it honored the legacy of African American Episcopalians and echoed the vision of beloved community. A few years later, in 1958, several years after the seminary merger, conversations about race had begun among faculty, and their thoughts became public. John Q. Beckwith, associate professor of homiletics, gave five presentations on racial discrimination in the "Christianity and Modern Man," series titling his talks "Race Problem and the South." He spoke in the terms of his day by calling for "integration." Beckwith also spoke ahead of his time by referring to "justice."[42] The tone of his address was personal and plaintive. He spoke clearly as a Southerner, but even more clearly as a Christian.

Then the tone of discussion intensified. In the wake of King's murder, the 1968 Workshop on Racial Conflict and Justice revealed deep perceptions and convictions among Black and white members of the Virginia Seminary community. Feelings of anger and fear were widespread and called for further measures that could surface both the full historical record and the nature of the present challenge. There was a widespread sense that a conference on racism early in 1970 had acknowledged the extent of the harsh reality without prompting consensus on addressing it. One outcome was the adoption of a seminary-focused Civil Rights Act in April 1970. In a sense, white leadership of all American institutions was beginning to grasp that the issue of justice for slavery and discrimination was more compelling and more resistant to being engaged than momentary warm words and a few events could resolve. It was increasingly the case that American society fell short, and the burden on the churches was considerable.

Increasingly institutional efforts were held in judgment by the activism that sprouted among some Episcopalians. Even as John Beckwith was writing about integration in 1959, two white priests, Cornelius Tarplee

---

41. Booty, *Mission and Ministry*, 130, 307.
42. Hein and Shattuck, *Episcopalians*, 134; Beckwith, "Race Problem."

and John B. Morris, founded ESCRU, the Episcopal Society for Cultural and Racial Unity.[43] It became a doorway to activism in the South. Some segments of the church's structure needed no prompting. By 1963, the House of Bishops endorsed civil rights legislation and urged church members to take part in the March on Washington, though the sentiment was not unanimous. In April 1964, the wives of three Episcopal bishops—one Black and two white—were arrested in St. Augustine, Florida, for challenging segregation laws at a restaurant. The episode drew admiration as well as surprise and dismay. Amid fresh commitment to social justice, fault lines were appearing like those in most American religious bodies.[44]

The extent of the resistance to confronting injustice was driven home in 1965, when an Episcopal Theological Seminary student, Jonathan Daniels, was murdered while working to register Black voters outside Selma, Alabama. He had gone to Alabama under the auspices of ESCRU.[45] His murder has symbolized sacrificial determination to correct historic wrongs. Soon the Episcopal Church debated sacrificial action when John Hines, the presiding bishop since 1965, called for special action by the General Convention. Hines, a Virginia Seminary graduate in the class of 1933, summoned the General Convention Special Program (GCSP) which would designate $9 million over three years for programs that would empower poor people. Hines's action and the church's response seemed to inaugurate a new era of mission.

However, as David Hein and Gardner Shattuck point out, Hines made tactical errors. He failed to consult African American clergy and he dismissed the senior Black member of the church's national staff. He also failed to anticipate that some bishops and dioceses would be resistant to GCSP. In other words, despite its daring vision, GCSP failed to advance beloved community. Habitual institutional assumptions diminished the good work. Fragmentation of the effort and the church became clear in 1969 at a special meeting of the General Convention intended to address unfinished church business. The issue became the GCSP, and conflict arose over how a program agenda had been set. After some African American deputies walked out, the agenda shifted from church business

43. Shattuck, *Episcopalians and Race.*
44. Hein and Shattuck, *Episcopalians*, 135.
45. Hein and Shattuck, *Episcopalians*, 136.

to social issues. After the convention, conservative sources challenged the GCSP, and it was curtailed by 1970.[46] The reality of division was apparent.

As the temperature rose in the Episcopal Church, Virginia Seminary took a measured approach. In 1976, Pauli Murray became the first Black woman student.[47] A noted attorney, she divided her theological education between Virginia and General Theological Seminary. She became the first Black woman to be ordained in the Episcopal Church and received an honorary doctoral degree from Virginia in 1980. In 1978, Lloyd Lewis, an alumnus of the class of 1972, became the first full-time Black faculty member and would serve for about thirty years over two stints. Part-time Black instructors already had included Henry B. Mitchell, class of 1957, and John C. Davis, from Bishop Payne Divinity School's 1936 class. In 1982, Norma Lee Blackwell would become the first Black woman to complete the master of divinity degree at Virginia Seminary.[48]

From the incremental changes in Alexandria to the more dramatic ones elsewhere in the church, a new vision of the church seemed to be on the horizon. As we shall see, the conduct of international mission and the domestic life of the church could not be distinguished. It became clear that missteps at the institutional level pointed to the nagging question that challenged even the most energetic pursuits of justice. In the words of Raphael Warnock, "What is the true nature and mission of the church? As a community formed in memory of Jesus Christ and informed by the gospels, what is it that makes it a faithful and authentic witness, what exactly is it called to do?"[49] All Christian communities must answer that question, Warnock adds pointedly.

For Walter Earl Fluker, the question of identity and mission in the Black church—and, in their own ways, all churches—is what he terms the "Dilemma."[50] Following King, there is the vision of beloved community uniting disparate people. An identity that invites a broad sense of joining in wide possibility must embrace unwieldy difference. Religious identity requires particularity, if only in terms of being rooted in one locality or another. The vision of community that thrives in a particular context may falter as it faces the vagaries of institutional process which tries to meld

46. Hein and Shattuck, *Episcopalians*, 136–39.

47. For a discussion of Pauli Murray's gender identity, see Cohen and West, *My Name Is Pauli Murray*.

48. Virginia Theological Seminary, "Explore Our 200 Years of History."

49. Warnock, *Divided Mind of the Black Church*, 1.

50. Fluker, *Ground Has Shifted*.

disparate styles and priorities. How does this become possible? If one size does not fit all, how can diversity enhance rather than blur the whole? This is especially the case when powerful, locally held visions differ, and when institutional efforts fail to grasp the gift that a particular vision offers. How can mission to many encourage unity for all?

Though there is hardly space to treat the subject adequately, the legacy of Black Episcopal life offers a noteworthy case study on the relation between identity and mission. As Harold Lewis has traced, Black Episcopalians have cultivated both their own religious culture and connection to a larger whole.[51] The formation of Black clergy, including bishops, in segregated facilities such as Bishop Payne Divinity School, encouraged a distinctive identity. As movement began in the church toward justice, Black voices called for their legacy and their leaders to be honored in the wider culture. The whole must honor the particular. A prime example is to be found in the work of James Theodore Holly, the first African American Episcopal bishop who spent most of his career in Haiti. Another example concerns the role of the Union of Black Episcopalians, formed in 1968. Confronting racism and giving a distinctive voice, the UBE has held being Episcopal as basic to its identity. The particular and the whole must seek affinity.

When such affinity arises, and when it approximates beloved community, it is more likely to arise personally in local settings, amid personal searches for meaning and belonging. In his sweeping study of the Black church, Henry Louis Gates Jr. includes reference to his own religious journey. He prefaces that account by describing the Black church viewed broadly as a cultural system with profound patterns of identity and participation. Mindful of King's dream, Gates speaks warmly of Black clerical pioneers such as Alexander Crummell with his strong commitment to mission in Liberia and the United States. It is telling that Gates cites Crummell.[52]

Gates's father was an Episcopalian grounded in the church's liturgy. That meant that Gates himself had been introduced but was not necessarily rooted. He had to make his own religious journey, which included time in Pentecostal circles. Ultimately this was not his home. He rediscovered the church of his father, becoming an Episcopalian drawn by the liturgy but being at home intellectually. It could not be the destination

---

51. Lewis, *Yet with a Steady Beat.*
52. Gates, *Black Church,* 210–13.

for all. No one place ever can be. In a way the Episcopal Church was incidental. Gates, like Warnock and Fluker, found that the church's mission must balance particularity and breadth, that which is distinctive and that which can encompass. In its own way too, Virginia Theological Seminary would plunge into facing this tension over the last quarter of the twentieth century.

9

Mission and Global Society

THE IMPACT OF ANGLICAN UPHEAVAL

By the time Raphael Warnock posed the question of identity and mission, it had gone through various iterations. For the historic Protestant churches, such as the Episcopal Church, the answer seemed evident. The task was to renounce racism in its own ranks. Episcopalians also broadly affirmed social justice across American society. There was little overt disagreement with this goal. Discussion concerned the means chosen to combat racism. Such preoccupation could conceal lingering prejudice, as well as a reluctance to change. Like the Alabama bishops in 1963, there were voices across the Episcopal Church who preferred a vague, institutional process that would slow the pace of change if not actually thwart it. The issue of racism compelled questions of Episcopal identity and mission that might become obscured by institutional procedures.

Hesitation to change did not always reflect racial animus. It would be difficult to quantify, but there were clergy and lay leaders who shuddered at any mention of change in the church or the world. As the nation was challenged by the Civil Rights Movement and by the war in Vietnam, concerned voices across the Episcopal Church hoped it could retain the imagined stasis of bygone eras. It became instinctive for some to idealize an imagined church in which faithful consensus prevailed. Unfortunately, there had rarely been such a time. The Episcopal Church, like all churches since Christianity's earliest years, has repeatedly been contested. Its identity and mission have found one or another form of clarity about its life through debate, producing partial consensus until new circumstances in the world produced new sorts of questions about the Christian life. Identity and mission must be pursued and are not readily secured. So it would be as the Episcopal Church moved into the late the twentieth century.

Beginning quietly in the 1950s and gaining momentum in the 1960s, there had been discussion in church leadership circles, such as the Standing Liturgical Commission, about revision of the Book of Common Prayer. The reference to Charles Price's leadership in the previous chapter illustrates that a broad and methodical approach had begun. Yet it should not be assumed that a consensus about the necessity and shape of Prayer Book revision had already been formed on the basis of Price's work, the work of various church bodies, and the work of other liturgical scholars such as Marion Hatchett, Massey Shepherd, and Louis Weil. In the 1960s, as trial liturgies appeared and revision gained institutional momentum, an affirming consensus indeed did appear, and the outcome could seem assured. However, a fervent body of opposition also appeared. It paid little attention to the stated rationale for revising worship.[1]

If opposition to Prayer Book revision hardened in the 1970s, such opposition featured a Virginia Seminary alumnus, Jerome F. Politzer, a parish priest in California who became a founder of the Society for the Preservation of the Book of Common Prayer. The book to be preserved was the Episcopal Church's 1928 version. Its Elizabethan cadences had become a widely presumed expression of Episcopal identity and mission. Despite years of discussion that was often coordinated with other branches of the Anglican Communion, final adoption of a new version of the Book of Common Prayer in 1979 seemed to be the abandonment of faithful grounding for the sake of superficial social relevance, or so opponents declared. An activist opposition grew among many who were troubled by revision. Its timing seemed to coincide with protest against the Vietnam War and the continued mobilization for the advance of social justice. America, and the Episcopal Church, were fracturing into politicized coteries of the left and the right.

Earlier in the 1970s, another seismic change in the church's life occurred—the ordination of women to the priesthood. The ordination of women as deacons occurred quietly and drew on the legacy of women serving as deaconesses. Admitting women to the priesthood, on the other hand, raised the likelihood of women becoming bishops, and more

---

1. Hein and Shattuck, *Episcopalians*, 147.

immediately, it ensured that women would perform key liturgical roles, including the celebration of the Eucharist. Virginia Seminary proved central to advancing the issue. Shortly before the church's General Convention of 1976 voted on admitting women to the priesthood, two faculty members, Marianne Micks and Charles Price, edited a volume of essays pointing toward a "new theology of ordination." It was symbolic that Marianne Micks was coeditor and professor of theology, though she was not the first woman to serve as a full-time faculty member. Marion Kelleran became professor of Pastoral Theology and Christian Education in 1962 after teaching part-time since 1949. Micks joined the faculty in 1974.

It was a propitious arrival. In July 1974, eleven women had been ordained as Episcopal priests by four bishops, three of them retired. Conducted at Church of the Advocate in Philadelphia, the unauthorized rite attracted widespread public interest.[2] Two of the eleven, Allison Cheek and Nancy Hatch Wittig, were recent Virginia Seminary graduates. The event galvanized both fervid supporters and dismayed opponents. It was impossible not to take a position because the issue was not abstract. Although debate tapped varied readings of Christian tradition and ideals of the church's mission, the issue was as visceral as it was intellectual. The book edited by Micks and Price enacted a deliberate strategy: it included voices appreciative of opposition to ordaining women, but Micks and Price intended to convince. Their overview ended with the conviction that the book's essays "will introduce its readers to some strong theological arguments in favor of ordaining, for roles of leadership in the church of Christ, some persons who happen to be female."[3]

The volume can be cited as a measure of new theological currents in the Episcopal Church; it also revealed that Virginia Seminary was shifting its theological direction. The construal of biblical interpretation and theological grounding relative to the ordination of women posed wider implications. For example, in discussing the biblical pros and cons of ordaining women, Reginald H. Fuller dealt fairly and thoroughly, but spoke of an "emergent Catholicism."[4] Recently arrived in Alexandria from Union Seminary in New York, Fuller was a highly respected scholar known for his book *The Foundations of New Testament Christology*. With Micks and Price, he concluded that the Christian ministry has been

2. Hein and Shattuck, *Episcopalians*, 141.
3. Micks and Price, introduction to *Toward a New Theology*, x.
4. Fuller, "Pro and Con," 8.

continuously adapted. He also declared that the New Testament does not lay down rules valid for all time.

Such a perspective brought dynamism and appreciation of changing realities and the possibilities inherent in them. Theological perspectives were enhanced by pastoral ones. Various essayists acknowledged the intricacies of tradition and authority, but, like the concluding essay by Henry Rightor, also of Virginia Seminary, all concluded that Anglican tradition possessed an inherent capacity for fresh consensus even about matters deemed historic and basic.[5] Still, even as it seemed to declare its progressive convictions, Virginia Seminary sought balance. Among faculty hired in the 1970s and 1980s, none was necessarily resistant to social justice, to revision of the Book of Common Prayer, or to the ordination of women. But some were troubled by what they saw as the progressive theological tendencies such changes appeared to foster.

The ground of faith was shifting and the implications for mission would be profound. Most immediately, it was apparent that the Episcopal Church, like all of the historic Protestant denominations, steadily included opposing factions that may be demarcated as "progressive" and "traditionalist." Such groupings did not represent all Episcopalians. At all levels of church life, there were clergy and laity who were troubled by this development and sought ways to address it. To further blur distinctions among Episcopalians, many sympathized with one or another feature of progressive or traditionalist conviction but hesitated to declare allegiance to a mobilized faction. Yet both progressives and traditionalists awakened sufficient purpose and even alarm that they gained momentum. Progressives felt their hold on the levers of power in the church expand. Traditionalists focused their energies on grassroots allegiance, some even anticipating a day when the extent of progressive influence would drive faithful people into new ecclesiastical bodies where historic belief and the uncorrupted practice of it would be preserved.

In more extensive ways, progressives translated the theological purview of Marianne Micks and Charles Price into politicized restatements of Christian faith and something of an agenda for the Episcopal Church. The progressive outlook should not be granted as much coherence as it sometimes appeared to possess. But progressives gathered loosely around the ideal of restating Christian belief for a world skeptical of historic faith and certain that religion proved socially repressive. Instead, progressives

5. Rightor, "Existing Canonical Authority," 101–10.

agreed that the faith must be read in modern and dynamic terms. The human meaning of the Bible must be uncovered and any use of it to support social injustice rejected. In short, the Bible must be freed, as lives must be freed, to move past distortion. Traditionalists believed the progressive juggernaut, as they saw it, abandoned the essentials of biblical faith and the church's tradition for the sake of "radical inclusion" and social relevance. More than revision of worship or admission of women to priesthood was entailed. For both sides, such issues dramatized the battle for Christian truth and the church's future.

There was sufficient assertiveness by progressive figures to explain traditionalist concern. In the 1960s, sometime bishop of California, James A. Pike, who had studied at Virginia Seminary, became synonymous with iconoclasm in the church. His confrontational style fostered talk of a bishop falling into heresy. His appearances on television seemed to confirm charges of heterodoxy. His tragic death in 1969 in an Israeli desert added to images of an incongruous life.[6] His seeming successor as Episcopal iconoclast had deep roots in Alexandria. John Shelby Spong, bishop of Newark from 1979 to 2000, had graduated from Virginia Seminary in 1955. He became a prolific author and public figure, regularly speaking and appearing on television for interviews and discussions. Tracing his stridency to a difficult childhood in a religiously conservative home, Spong challenged literalism to "rescue the Bible from fundamentalism," as one of his books declared.[7] Uncongenially, for those drawn to traditionalism, Spong attacked habitual moral precepts based on the Bible. Like Pike, Spong cultivated a defiant style that encouraged supporters and energized opponents. He readily offended sensibilities, especially as he became an advocate for acceptance of homosexual persons in the Episcopal Church.[8]

The story of the church's culture wars is unfinished and larger than this narrative can address. The issues and personalities cited here merit further consideration. It suffices to say that the Episcopal Church became mired in conflict that most church members likely did not want. At first, the issues that mobilized progressives seemed to advance. Loud voices such as those of Pike and Spong enhanced the image of a progressive phalanx confronting historic Christian belief and biblical interpretation.

6. Robertson, *Passionate Pilgrim.*
7. Spong, *Rescuing the Bible from Fundamentalism.*
8. Spong, *Here I Stand.*

But traditionalists proved just as committed and arguably more theologically focused. They resolved to retrieve what they were assured was the church's essential core of faith. Thus, both parties in the church's culture wars believed they were addressing core issues in ways that secured the church's identity and advanced its mission.

A benchmark in the unfolding debate came in 1993 with the publication of *Reclaiming Faith*, a multiauthored book intended to restate Christianity's essential doctrines and to frame the progressive-traditionalist tension in the Episcopal Church. The work was coedited by two Yale graduate students in theology whose profiles would rise in the church. Ephraim Radner and George R. Sumner gave the book a Yale imprint by including essays authored by senior Yale faculty in biblical and theological studies. The occasion for this work was the appearance in 1991 of the "Baltimore Declaration," a statement of traditionalist conviction by six Episcopal priests in Maryland. Alvin F. Kimel Jr., lead author of the Declaration, added remarks that buttressed the Radner and Sumner volume. The Declaration declared that "a revision of our faith inconsistent with Holy Scripture and the Creeds has been gaining ascendancy in our Church, and . . . a bold stand against such teachings must be taken."[9]

In seven articles, the Declaration emphasized the following beliefs: belief in the Trinity; God is Creator; Jesus is God incarnate; Jesus is the Way, the Truth, and the Life; the Jewish people are "a chosen and blessed people"; salvation is "solely by grace through faith"; and the Holy Spirit is "the ultimate author of Holy Scripture." The core of a traditionalist faith was posed, and *Redeeming Faith* gave it an exposition. More than a particular moral issue was at stake. The faith seemed under assault. The point was made in Robert Prichard's chapter. He saw a loss of consensus about the nature of doctrine and its place in the church.[10] It would be a theme in his writing. Radner and Sumner were also concerned for the church's mission. Alluding to the church in Africa, they foresaw the fracture of the Anglican world. "The Christian church of the West needs to see itself through the eyes of Christians from the younger churches of the world, from Africa and Asia."[11]

The church's "primary mission," they continued, is "to equip the laity to understand, articulate, and act upon their Christian faith." But

9. Kimel, "Confessing Faith" 276–83.

10. Prichard, "Place of Doctrine in the Episcopal Church," 13–45.

11. Radner and Sumner, "Reclaiming," 1.

"many priests . . . have been profoundly and inescapably formed by the worldview of a completely secularized society and educational system. Too many of these ministers are either intimidated by the claims of modernity or sufficiently confused by them that they cannot pedagogically appropriate the Christian Scriptures, doctrinally interpreted by the traditions of the church."[12] This point would arise repeatedly. The theological and institutional assumptions of the Episcopal Church were facing off with the Christianity of the Global South. Virginia Seminary was one meeting ground. What would become of such encounters? Who would instruct and who would require instruction?

The recognition of gay people in the Episcopal Church, and their full acceptance in ordained and lay leadership roles, had long been anticipated or dreaded. The Episcopal Church's General Convention of 2003 approved the election of Gene Robinson, a partnered gay man, as bishop of New Hampshire. But it was not universally celebrated.[13] This event proved to be as much of a beginning as it was a conclusion. Virginia Seminary, the Episcopal Church, and the Anglican world were cast into ongoing dispute and faced with the rupture of "Communion" as ideological clusters among Anglicans hardened.[14] Clergy and lay persons of traditionalist loyalties saw the Robinson confirmation as final proof that the Episcopal Church had abandoned its biblical roots and theological mandate. Prominent figures in North American traditionalist groups found consecration as bishops in sympathetic Anglican churches, especially in Africa. By 2007, dissenters had begun to coalesce into the Anglican Church of North America, which claimed to uphold biblical faith and Anglican identity. A struggle to be the true expression of Anglicanism erupted and divided the world into alienated factions. Two distinct views of faith, the church, and mission had arisen with no apparent means of reconciliation.

CONVENING CRITICAL REFLECTION ON THE CHURCH

Though the election of Gene Robinson as bishop in New Hampshire could not have been foreseen, debate over the rectitude of recognizing gay people in the church had been ongoing for some years and the fault lines which would divide Anglicans had long been apparent. So too, there

12. Radner and Sumner, "Reclaiming," 3.

13. Sachs, *Homosexuality and the Crisis of Anglicanism*, 1.

14. Radner and Turner, *Fate of Communion*.

had been recognition that the issue had significant implications for the church's mission and for the cross-cultural relations mission entailed. Debate about the legacy of colonialism and the nature of the post-colonial world added another, complex dimension. For Virginia Seminary, these matters had become acute concerns before 2003. The seminary's relation to the Global South and its efforts to foster faithful and enduring relations became urgent matters. How relations across the Anglican world could be built and in what sense they might be cosmopolitan, that is reciprocal and equitable, became the central question. The course of discussion at the seminary, before and after 2003, proves illuminating. In effect, Virginia Seminary worked to be a meeting ground for disparate outlooks. It tried to bridge the chasm that loomed.

By the early 1990s, there were faculty at Virginia Seminary who held, or were responsive to, traditionalist views. They took no steps to break with seminary or the church in the wake of 2003. Their concern, long before Gene Robinson's election, was broader. They perceived the erosion of essential aspects of Christian belief, and they explained the acceptance of gay people in such terms. To this outlook, church and seminary leaders were willing to alter historic belief and practice for the sake of favorable recognition in contemporary secular culture. Several Virginia faculty members joined an assertive group of young scholars who were intent on driving home this point. They sought intellectual as well as spiritual grounding for a renewal of Christian orthodoxy. As they did so, they nurtured a revised sense of Christian mission.

More than a decade before the consecration of Gene Robinson as bishop, several seminary faculty members helped to launch SEAD, or Scholarly Engagement with Anglican Doctrine. A cluster of scholars organized a periodic newsletter and an annual conference where they would promote a widespread return to "classical Christian teaching" as a "community of theological discourse."[15] Christopher Hancock of Virginia Seminary became cochair and SEAD's mailing address was the seminary's, though formal recognition as an aspect of seminary life was not forthcoming. Nevertheless, Hancock's leadership role and that of David Scott, faculty colleague and also a SEAD cochair, made plain that SEAD was at home on Seminary Road.

In 1993, Hancock outlined the new organization's convictions. He termed them "Dynamic Orthodoxy" and depicted them as "a

---

15. Scott, "Vision for SEAD," 1–3.

compellingly attractive alternative to the existing theological *status quo.*" He added that "if SEAD is indeed to stimulate the healthful renewal of the mind of the Church it must encourage among its members a sense of the 'viability of tradition.'" Thus focused, Hancock outlined the hallmarks of a dynamic orthodoxy, depicting Christian belief as historic, open to doubt, witness to Christ's resurrection, offering lively praise, resulting in Christian living, and mindful of contemporary life.[16] In other words, Hancock attempted to hold essential aspects of Christian faith in constructive tension with the secular world. David Scott added an emphasis on theological discourse in a subsequent essay. In that essay, the section titles gave a summary of SEAD's purpose: "Loving God with the Mind," "Giving Voice to Classical Orthodoxy," and "Being a Community of Theological Discourse." From a traditionalist rootage, SEAD seemed to strike a mediating option.[17]

The issue of human sexuality would narrow the possibility of finding common ground and eliminate the possibility of remaining above the fray. Even as SEAD began, David Scott took a traditionalist position on sexuality. He was aware that traditional moral teaching was being rejected in the lives of many people. Sexual relations outside of marriage were commonplace. Homosexuality was openly acknowledged, and its affirmation by the church fervently sought in some circles. Something of a mediating position was needed, and Scott posed one. "Christian faith should give believers the courage to face and engage people who think and act differently from traditional Christian teaching. Closed-mindedness is not a Christian virtue."[18] Such an inviting stance proved to be little more than a holding pattern. Yet Scott, Hancock, and other voices in SEAD continued to think about mission amid theological change in what was seen as a post-Christian culture. But human sexuality proved to be the issue where Episcopalians had difficulty rising above dispute and finding unity. No aspect of church life would escape the challenge.

Scott wondered in print if a center of Anglican theology could be found. The mere asking of the question acknowledged the difficulty of the times, and Scott's framing of a response made such difficulty plain. He wrote wistfully of an Anglican historical legacy in which certain core assumptions could be shared. The farther back one goes, "the more certainly

16. Hancock, "Dynamic Orthodoxy," 1–3.

17. Scott, "Vision for SEAD," 1–3.

18. Scott and Griffith, "Christian Response to Human Sexuality," 3.

one can affirm a center to Anglican doctrine." But, informed by the exploratory work of Stephen Sykes, Scott noted that Anglicans have given different meanings to doctrines "in different frameworks or contexts."[19] Noting that it was easier to make the case for distinctively Anglican doctrine if certain contemporary thinks were excluded, Scott determined that the historic center was framed by the Trinity and by the incarnation of the Word, as well as the Apostles' and Nicene Creeds. He also noted that the creedal reference invoked the importance of giving praise and thanks in worship. He did not draw sharp boundaries around the center he defined, for he also urged that the *Anglican Theological Review*, for which he was writing, should publish disparate points of view while holding to an historic sense of Anglican affirmations as he had outlined. Thus, he tried to hold to tradition and allow for its multifaceted expressions.[20]

Yet the challenge before the Episcopal Church and Virginia Seminary remained. It required informed positions, but the deeper issue could not be resolved confessionally. The issue of the church's relation to culture was surfacing again, this time with a vengeance. It arose starkly with different outlooks asserted stridently. These outlooks hardened as authenticity of belief and life were sought on the basis of conflicting convictions. Increasingly, confessional positions were supplemented by personal experience, which could be used as a trump card to justify rigidly held theological and moral stances. The culture wars in all the churches reflected the widening view that ambiguity could not be tolerated, and any suggestion of a mediating position could come across as ambiguity. Particularity of outlook and alignment into like-minded factions became prized. In that sense, Virginia Seminary was swept up in larger religious and social dynamics. Yet by giving different voices their due, Virginia Seminary sought to mediate among its own, increasingly varied constituencies. The seminary's emerging approach to mission sought to create breadth while transcending division.

It should be apparent at this stage of the history of Virginia Seminary that mission could not be seen as just one aspect of seminary life. Mission had been a recurring reference point, seen in disparate ways as the organizing principle. In the late twentieth century, that ideal was challenged as it had not been since the American Civil War. Yet, Virginia Seminary was not unique. The history of this institution, like that of all

19. Scott, "Concerning a Center of Anglican Theology," 91.
20. Scott, "Concerning a Center of Anglican Theology," 91.

seminaries, must be read in terms of its relation to larger social and religious dynamics. Often the history of an educational institution has been depicted in isolation from the forces that actually shaped it. The impact of the American conflict over sexuality became a prominent instance. It became an issue on which there was no neutral ground, even as the ideal of a center to gather disparate voices was debated. Even as Virginia Seminary sought allegiance to its faith and its past, the social realities it faced compelled a stance.

On January 22, 1997, the Board of Trustees of Virginia Theological Seminary confirmed publication of "A Call to a Holy Life." It was a revised statement of the seminary's policy on human sexuality. The kernel of the document was its direct affirmation that "the absolute ban, under all circumstances, on the admission of non-celibate gay and lesbian persons be lifted."[21] Discussion at the board level prior to the vote had abundant precedent. Quietly the seminary's faculty had discussed the matter, with several members publishing papers that were both pro and con, and some in between. The shape of the divide among faculty and board was familiar. Opponents cited the Bible and tradition as well as wary perceptions of modern culture. Advocates spoke of the seminary leading the church to a new, generative affirmation of the intention of tradition and of human relations. Yet faculty members found sufficient clarity to outline their points of agreement and disagreement. They also committed to continued dialogue. There was a degree of unity, especially on the theme of remaining together.[22]

The faculty statement had reviewed past discussions and prior statements of behavioral standards and their basis. Thus, the matter was framed historically and theologically. But the board's mind was clear. Among members of the board, bishops were among the most vigorous proponents of a revised policy. One bishop cited William Sparrow's maxim, "Seek ye the truth, come whence it may, cost what it will." Others spoke of the authority of Scripture on the one hand, or the task of interpreting Scripture consistently. Some spoke of offending the seminary's constituencies, others of expanding the seminary's base of support. Concern also was voiced about the impact of such a step on the seminary's relation to the church and to the wider Anglican Communion. With the

21. Episcopal News Service, "Virginia Seminary Revises Policy on Sexual Behavior."
22. Faculty of Virginia Theological Seminary, "Statement of Agreement."

issue broached, the minds of the faculty and of the board were not entirely united. There was more faculty caution than was evident on the board.

Nevertheless, the board acted. Soundly defeating a substitute motion, the board adopted "A Call to a Holy Life" by a vote of 31 to 3. With
this action, the seminary endorsed removal of a ban on the participation
of non-celibate gay persons in seminary life. This would include faculty
as well as students and would presume that some would live in partnered
relations at the seminary. Some affirmative board votes had hinged on the
document offering a broadly applicable statement on the quality of life
expected of those associated with the seminary. Thus, those of traditionalist sympathies found a way to be supportive. Those who were inclined
to be progressive in their views found the dismissal of theological and
psychological stigma imposed on homosexual persons to be key. In other
words, support was not uniform and neither was the opposition. A consensus had emerged. Its fluidity was presumed. How seminary life would
be affected remained to be seen. Some board members noted that the
true work was only beginning.[23]

The scope of the work that was needed became apparent with the
publication of "Strategic Objectives for the 21st Century," a report of the
Strategic Planning Committee to the Board of Trustees, in November
1998. It emphasized that the seminary possessed a "strong historic base
of theological education focused on scripture, mission, and evangelism
with its emphasis on a residential body of students and faculty, living
in community and centered on worship, faith formation, face-to-face
interaction, academic study, and learning." The report's summary also
emphasized continued partnerships with dioceses, parishes, and other
institutions "to enhance theological education" and to provide resources
for theological education "to the wider church." To be explicit about the
report's emphasis, "this call for mission to the world is also within the
proud tradition of the seminary."[24]

The renewed mission emphasis was manifest in the creation of the
Center for Anglican Communion Studies to "foster theological research,
encounter and reflection within the Anglican Communion." In other
words, even as the wider church struggled with difficult issues, and Virginia Seminary was compelled to declare its position on human sexuality, there was resolve to embrace mission on fresh terms. For example,

23. Board of Trustees, "Report to the Board," May 14, 1997.
24. Strategic Planning Committee, "Strategic Objectives."

a fourth strategic objective of the Center "is to broaden and strengthen VTS partnerships with dioceses, parishes and other institutions for mutual learning and sharing of theological education resources." Reiteration of this point, with the addition of reference to "mutual learning," signaled the dawn of a new approach to mission. Such a call was consistent "with the Seminary's evangelical and missionary heritage," the report added, perhaps on a cautionary note. But a new day was dawning. In new and expanded ways, Alexandria not only would go to the Anglican Communion; the Anglican Communion would come to Alexandria.[25]

THE COMMUNION COMES TO ALEXANDRIA

As conflict erupted within the Episcopal Church and across other American churches, it was not readily acknowledged that Virginia Theological Seminary had been sending its graduates into the work of mission for over a century and a half. Broadly speaking, mission had been the theme which framed theological education at the seminary. Even among clergy whose ministries unfolded in close proximity to the campus, mission was the priority. That is, Virginia-trained clergy intended to awaken lively Christian faith and to build the church. They placed particular emphasis on worship and Christian education. Over time they sharpened their skills in pastoral care and leadership formation. Often, they were prominent moral voices in their local contexts and so stamped the Episcopal Church as tradition-minded yet accessible, faithful, and adaptable. Certainly, there were occasions when the outcomes of a given ministry failed to live up to this high calling. But the instances of ideals becoming realities were sufficient to enhance the legacy of the seminary. Many seminary alumni became renowned for faithful service.

They were hardly a majority of seminary graduates, but a steady and at times striking number of alumni spent at least a portion of their ministries in overseas mission. As this account has described, Virginia Seminary alumni were prominent in founding the Episcopal Church in Liberia, China, Japan, and Brazil. In each of these settings, the first bishop was a Virginia graduate, and in each instance, the contingent of missionaries included large numbers of seminary alumni. Continuing relations with the church as it developed also reflected Virginia Seminary's continuing mission commitment.

25. Strategic Planning Committee, "Strategic Objectives," 3–4.

That commitment could also be seen in a legacy of international visitors to Alexandria. Some of these visitors have been American missionaries on sabbatical, working to raise funds for mission and to recruit new clergy and lay missionaries. It has been noted that interest in mission has been extensive beyond the seminary campus. The Diocese of Virginia, for example, built rural congregations that proved illustrative of the importance of local mission. In addition, Virginia was fertile ground for recruiting lay missionaries. Dr. Rudolph Teusler, physician and lay Episcopalian from Richmond, played a prominent role in the growth of St. Luke's Hospital in Tokyo, a prominent aspect of Episcopal mission in Japan. Thus, Virginia Seminary participated in a larger culture of mission which shaped it and which it helped to shape.

It wasn't just returning missionaries who visited the seminary's campus. There had been periodic enrollments of international students, and those numbers grew in the twentieth century. Japan was a prominent source of such students for a time. In the first half of the twentieth century, there were eight Japanese students, including Takeshi Naide, who became bishop of Osaka in 1922. In the 1950s and 1960s, a total of seventeen students from Japan spent part of their theological education in Alexandria. In addition, by the 1960s, there had been eight students from Brazil and seven each from Cuba and Mexico. Missionaries from Virginia took prominent roles in these countries, notably A. Hugo Blankingship, the last American bishop in Havana, and Robert F. Gibson, later a seminary faculty member and then bishop of Virginia, who served in Mexico. By the second half of the twentieth century, the legacy was substantial.[26]

Then the profile of international students changed. From his study of international students at Virginia Seminary, Troy Mendez concluded that "a major paradigm shift occurred in the later 1960s / early 1970s at Virginia Theological Seminary. Students from overseas started to originate from countries where the Episcopal Church and Virginia Theological Seminary did not historically have missions."[27] The seminary's reputed emphasis on mission and on theological breadth helped to widen its geographic reach. By the end of the twentieth century students from an additional twenty-two countries had studied at the seminary. These included various African nations, notably Uganda, Nigeria, Kenya, South Africa, and Tanzania. In the wake of the confirmation of a gay bishop for

26. Mendez, "History of Mission."
27. Mendez, "History of Mission," 23.

New Hampshire in 2003, Uganda and Nigeria suspended relations with the Episcopal Church and Virginia Seminary in particular.

But relations between Virginia Seminary and the church in Tanzania grew appreciably. One of the first students from there was Alpha Mohamed, already a bishop when he enrolled in 1976. By 2008, there had been twenty-one Tanzanian students. By comparison, over the same period, there were nine students from Sudan. They joined students from Myanmar, Israel, and Palestine who further stimulated cross-cultural conversations and challenged presumptions about mission. A brief survey conducted by Mendez gave insights. He explored the attitudes of the international students in 2008 and of some alumni from overseas. The assessments of Virginia Seminary were quite positive. It was notable that current international students were inclined to feel that aspects of American culture were incompatible with their own cultural contexts.[28]

The presence of international students, especially from east Africa, was not without its tensions and even an instance of abusive behavior. On May 16, 2000, faculty member Robert Prichard wrote to the seminary's Community Life Committee to report that several students from Africa had received harassing telephone calls in recent years. It appeared that the students who were harassed had spoken critically in their classes about the ordination of gay and lesbian persons. The students who were singled out did feel supported when a petition against such harassing behavior circulated through the student body in April 1999. Prichard's letter a year later summarized the situation and represented an apparent conclusion to it.[29]

The path toward a cosmopolitan approach to mission at Virginia Seminary was not without its obstacles. The intrusive and insulting behavior leveled against certain students because of how they read the Bible had no apparent recurrence. But in an overt way, it harkened to Western cultural assumptions, racist implications, and patronizing behavior that had surfaced at times in the circumstances of mission up to the second half of the twentieth century. Again, the history of Virginia Seminary must be understood in a larger context. Virginia Seminary has been exceptional in its emphasis on mission and on the number of its alumni who have spent time as missionaries. But the issues surrounding their service were not unique to the seminary or to the Episcopal Church. They were

28. Mendez, "Survey of Current International Students."
29. Prichard to the Community Life Committee, May 16, 2000.

continuous with the experience of mission undertaken by mainstream American Protestant churches. Foremost among these issues were the cultural and institutional assumptions most missionaries brought and the frequent assumption of the need for their continuing presence. It was difficult to shed the Western point of view.

Yet, perhaps more than most missionaries, those who had been educated in Alexandria, Virginia, began to grasp the realities they faced, including their own foibles. At points in this narrative, accounts of cultural as well as religious awakening in the lives of mission workers have been cited. The experience of faith and life in a difficult context encouraged the sensibility we have termed cosmopolitan. In turn, hints of that sensibility returned to Alexandria. In the late twentieth century, amid the furor of dispute over various issues, Virginia Seminary took concrete steps to advance a cosmopolitan approach to mission.

An obvious step in this direction was the appointment of Richard Jones as the first faculty member strictly teaching mission since Robert K. Massie early in the twentieth century. Jones joined the faculty in 1988 and would serve until his retirement in 2009. An alumnus of the seminary in the class of 1972, he had served as a missionary in Ecuador as well as in parish ministry, then completing doctoral studies. A one-man department of "Mission and World Religions," Jones taught mission from both historical and theological perspectives, bringing appreciation for non-Western cultures. His doctoral work had been on Islam, and after his seminary retirement he remained active in Christian-Muslim dialogue, even teaching at an Islamic faculty in the Washington, DC, area. He left an enduring imprint upon the understanding of mission by moving it in the direction of cosmopolitanism.

That contribution was made plain at Jones's retirement. An article in the *Virginia Seminary Journal* in the spring of 2009 summarized a symposium held in his honor. The theme was "The Unfinished Business of Mission." The *Journal* observed that in 1969, when Jones entered Virginia Seminary as a student, "interest in overseas mission was at a low ebb in the national church and at the Seminary. The focus in the Episcopal Church was on the turmoil in the inner cities, and funding for the overseas work of the church was greatly reduced."[30] It could be added that recognition of the impact of colonialism raised probing questions about the study of mission as well as its practice. At Virginia Seminary, as at various other

30. "Unfinished Business of Mission," 21.

theological institutions, mission for some years had only been taught in ways incidental to larger topics, such as the history of the church. Thus, it would continue until Jones returned as a faculty member in 1988.

Clearly alumni had gone forth in mission, Jones among them. Clearly international students had continued to enroll. But the teaching of mission lacked coherence, a fact that the symposium honoring Richard Jones addressed. The noted Roman Catholic theologian of mission, Robert Schreiter, keynoted the event. He summarized the obvious challenges, such as colonialism, which had combined to place the "concept of mission and mission studies in flux." Yet this was no reactive or one-sided discussion. Substantive questions had arisen about whether "missiology" constituted a distinctive field or whether "it is an arena of study where many disciplines come together."[31] The conservatism among former colonial churches compounded lingering forms of paternalism among North American and European churches. The intention of mission and the relations it encouraged among Christians cross-culturally remained in doubt.

Updating a theme which had gained traction in mission discussions, Schreiter identified the "principal ways that the Church and its members are called upon today to participate in the *missio Dei.*" He cited witness, dialogue, and reconciliation. He defined witness as testimony which "recalls and reminds us of how an event in the past endures into the present." In word and deed, witness points to God's activity in the world. Dialogue is more than communication. It reflects human interdependence and engages the ideal of communion which Anglicans prize. It honors the reality of difference and poses the hope of building ties among disparate peoples. Reconciliation builds on witness and dialogue. Citing 2 Corinthians 5:17–20, Schreiter noted that when one is in Christ "there is a new creation: everything old has passed away; see, everything has become new!" Becoming a new creation is emblematic of reconciliation.[32]

Schreiter introduced the idea of cosmopolitanism without naming it as such. He used a contrast in historical contexts between past and present to make this move: "If colonization was the inevitable context of mission through the past two centuries, bringing with it a very mixed set of results, today that context is globalization, which is yielding up its own

---

31. Schreiter, "What Is the Church's Enduring Mission," 24.
32. Schreiter, "What Is the Church's Enduring Mission," 29–31.

ambivalences."[33] On the one hand, people are being linked more closely. On the other hand, the wedge between economic haves and have-nots has deepened. In such a time of global connection, some denominations look inward, compelled to shore themselves up amid decline. Rather than an inward turn, the churches must look outward in mission. Schreiter cited the evangelical legacy of Anglicanism as precedent. Evangelicalism was a prominent basis upon which a national church became global and developed profound, enduring moral witness. Mission awakens the church's possibility, just as it energized Virginia Seminary. By the time a symposium honored Richard Jones, Virginia Seminary had begun to move outward in innovative ways. By the early 1990s, Frank Van Develder, faculty member in Old Testament, regularly took students on May study tours to Jerusalem. These academic and spiritual pilgrimages deepened a tie to St. George's College, the Anglican study center in Jerusalem offering short-term, residential programs. Most attendees sought no academic credit, but students did so because they had enrolled in a seminary course.

Thus, the arrival of Richard Jones in 1988 was one aspect of a revision and renewal of the seminary's emphasis on mission. The inception of regular immersion experiences in Jerusalem accompanied fresh interest in Latin America. Also in 1988, Robert Prichard described his recent visit to the Episcopal Church in Colombia. Even "that brief immersion in Latin American culture has helped me to rethink some of my premises about the Episcopal Church." Prichard gained ready entrée through his facility in the Spanish language and because his brother, Tom, a Virginia graduate, was serving in mission in Colombia. In summarizing the visit, Prichard spoke little of how mission would change Colombians. Instead, he described what he gained through local, person-to-person moments as well as through worship and a conference. In other words, he reflected on what he gained rather than on what he gave.[34] A shift in the meaning of mission was occurring. This shift was enhanced as Jacques Hadler and Richard Jones joined their colleagues, Prichard and Van Develder, in considering the cross-cultural dimensions of their work.

In 2001, Hadler and Jones published an article that described the "Cross-Cultural Colloquy" which they had launched at the seminary. The sorts of questions Troy Mendez later utilized were already on the table.

33. Schreiter, "What Is the Church's Enduring Mission," 32.
34. Prichard, "Latin American Anglicanism."

Hadler and Jones credited Van Develder with having surfaced them. The issues focused on appreciation and negotiation across differences and on engaging the unique facets of American life and life at Virginia Seminary in particular. Van Develder had raised the idea of "theological transfer," that is, applying theologically what is learned in one culture to a different context.[35] As an ongoing colloquy began, Hadler and Jones served as mentors. Like Jones, who had served in mission in Ecuador, Hadler had spent several years in Tanzania. They launched the colloquy as an opportunity for international students to "reflect on their experience in the Episcopal Church in the United States and begin to translate that experience for application in their home church," thus following Van Develder's ideal.[36] Begun in 1994, the colloquy assumed the central effects of culture upon church life in any setting. The colloquy also viewed "action-reflection learning" as a "method of education which the church in the United States can offer to sister churches."[37]

The door to cosmopolitanism was opening plainly and widely. Hadler and Jones traced the colloquy's development over several academic years. From the outset, participants took turns presenting brief, written accounts of issues they faced either at Virginia Seminary or at home. The presenters included cultural concerns and theological resources to frame their analyses. As the group's life deepened conflict could arise around several themes: first, the applicability of norms from one's home, especially one's church origin; second, friction between one's religious and cultural values and aspects of American life. The issue of sexual norms, especially around homosexuality, could be a flash point. Thus, a recurring focus was the relation of the church to culture. This issue has proven pivotal to mission in every generation. For international students and Virginia Seminary's commitment to mission, the issue became acute. The Cross-Cultural Colloquy offered a valuable setting for disciplined, respectful reflection. Sharpened questions surfaced as the colloquy developed. One question concerned the adaptation of the gospel and church life to local culture. When is adaptation "a necessary and faithful translation? When is it syncretistic, an unfaithful distortion of the Gospel?" Indeed, "what is the essence of the Gospel?"[38]

35. Hadler and Jones, "Two-Way Bridge," 102.
36. Hadler and Jones, "Two-Way Bridge," 103.
37. Hadler and Jones, "Two-Way Bridge," 103.
38. Hadler and Jones, "Two-Way Bridge," 104.

The colloquy set an important tone for the seminary's approach to mission. Conversation no longer was solely by missionaries seeking conversion. Conversation now flowed across cultures, seeking a meeting ground enlivened by the Christian faith. The approach to such mutuality happened as faculty and students went outward as well as when they welcomed international students to Alexandria. Thus, in 2000, Richard Jones reported on travels that included Uganda and Sudan. He went outward to trace aspects of mission history and to engage contemporary contextual realities. He was especially interested in Archibald Shaw, English missionary in Sudan in the early twentieth century. Jones cited more than Shaw's persistence. As Jones reported, in an era of colonial racism, "Shaw went among the southern Sudan seeking friends."[39] He engaged people and contexts on their own terms. It was an apt illustration for a new era of mission characterized by cosmopolitanism.

The most tangible sign of a new approach to mission was the creation of the Center for Anglican Communion Studies. The seminary's board voted in November 1997 to create a means of serving Anglican leaders and scholars with resources available at the seminary. Then Virginia Seminary's dean, Martha Horne, articulated the cosmopolitan hope in an interview in June 1998. The seminary's readiness to give was matched by its receptivity. "At the same time, we know that our own community will learn a great deal from the insights and experiences of those who come here." It was an idea Martha Horne inherited but one which she and Bishop Peter James Lee, chair of the board, brought to fruition. The founding vision was to encourage scholarly engagement among Anglicans, to house materials and host scholars, and to assist reflection on "the historic nature and contemporary possibilities of the Anglican Christian tradition."[40]

The new center's viability was demonstrated before its actual launch. In 1991, 1994, and 1996, the seminary hosted sessions of the Inter-Anglican Theological and Doctrinal Commission. This body included bishops, theologians, and lay leaders from across the Anglican Communion. Papers from its meetings in Alexandria were refined into a report to the Lambeth Conference of the world's Anglican bishops in 1998. Soon known as the "Virginia Report," this document became a benchmark for

---

39. Jones, "From Uganda Martyrs to Sudan Ox" 19.
40. Stafford, "Virginia Theological Seminary," 15–19.

the Anglican understanding of being in communion.[41] That ideal would be tested by subsequent Anglican division over sexuality. But it remains a reference point. In the process of its formulation, the "Virginia Report" encouraged the vision of a center located at the seminary. Faculty met with commission members to refine thoughts about what was possible. The commission's presence and the conversations that ensued gave major impetus to the center.

By various steps the seminary turned a corner in its approach to mission. The presence of Anglican doctrinal discussions followed by the founding of the Center for Anglican Communion Studies consolidated the disparate initiatives of various faculty members and drew in the student-led Missionary Society. Later renamed the Mission Society, this body continued its traditional activities of raising monies for grants toward mission projects and hosting notable speakers and preachers. With a professor of mission, the seminary's approach became more coherent and emphatic than it had ever been. The seminary's strategic plan of 1998 secured this clarity. As if to underscore the cosmopolitan turn, the plan also stressed the seminary's "partnerships with dioceses, parishes and other institutions for mutual learning and sharing of theological education resources." In the plan's details, "cross-cultural internships and/or immersion experiences" received specific reference. Possible sites for such exchange in Africa and Latin America were named. The report also articulated the goal of offering the seminary as "a place for church leaders to assemble for study, prayer, and consultation on issues of importance to the Anglican Communion and the church universal."[42] The renewed emphasis on mission featured reciprocal ties as its hallmark. The meaning of mission had become cosmopolitan.

41. Anglican Consultative Council, "Virginia Report."
42. Strategic Planning Committee, "Strategic Objectives," 3–4.

10

Toward Mutual Benefit

AMBASSADORS OF HUMAN FLOURISHING

On April 6, 2021, the president of the United States, Joseph Biden, visited a COVID-19 vaccination site at Virginia Seminary. Neighborhood Health had opened in the Immanuel Chapel as a community clinic to serve low-income communities. By the time of the president's visit, the site had vaccinated over twenty thousand people. Biden used the occasion to announce that over 150 million vaccine doses had been administered nationwide. "People are coming together across the different faiths to serve those most in need, with a special focus on vaccinating seniors from all races, backgrounds, and walks of life," he said. "It's an example of America at its finest."[1]

This presidential visit is emblematic. Located a short drive from the nation's capital, Virginia Seminary looms large in American history and on the global stage. As a seminary of the Episcopal Church, it has been both blessed and challenged by social privilege. Episcopal history reaches back to the founding of the republic. It has been the church of more presidents than any other denomination. It has enjoyed power on Wall Street and Main Street. Its legacy includes spectacular church buildings and fine colleges and universities. There are social service centers, schools, and hospital systems that reflect the Episcopal Church's imprint. A variety of initiatives have conveyed the Episcopal expression of Christianity around the world. There also is abundant evidence that Episcopal

---

1. Banks, "Biden Says," para. 8.

experience reflects the cosmopolitan turn toward all humanity. Christian mission now is driven by a compassionate re-reading of social challenges at home and abroad. COVID-19 itself was a national and international crisis. In the seminary's chapel-turned-health-clinic, the presence of the American president represents mission gone to the world and returned home. The In Trust Center for Theological Schools, a resource organization, ascribed a "redemptive significance" to the presidential visit.[2] Dean Ian Markham affirmed the seminary's commitment to peacemaking and alleviating suffering. To him, connections between the seminary and its neighboring community are at the heart of the seminary's mission. For this reason, the board of trustees made community links a strategic part of seminary life, complete with a position of associate dean for church and community engagement in 2012.

Privileging compassionate mission to the poor seals the cosmopolitan leitmotif in mission that has been considered in previous chapters. Although missionaries went to particular geographical locations, becoming cosmopolitan suggests that mission itself is not about a fixed resolve to "convert the whole world." Rather, mission is a vocational quest to "bear witness to Christ," as we read in the Gospel of Luke: "You are witnesses to these things" (24:48), Jesus told his disciples as he commissioned them to bear the good news in their world. Disciples are to testify to what they have witnessed. Witness leads to engagement in the face of material and physical needs. Thus, mission is both contingent and developed: contingent on communities of participation at home and abroad; developed with discerning leadership that is intent on human flourishing. Michael B. Curry has been illustrative in his leadership. Elected as the Episcopal Church's presiding bishop in 2015, Curry has preached a revolution of love.[3] Speaking after the Anglican primates' meeting in 2016, he observed that the Anglican Communion is a network of relationships that have been built on mission partnerships, grounded in a common faith.[4] Robert Heaney affirms that, because of the mission of God, there is a worldwide Anglican Communion. The communion challenges the isolation and reaction that would threaten otherwise productive relationships, fellowship, and partnerships.[5]

2. In Trust Center for Theological Schools, "All People Considered."
3. See Curry, *Love Is the Way.*
4. Davies, "Presiding Bishop."
5. *News on the Hill* (2016) 20.

What does this outlook mean for Virginia Seminary in the twenty-first century? The outlook that has been cited as cosmopolitan has shaped the seminary's commitment to human flourishing. The meaning of mission has been transformed. Once foreign mission was the locus of immense energies of mobilization and resourcing. These now are subsumed in a model of theological education and community that seeks something fuller: mission involves responding to challenges that confront society. Curriculum, programs, projects, and activities now reflect the realization that the arena has become the whole of human experience. Such impetus entails views of human flourishing that regularly include religion. This is striking because studies of human flourishing now emanate from scientific sources. One study aligns religious community with family, work, and education as sources of flourishing.[6] Another study, by Andrew Briggs and Michael Reiss, discusses human flourishing in three dimensions: the yearnings for material goods, successful relationships, and a search for something greater, i.e., embrace of the human family within a learning community.[7] Such views of human flourishing resonate with the cosmopolitan focus of this book. The advance of cosmopolitan sensibility has enhanced the link between mission and the church's ability to embellish human life. Similarly, the advance of cosmopolitanism in the context of mission has influenced theological education. A circle of mutuality and learning has been created.

Under the leadership of Ian Markham, Virginia Seminary pursues human flourishing. Established in an age of educational innovation, the seminary adopted a formative approach to theological education that planted the seed of cosmopolitan vision. This seed was nurtured throughout the history of the seminary by cultural encounter, making the seminary a community of memory in which history and tradition shape perspectives on mission. Distinction is not lost, but the tent is enlarged. In recent decades, the work of various leaders of Virginia Seminary, in conversation with such figures as Michael Curry, Rowan Williams, Justin Welby, and Desmond Tutu, among others, has encouraged the seminary to serve as "a big tent." It is a welcoming space that pursues human flourishing, at home and abroad. Mission becoming cosmopolitan has a homing instinct, an emphasis on the love of Christ. Morphing out of insularity and provinciality, cosmopolitanism represents genuine

---

6. VanderWeele, "On the Promotion of Human Flourishing."
7. Briggs and Reiss, *Human Flourishing*, vii–viii.

belonging in a transnational world. Rather than fixing the world in the image of the West, mission must encourage complex attachments and tap the possibilities they bring for mutual enhancement. This is the intention of cosmopolitanism.

PATTERNS OF CONSTRUCTIVE EXCHANGE

The emphasis on flourishing became explicit during the tenure of Martha Horne as dean and president from 1993 to 2007. Her leadership coincided with a period of dynamic theological contention in the Anglican Communion. The clash of cultural and religious identities brought into focus questions of Anglican distinctiveness and theological integrity. Pressing leadership questions surfaced. How could the seminary's leadership address deep-rooted disagreements among faculty, students, and staff? What kinds of policies, curriculum, and programs could be accommodated? As the conversations from those years reveal, there was a temptation to evade theological reflection and dialogue by responding superficially. But thoughtful leadership prevailed. Taking deep-rooted disagreements in stride, Horne pursued comity among trustees, faculty and staff, students and alumni. She fostered a culture of theological pluralism and embraced diversity in matters of gender, race, and culture. Her years were characterized by appreciation of the wider Anglican world's history and dynamics. She refocused the seminary's gaze on the larger Episcopal Church and the Anglican Communion.[8] One outcome was creation of the Center for Anglican Communion (CACS). It has become a catalyst for reconciliation and mission even as Anglican splinter groups have asserted particular agendas.

When Robert Heaney became director of CACS and assistant professor of mission in 2013, the seminary's international profile advanced. By 2021, CACS had focused its work on "Equipping International Community," "Empowering International Leaders," and "Enriching Episcopal-Anglican Identity."[9] It addressed these goals through various projects. One was to coordinate and nurture scholarly engagement among Anglicans worldwide by bringing people of faith together through public events, lectures, and conferences. The second was to house Anglican materials

8. Jones and Hawkins, *Staying One, Remaining Open.*

9. Center for Anglican Communion Studies, "Resourcing Practices of Reconciliation," 5–8.

and host Anglican scholars through consultations and the promotion and publication of reports, research, and books. Third, CACS would devote time, money, and energy toward assisting individuals and groups around the world to reflect on the historic nature and contemporary possibilities of Anglicanism engaging in intercultural and interreligious partnership. With these purposes in mind, CACS has facilitated the seminary's reach into the Anglican Communion and the wider world through mission-oriented initiatives.

Ian Markham has reinforced the seminary's responsibility to the Communion. A shared liturgy and theological disposition make outreach a priority. Because the seminary is connected in tangible ways to those who live in some of the poorest countries in the world, the seminary must be attentive to life's material realities. Such attention is possible because Markham and the seminary's leadership retain a dynamic sense of identity. In his address to the 2015 General Convention of the Episcopal Church, Markham listed three aspects of identity: the seminary is Episcopal, residential, and global. The seminary serves the Episcopal tradition while being connected to wider religious worlds. CACS's cross-cultural and interreligious efforts make this commitment plain.

In 2010, CACS organized and coordinated a preliminary "Interreligious Conference on Conflict Analysis and Peacebuilding" in Dodoma, Tanzania. In 2014, CACS offered a second interfaith conference at Msalato Theological College in Dodoma, Tanzania. This was funded by the Luce Foundation.[10] More than sixty Christian and Muslim faith leaders from Kenya, Malawi, South Africa, the United States and Tanzania explored the theme "Understanding Ourselves, Our Faiths, Our World." The Tanzanian host, Jacob Chimeledya, a 2003 alumni of VTS and then archbishop of Tanzania, was joined by Sheikh Mustapha, regional Muslim leader of the Dodoma. Both men were enthusiastic about the potential for the gathering to achieve mutual respect and compassion between the faiths. They led participants through dialogue on effective interreligious engagement. As the chief architect of the event, Robert Heaney affirmed the collegiality between Anglicanism and other religious. The culmination was "The Dodoma Statement 2014," which reflected the gathering of Muslim and Christian leaders and interreligious workers and peace builders in common accord. It refers to all as "descendants of Abraham" who "believe in one creator God who has called us to be caretakers of

---

10. Virginia's ability to network with grant-funding organizations forms a key pillar of its cosmopolitan outreach.

creation, to work for the common good, and to promote and practice peace."[11] The document shows how participants represented, listened, and engaged from their religious heritages without acquiescing to a watered-down middle ground. In enumerating the encounters, one sees a running theme. The reciprocal communities recognize the shared human experience that overrides prevalent strife. Both Christianity and Islam in Tanzania lack sufficient resources. Both confront secularism, poverty, environmental degradation, corruption, mistrust, and misrepresentation of their respective faiths. Social disruptions affect the followers of both faiths. In the end, both religions must face painful, shared realities.

For Virginia Seminary, participation in interreligious dialogue is not divorced from overseas mission; often, the one facilitates the other. One coordinator of the Dodoma Conference was Sandra McCann, then a missionary in Tanzania. Trained as a medical professional, she later attended the seminary where she wondered if she was too old to study with younger students. After graduation in 2003, she became so accomplished that she was awarded an honorary doctoral degree in 2017.[12] Ordained in the Diocese of Atlanta, she and her husband, Martin, were appointed as missionaries of the Episcopal Church and served in Dodoma, Tanzania. She worked in various capacities for twelve years, including teaching and being communications director at Msalato Theological College and at St. Philips Theological College in Maseno, Kenya. She and her husband utilized their medical skills in a clinic with meager resources in rural Tanzania. As cosmopolitans, missionaries must discern how tradition, social change and culture shape daily experience in diverse societies.

For McCann, serving in Tanzania erased lingering assumptions about progress and piety. Spiritual discourse in missionary service must navigate issues of literacy. First world notions of equality of men and women do not translate easily in societies that are heavily patriarchal. Living in quarters without running water shifts priorities of what conversations are valuable to the moment. Women who must walk long distances to fetch water from the river will have a different notion of rights and privileges than women in the United States advocating for equal pay. Cross-cultural differences are not erased by missionary collegiality. McCann encourages students at Virginia Seminary to gain cross-cultural encounters before venturing abroad. The seminary campus abounds

11. "'Descendants of Abraham' Unite," *Living Church*, June 27, 2017.
12. "Virginia Theological Seminary Awards Five Honorary Degrees," 25.

with intercultural possibilities. "To serve God in many communities and schools in the US requires crossing language and cultural barriers," she adds.[13] She observes how once abroad, outsiders may struggle to grasp cultural differences. In Tanzania, traditional religion and customs continue to influence this modernizing society. Approaches to problem solving, sources of patronage and authority, and the lens through which scripture is read differ in perplexing ways. To eschew cynicism, boundary-crossing mission requires wisdom and prayer.

Complex intercultural and interreligious issues are at the heart of mission. This has always been the case, but in the United States, interfaith matters became even more important after the attack on the World Trade Center on September 11, 2001. Christian-Muslim relations became fraught with mistrust and divisive diatribe. Over the next decade, various religious communities would hold consultations on religion and politics. In 2010, John Chane, then bishop of Washington and advisor for interfaith relations at the Washington National Cathedral, observed that Christianity and Islam had "a great opportunity to work together effectively with governments and civil societies currently in turmoil."[14] The National Cathedral has worked closely with the seminary. In 2014, CACS hosted Muslim and Christian scholars and leaders from across Northern Virginia for a two-day conference titled "Faithful Neighbors: Transforming Attitudes." United by their love for God, participants met to examine the state of interreligious cooperation, to discuss the intercultural dimensions at work in such cooperation, and to develop resources to build better understanding and practice. Deepened understanding of the need for healthy interreligious dialogue in the public arena prompted the gathering. The importance of developing personal relationships across faith and cultural boundaries was an insight that helped to form cross-faith groups to focus on social action projects, another dimension of CACS's work.

As it hosted various gatherings, CACS recruited Zeyneb Sayilgan to be the Luce Muslim Visiting Professor and Senior Fellow in Peace and Reconciliation. She is the consummate cosmopolitan, fluent in Turkish, Kurdish, German, and English. She has additional reading skills in Arabic and Farsi, and she has traveled throughout the Middle East, Asia, and Europe to explore interfaith dynamics in these regions. She is known for writing on matters concerning Muslim immigrants in Europe. She brought insight

13. "Virginia Theological Seminary Awards Five Honorary Degrees," 25.
14. Washington National Cathedral, "Third Summit."

from her research on Islamic mosques, their leadership, and factors sur-rounding their cross-cultural and cross-faith engagement. Granted that the sociopolitical discourse can still vilify Muslim presence in American public life, extending such interfaith hospitality brought some criticism to Virginia Seminary. In 2017, Ian Markham told the community about an email that was sent to his office in protest of her residency.

> As a Christian Seminary we are already receiving attention for our relationship with Dr. Sayilgan. Soon after the March 2017 eNews was sent out, we received the following email: "I'm sure that I will get the usual wishy-washy response, but why would you invite a hijab wearing Quran sworn enemy into our midst? Any answer other than know your enemy reeks of the PC non-sense that is rotting us from within?"[15]

Dean Markham's response was both conciliatory and discerning. He affirmed the approach Zeyneb Sayilgan represents. Her interest was not in a syncretistic amalgam of the Christian and Muslim traditions, but in an encounter that comes grounded and committed to the particular focus of the two religious traditions. Sayilgan understands that there are groups committing atrocities based on their flawed reading of the Quran. Their victims include Christians, secularists, gay people, Jews, Buddhists, Hindus, and, of course, Muslims. It could be argued that Muslims make up the majority of victims of religious hatred. A cosmopolitan view re-sists outright rejection of Muslims or any particular group as a whole. The Islamic tradition out of which Dr. Sayilgan comes is committed to nonviolence, treats the five pillars as vehicles for a transformed human life that is grounded in God, and seeks to have good relationships widely. Her response to the biased missive is telling:

> Dean Markham has passed along your message expressing your disquiet that Virginia Seminary has "a hijab wearing Quran sworn enemy in our midst." So please allow me to respond. I was born and raised in Germany. I have spent my whole life liv-ing and studying with Christians. I have obtained my graduate degrees at the Johannes Gutenberg University in Mainz, Germa-ny—the city which I always fondly describe as my home where the Bible was first printed. I came to the United States in 2006 to study my Master of Arts in Christian-Muslim Relations at Hart-ford Seminary in Connecticut. I then received my doctorate in the Department of Theology at Georgetown University. I have

15. Markham, "Reaffirming Our Baptismal Promise," 5.

always been committed to peaceful relations between Christians and Muslims. I am persuaded that the witness of the Qur'an and the Prophet Muhammad is that we need to be at peace with our neighbor. I am dismayed by any Muslim who says otherwise. I would be pleased to meet with you on your next visit to VTS, where we both could share our concerns with one another.

Yours, Dr. Zeyneb Sayilgan[16]

In 2016 CACS published *Faithful Neighbors: Christian-Muslim Vision and Practice*, edited by Robert Heaney and Zeyneb Sayilgan. Reading this volume from a cosmopolitan norm, the clarion call is for human communities to live in one accord. Both Christians and Muslims love their faith and naturally want to share it with others. While conversion as a theme of interfaith conversation cannot be avoided, it is not the end game. True evangelism seeks to discover the holiness in fellow human beings by listening attentively, sharing one's own voice, then cultivating interfaith relations.

In the foreword, Ian Markham lauds the volume for charting this middle pathway.[17] When some advocates of different traditions come together, they may tend to float increasingly adrift from the communities they represent. The professional dialogue participants are often critical of conservative coreligionists. If the challenge is living with religious diversity, then the solution is not to disparage those who are most committed. As Zeyneb Sayilgan states in her chapter, one starts with exegesis of one's own scriptures, in faithfulness to the text that one believes is the word of God.[18] Another approach is to enter the interfaith conversation through stories of the journey that portray a humanity yearning for connectivity and affection. In the end, Sayilgan and Heaney catalogue the features of interfaith conversations, namely self-discovery, relationships, generosity, recognition of difference and power relations, contextualism, and humility. These emerge from their book and from the work of the Center for Anglican Communion Studies.

Virginia Seminary has also reimagined mission through being a hospitable place for inter-Anglican discussion, for ecumenical dialogue, and international discernment on topics of twenty-first century world Christianity. CACS has hosted fellows in residence, organized

16. Markham, "Reaffirming Our Baptismal Promise," 5.
17. Heaney and Sayilgan, *Faithful Neighbors*, vii–viii.
18. Heaney and Sayilgan, *Faithful Neighbors*, 20–36.

ecumenical meetings, and supported international students studying at the seminary. Nurturing a sense of catholicity is core to a mission ethos at Virginia Seminary. This has been apparent through a partnership of two programs to enrich the curriculum. The Washington Theological Union (WTU), founded at a Roman Catholic Seminary in Washington, DC, in 1968, educated members of many religious orders and traditions. The program had developed a unique doctor of ministry program in Christian spirituality drawing on the traditions of its founding religious orders brought into conversation with ministry through its curriculum. Resource constraints compelled WTU to close its operations by 2010. The board, administration, and faculty of Virginia Seminary agreed to adopt WTU's program as a part of Virginia's doctor of ministry concentration in what was termed as an ecumenical "exchange of gifts."[19] When brought together, the Catholic, Anglican, and Reformed traditions offer a rich perspective on the spiritual journey, offering a new step toward forming religious cosmopolitans. Biblical spirituality is a foundation shared across Christian traditions. The new degree offered a template for redesigning curricula of other concentrations. Virginia Seminary adopted the program for its ecumenical focus and international reach. Students come from congregational ministries, hospital and prison chaplaincies, ministries to ethnic and native communities in the US, spiritual direction and pastoral care. Reflecting on this exchange, Kathleen Hope Brown, associate director of the doctor of ministry program, observed that religious traditions represent gifts, one Catholic and the other Anglican. Ecumenism requires diplomacy, dialogue, social involvement, pastoral cooperation, and recognition of the Holy Spirit in both traditions.

Another way the spirit of catholicity and ecumenism is nurtured is by bringing international community into relationships of dialogue, collaboration, and partnerships on the priorities for Christian ministry. In 2015, CACS hosted "The Mission of God and the Future of the Anglican Communion." At the event, Anglican mission theologian Graham Kings, another frequent seminary guest, defined his role as promoting awareness about world Christianity. Kings reminded those present that mission is God centered. The communion's future is "in the hands of God," who calls us to be catholic, evangelical and ecumenical.[20] That calling is theological by definition, and intercultural by necessity. King's words

---

19. Brown, "Exchange of Gifts," 16–17.
20. Virginia Theological Seminary, "Dr. Kings."

challenged his hearers and revealed his intentions for his new position. These included convening a network of theologians as "doctors of the church," online intercultural reflection, and coordinating published resources from Africa, Asia, and Latin America.

The polarities tugging at the Anglican world do not fade easily. Virginia Seminary has worked hard to be a mediator. In 2016, Virginia Seminary participated in the Anglican Consultative Council Meeting. The contestations of the living tradition of Anglicanism were illustrated in Lusaka through key contributions from the archbishop of Canterbury, the secretary general, and the chairman of the ACC; the meeting also included numerous reports from the Anglican Communion Office staff, greetings and reports from ecumenical partners, small group discussions, and numerous informal conversations. Each of these vital components of the conference emphasized that being in communion takes work. Catholicity is a gift, and it is a calling that must be nurtured. This reality was underlined by the absence of Uganda, Nigeria, and Rwanda and by the controversy caused by the General Convention's decision to change the canonical language on marriage in the Episcopal Church.

The Anglican debate over sexuality, on the heels of debate over the ordination of women, represents a legacy of contestation. That is, Anglicans have debated the necessary norms that should structure church life and even the appropriate modes of discourse about such norms. One theorist sees contestation as a path toward cosmopolitanism. Thus, contestation is seen in relational terms regardless of how tenuous the relations have become.[21] A prominent instance concerns the history of slavery in America. The question of how to make amends for the enslavement of Africans is an issue that remains mired in controversy. Talk of reparations elicits strong emotions tinged with complex economic, political, and social implications. In 2006, the General Convention passed a resolution supporting federal legislation to confront the country's legacy of slavery, proposing monetary and non-monetary reparations to the descendants of the victims. The Episcopal Church was slow to take practical steps until Virginia Seminary acted.

In the political climate of the last few decades, some colleges and universities that were founded before the Civil War grappled with their histories of racial injustice. At least fifty of them formed a coalition of

---

21. Wiener, "Theory of Contestation," 109–12.

universities to study slavery and research that history.[22] In 2009, Ian Markham issued a public apology for the seminary's complicity in slavery. In 2019, Virginia Seminary took an unprecedented step. Amid a national conversation over reparations, it set aside $1.7 million for a slavery reparations fund. Markham noted the moral responsibility involved. The seminary recognized that repentance for past sins requires action. Enslaved African Americans worked on the campus of Virginia Theological Seminary. As many as three hundred people may have been enslaved over time at the seminary. Black students were excluded from attending the seminary until the 1950s. The reparations endowment fund is meant to atone for injustice.

The seminary's Office of Multicultural Ministries administers the fund. Income from the endowment fund for reparations is being used in five ways. One is to meet the needs identified by local congregations with ties to Virginia Seminary. Second is to issue funds to meet the needs of descendants of enslaved people who worked at Virginia. Third is to support the work of Black alumni at historically Black congregations. Fourth is to encourage African American clergy in the Episcopal church to study to serve the church. Fifth is to fund activities that promote justice and inclusion. The commitment of financial resources brings significant public impact.

Joseph Thompson is a faculty member and Associate Dean of Multicultural Ministries. He observes that there is a fascinating juxtaposition of past and present at Virginia Seminary. The Seminary Covenant, published in 2019 after several years of discussion, affirms that diversity must be definitive of the seminary's life. Study of the past elicits instances

22. The Universities Studying Slavery (USS) consortium, created and led by the University of Virginia, represents a multi-institutional collaboration focused on sharing best practices and guiding principles about truth-telling projects addressing human bondage and racism in institutional histories. Member schools are all committed to research, acknowledgment, and atonement regarding institutional ties to the slave trade, to enslavement on campus or abroad, and to enduring racism in school history and practice. USS additionally allows participating institutions to work together as they address both historical and contemporary issues dealing with race and inequality in higher education and in university communities. Together, the growing movement of schools committed to this work seek to address the complicated legacies of slavery in the modern world. Member institutions also work together on developing ways for individual institutions to commit school resources to addressing equity in the twenty-first century. Finally, USS hosts semiannual meetings to discuss strategies, collaborate on research, and learn from one another. For further information, visit https://slavery.virginia.edu/universities-studying-slavery/.

of disparaging discrimination and even enslavement. However, Thompson affirms how far the seminary has come. In June 2022, the seminary's intention to become a prominent Anglican meeting place took on new meaning. Over two hundred descendants of those who had been enslaved at the seminary gathered on campus to remember and to affirm the advance of justice. It is "the relational piece," Thompson said.[23] His emphasis pointed to the cosmopolitan sensibility that has unfolded. Mission and seminary life generally must center on mutuality and reciprocity. It is an ongoing pursuit.

MISSION AS A LIVING TRADITION

Institutions that mark two hundred years of experience can often point to one or another treasured aspect of their identity. Discussion of the history of Virginia Theological Seminary soon adverts to the theme of mission, which has been presumed to be prominent. This book has documented the place of mission in the seminary's life especially with regard to initiatives abroad. The mission emphasis has been dynamic, unfolding over time to become a key reference point. Given such centrality and continuity, mission in the seminary's life can be termed a "tradition." But such a reference cannot presume a static quality. Tradition must be lived, it must adapt and change if it, and the institution in which it is rooted, are to thrive.

Tradition at Virginia Seminary or any other institution may not seem dynamic. The word "tradition" refers to the transmission or passing on of customs from one generation to the next. Traditions seem to be treasured artifacts possessing authority and curiosity. They commonly offer guidance and clarity of belief and practice from past to present. Charles Price suggested as much in 1988 when he described "The Virginia Seminary Liturgical Tradition." In general terms Price described tradition as necessary. It draws its hearers into lived experience, possessing wisdom, bridging past and present. For Christians, it creates ways of receiving the gospel. "The gospel has to be traditioned. Traditions are necessary."[24]

Comparing the transmission of tradition to a runner passing a baton in a relay race, Price then affirmed that tradition is dynamic. Unlike the baton being passed, tradition is modified, even reshaped, by being

23. Joseph Thompson in an interview with the author, September 6, 2022.
24. Price, "Virginia Seminary Liturgical Tradition," 24.

passed on. In effect, tradition is modified by the runner carrying it. Paradoxically, traditions "have to change so that their meaning can remain unchanged through changing epochs of time." That "complex and dynamic process . . . involves the interactions of persons in the process of telling and hearing." In a word, tradition involves relations. Price adds that "this process lies in the background of any discussion of a liturgical tradition." His depiction could be enlarged to encompass mission, of which the relational aspect is pivotal and in which liturgy is prominent. Price sensed this relation. He emphasized that tradition points to "a way of life and thought, and worship. It's all one ball of wax, though it has many interrelated elements."[25]

From a broad framing of tradition, Price moved to an outline of Virginia Seminary's particular approach to worship at the time, for tradition consists of particular practices in particular settings, grounding identity in time and space. The seminary's tradition in Price's hands has been a communal activity set by the Book of Common Prayer, regularly using the Daily Offices while making the Eucharist central. Invoking the Protestant dimension of the English Reformation, Price allowed that ceremonial in worship should be "as simple and direct as possible." In other words, "we try to keep services uncluttered." This seemed to be the best way to secure worship that is "filled with the glory of God."[26] Price's description blended preferred patterns of practice and intention with a broad, dynamic depiction of them. He might have added that tradition is never complete, the baton is ever being passed and so adapted. The same could be said of the teaching and practice of mission emanating from the seminary.

The shape of Virginia Seminary's commitment to mission has been set in larger contexts by this book. This commitment, and the founding of the seminary itself, arose during America's Second Great Awakening, by which a blend of evangelical character and Episcopal expression were wed. Evangelism was prominent, and the Missionary Society made this plain. Evangelism became the translation of conviction into practice as missionaries went forth to convert and to enliven religious life in various contexts. In Greece, a predominantly Christian nation, the goal became spiritual enlivening focused on equipping young women for service in their society. Even in Africa, China, and later Japan, conversion was only a first step. The liturgical tradition of which Charles Price wrote became

25. Price, "Virginia Seminary Liturgical Tradition," 24.
26. Price, "Virginia Seminary Liturgical Tradition," 26.

the basis of church life alongside translation and study of the Bible. Schools were founded and then colleges. It became possible to envision the emergence of modern, Christian societies, until social currents and political events diminished this naïve intention. Trial and error are part of the transmission of tradition.

A body of critical literature has spoken of "the invention of tradition" to criticize the work of mission and the veracity of the religious life it attempts to implant in new settings.[27] Mission has seemed to collude in the creation of unholy order. Such themes as "imperialism" and "colonialism" as well as "racism" reflect basic realities in the history of both empire and mission. For some critics, the two are fatefully entwined. Missionaries participated in the invention of tradition which bore the marks of Western societies. Patterns of economic, cultural, political, and military activity cannot be fully distinguished from the work of mission in all circumstances. Yet it must be emphasized that missionaries often consciously countered the worst of imperial and colonial designs and worked hard to distinguish themselves and their intentions from other, secular agents.[28] In speaking of the "invention of tradition," one is apt to speak of mission as offering adaptive strategies that guided cultural change. This narrative has shown that mission led to dialogical and multidimensional relations. Thus, tradition provides identity and direction.

In speaking of tradition, Edward Shils wrote that "traditions are indispensable; they are also very seldom entirely adequate." The spread of societies "from one part of the earth's surface to areas where they were previously unknown" created instances of encounter by which various traditions influenced one another. "Every society which becomes an empire, or which sends its members as explorers, merchants, soldiers, missionaries, and administrators experiences this juxtaposition of its own tradition with the traditions of the indigenous societies upon which it comes."[29] Experience instructs, Shils observed, especially when traditions encounter each other. What is learned from experience "leads both to confirmation and revision of what was previously believed," neither tradition remaining unchanged.[30] Both are modified and, for the tradi-

27. Hobsbawm and Ranger, *Invention of Tradition.*

28. Porter, *Religion versus Empire?*

29. Shils, *Tradition*, 240.

30. Shils, *Tradition*, 203.

tion from outside to endure, it must adapt, that is, become enculturated.[31] The mark of being enculturated, an enhanced way of speaking of "indigenous" life, is the emergence of new identity.

Over thirty years after Price spoke of Virginia Seminary's liturgical tradition, Archbishop Hosam Naoum of Jerusalem, an alumnus of Virginia Seminary, addressed the theme of Anglican identity. Though the occasion was the Lambeth Conference of 2022, Naoum's thoughts were not time-bound. He spoke first of basic, Christian identity, the "Body of Christ," rooted in "the Person of Jesus Christ." He then drew on the life of Anglican Christians in the Jerusalem church, who are speaking to Christian tradition's roots in a distinctive and powerful setting. The identity Naoum posed is dynamic. It is the way of pilgrims, an image drawn from centuries of faithful persons walking in holy footsteps and seeking to be reshaped in their own lives as a result. Naoum could speak of his ancestors embodying the faith and keeping it alive for two thousand years.[32] They did so relationally by inviting and welcoming. This image of pilgrimage shaped his view of Anglicans being in communion. Amid the Communion's fractured circumstances, the possibility of embodying its intention more fully became a pressing demand. Because of mission, the faith and the church became enculturated, and Naoum could speak as he did. Tradition had been passed on, and the church was poised to realize its cosmopolitan calling.

There have been multiple examples of the development of cosmopolitanism as a key feature of the life of Virginia Theological Seminary. The Christian faith has been proclaimed and the church built in various locations. Tradition has been adapted without being diluted. Identity, as Christians and as Anglicans, remains paramount. In fact, identity has unfolded to the extent that it is reflective of particular contexts without being dependent on them. As this book has explained, at the core of mission we find dynamic relations uniting peoples across the chasms that have separated them. The sense of being in communion has become vivid and durable, even as the institutional structures that proclaim communion have faltered.

Evidence of cosmopolitanism is not difficult to find. It is apparent in the international students who have studied and worshiped in Alexandria. It is unmistakable as seminary students have paid guided visits

31. Sachs, introduction to *The Oxford History of Anglicanism*, 13–19.

32. Naoum, "Lambeth Call."

to the church in such places as Jerusalem and Tanzania. The ties made have been personal and often informal. Yet tangible qualities appear on the basis of mutual recognition and respect. Herman Browne of Liberia speaks of sharing such resources, exchanging expertise in various fields, and building networks for patterns of assistance.[33] Basic tasks are inherent in this approach to mission, including proclamation of the Christian faith and the equipping of new lay and ordained leaders. Mission as a tradition possesses consistent qualities even as it unfolds.

When the intention of mission is described as cosmopolitan, an emphasis on equipping people for faithful living becomes plain. Mission is enhanced by an emphasis on mutuality and reciprocity that embodies cosmopolitanism. Over the course of Virginia Seminary's history, the intentions of being both faithful and cosmopolitan have cross-fertilized. The intention has not been fully realized, and, in a sense, it will not be. Mission remains a dynamic, unending pursuit. The cultivation of cosmopolitanism as definitive of mission must never abate. Thus, along the wide arc of Virginia Seminary's influence, the truth must be sought, come whence it may, cost what it will.

33. Browne, interview with the author, March 23, 2022.

Bibliography

Addams, Jane. *Democracy and Social Ethics*. New York: Macmillan, 1902.

Allison, C. Fitzsimons. "Go Ye into All the World and Preach the Gospel." *Virginia Seminary Journal* 23 (January 1971) 6–9.

Anglican Consultative Council. "The Virginia Report: The Report of the Inter-Anglican Theological and Doctrinal Commission." London: Secretary General of the Anglican Consultative Council, 1997.

Appiah, Kwame Anthony. *Cosmopolitanism: Ethics in a World of Strangers*. New York: Norton, 2007.

"Backward or Forward in Japan?" *Japan Missions* 6 (Winter 1956) 1–2.

Banks, Adelle M. "Biden Says VTS COVID-19 Vaccine Clinic Is Example of 'America at Its Finest.'" Episcopal News Service. April 8, 2021. https://www.episcopalnewsservice.org/2021/04/08/biden-says-vts-covid-19-vaccine-clinic-is-example-of-america-at-its-finest/.

Bass, Diana Butler. *Standing Against the Whirlwind: Evangelical Episcopalians in Nineteenth-Century America*. New York: Oxford University Press, 1995.

Bass, Jonathan S. *Blessed Are the Peacemakers: Martin Luther King Jr., Eight White Religious Leaders, and the "Letter from Birmingham Jail."* Baton Rouge: Louisiana State University Press, 2001.

Beckwith, John Q. "The Race Problem and the South." Five lectures. Washington, DC: Henderson Services, 1958.

Bell, W. Cosby. *The Making of Man*. New York: Macmillan, 1931.

Bender, Thomas. *Community and Social Change in America*. Baltimore: Johns Hopkins University Press, 2000.

———. "The Cosmopolitan Experience and Its Uses." In *Cosmopolitanisms*, edited by Bruce Robbins and Paulo Lemos Horta, 116–26. New York: New York University Press, 2017.

Bergo, Bettina. "Emmanuel Levinas." In *The Stanford Encyclopedia of Philosophy*, edited by Edward N. Zalta. Fall 2019 ed. https://plato.stanford.edu/archives/fall2019/entries/levinas/.

Bess, Douglas. *Divided We Stand*. Berkeley: Apocryphile, 2006.

Block, James E. *A Nation of Agents*. Cambridge: Belknap, 2002.

Board of Trustees, Virginia Theological Seminary. "Report." May 14, 1997. Seminary Archives, Virginia Theological Seminary.

Boone, Muriel. *The Seed of the Church in China.* Philadelphia: Pilgrim, 1973.

Booty, John E. *Mission and Ministry: A History of the Virginia Theological Seminary.* Harrisburg, PA: Morehouse, 1995.

Briggs, Andrew, and Michael Reiss. *Human Flourishing: Scientific Insight and Spiritual Wisdom in Uncertain Times.* Oxford: Oxford University Press, 2021.

Brown, Kathleen Hope. "An Exchange of Gifts." *News from the Hill* (Virginia Theological Seminary), Winter 2015, 16–17. https://vts.edu/wp-content/uploads/2015/12/VTS_Winter_2015_web-ready.pdf.

Browne, Herman. Interview with the author, March 23, 2022. Notes in the author's possession.

Bulletin of the Protestant Episcopal Theological Seminary in Virginia. June 1914.

Bulletin of the Protestant Episcopal Theological Seminary in Virginia. 1927–1928.

Carson, D. A. *Christ and Culture Revisited.* Grand Rapids: Eerdmans, 2008.

Center for Anglican Communion Studies. "Resourcing Practices of Reconciliation." Brochure. Alexandria: Virginia Theological Seminary, 2021.

Ciment, James. *Another America: The Story of Liberia and the Former Slaves Who Ruled It.* New York: Hill & Wang, 2014.

Cleaveland, George J. "VTS Graduates and the Nippon SeiKoKwai." *Seminary Journal* (March 1959) 26–31.

Cohen, Julie, and Betsy West, directors. *My Name Is Pauli Murray.* Documentary film. 91 minutes. Produced by Participant; Storyville Films; and Drexler Films. Distributed by Amazon Studios, 2021.

Constant, Joseph M. *No Turning Back: The Black Presence at Virginia Theological Seminary.* Brainerd, MN: Evergreen, 2009.

Craighill, Marian G. *The Craighills of China.* Ambler, PA: Trinity, 1972.

Curry, Michael B. *Love Is the Way: Holding onto Hope in Troubling Times.* London: Hodder & Stoughton, 2020.

Dame, William. "Reminiscences." In Goodwin, *History of the Theological Seminary in Virginia*, 1:451–71.

Danaher, William J. "Beyond Imagination." *Anglican Theological Review* 93 (2011) 219–41.

Davies, Matthew. "Presiding Bishop Responds to Primates' Actions, Stresses Relationships." Video, 5:56. *Episcopal News Service*, January 15, 2016. https://www.episcopalnewsservice.org/2016/01/15/video-presiding-bishop-responds-to-primates-actions-stresses-relationships/.

Dejung, Christof, et al., eds. *The Global Bourgeoisie.* Princeton: Princeton University Press, 2019.

Denison, S. D. *A History of the Foreign Missionary Work of the Protestant Episcopal Church.* New York: Foreign Committee of the Board of Missions, 1871.

"'Descendants of Abraham' Unite." *Living Church* (magazine), June 27, 2014. https://livingchurch.org/2014/06/27/descendants-abraham-unite/.

"Diocesan Nation-Wide Campaign." *Hawaiian Church Chronicle* 12 (January 1920) 4.

Douglas, Ian T. *Fling Out the Banner! The National Church Ideal and the Foreign Mission of the Episcopal Church.* New York: Church Hymnal, 1996.

Due, Paul. "The Work of the Seminary in Liberia." In Goodwin, *History of the Theological Seminary in Virginia*, 2:295–323.

Dunn, D. Elwood. *A History of the Episcopal Church in Liberia, 1821–1980.* ATLA Monograph Series 30. Metuchen, NJ: Scarecrow, 1992.

Eddy, William D. "Is There a Continuing Role for the U.S. Missionary?" *Virginia Seminary Journal* 23 (January 1971) 24.

———. Letter to Mary Dillon, April 29, 1954. Seminary Archives, Virginia Theological Seminary, Papers of William Eddy.

———. Letter to Mary Dillon, July 20, 1954. Seminary Archives, Virginia Theological Seminary, Papers of William Eddy.

Emery, Julia C. *A Century of Endeavor, 1821–1921*. New York: Department of Missions, 1921.

Episcopal News Service. "Virginia Seminary Revises Policy on Sexual Behavior." Archives of the Episcopal Church. February 13, 1997. https://episcopalarchives. org/cgi-bin/ENS/ENSpress_release.pl?pr_number=97-1690.

Every, Edward Francis. *The Anglican Church in South America*. London: SPCK, 1915.

———. "Some Impressions of the Brazilian Episcopal Church." *Spirit of Missions* 71 (November 1906) 922–24.

Faculty of Virginia Theological Seminary. "Statement of Agreement." September 25, 1996. Seminary Archives, Virginia Theological Seminary.

Flinn, J. Seymour. Letter from J. Seymour Flinn to Paul Lehman, July 7, 1953. Seminary Archives, Virginia Theological Seminary.

———. Letter from J. Seymour Flinn to Paul Lehman, April 2, 1954. Seminary Archives, Virginia Theological Seminary.

Fluker, Walter Earl. *The Ground Has Shifted*. New York: New York University Press, 2016.

Fuller, Reginald H. "Pro and Con: The Ordination of Women in the New Testament." In *Toward a New Theology of Ordination*, edited by Marianne H. Micks and Charles P. Price, 1–11. Somerville, MA: Greeno, Hadden, 1976.

Gates, Henry Louis, Jr. *The Black Church*. New York: Penguin, 2021.

Goetchius, Eugene Van Ness, and Charles P. Price. *The Gifts of God*. Harrisburg, PA: Morehouse-Barlow, 1984.

Goodwin, William Archer Rutherfoord, ed. *History of the Theological Seminary in Virginia and Its Historical Background*. 2 vols. New York: Gosham, 1923.

Grammer, Carl E. "The Virginia Seminary and the Origin of the Brazil Mission." In Goodwin, *History of the Theological Seminary in Virginia*, 2:349–70.

Hadler, Jacques B., Jr., and Richard J. Jones, "Two-Way Bridge: The Cross-Cultural Colloquy at Virginia Seminary." *Teaching Theology and Religion* 4 (2001) 102–7.

Hanciles, Jehu. *Euthanasia of Mission: African Church Autonomy in a Colonial Context*. Westport, CT: Praeger, 2002.

Hancock, Christopher. "Dynamic Orthodoxy." *SEAD* 3 (September 1993) 1–3.

Harrison, Robert. *Transformed By the Love of God*. Cincinnati: Forward Movement, 2004.

Hassett, Miranda. *Anglican Communion in Crisis*. Princeton: Princeton University Press, 2007.

Hawaiian Church Chronicle 12 (1920). Honolulu: Episcopal Diocese of Hawaii.

Hawkins, J. Barney, IV. "International Students at Virginia Seminary: A Long History with a Rich and Transformative Practice." In *Staying One, Remaining Open*, edited by Richard J. Jones and J. Barney Hawkins IV. Harrisburg, PA: Morehouse, 2010.

Heaney, Robert S., and William L. Sachs. *The Promise of Anglicanism*. London: SCM, 2019.

Heaney, Robert S., and Zeyneb Sayilgan, eds. *Faithful Neighbors: Christian-Muslim Vision and Practice*. New York: Morehouse, 2016.

Heim, Kenneth E., and Albert T. Mollegen. "Christianity and History." In *Christianity and Modern Man. Course 3*, Part 2. Washington: Washington Cathedral, 1949.

Hein, David, and Gardiner H. Shattuck, Jr. *The Episcopalians*. Westport, CT: Praeger, 2004.

Heitzenrater, Richard P. *Wesley and the People Called Methodists*. Nashville: Abingdon, 2013.

An Historical Sketch of the China Mission of the Protestant Episcopal Church in the U.S.A. New York: Domestic and Foreign Missionary Society, 1893.

Hobsbawm, Eric, and Terence Ranger, eds. *The Invention of Tradition*. Cambridge: Cambridge University Press, 1983.

Holifield, E. Brooks. *God's Ambassadors: A History of the Christian Clergy in America*. Grand Rapids: Eerdmans, 2007.

Hollinger, David A. *Protestants Abroad: How Missionaries Tried to Change the World but Changed America*. Princeton: Princeton University Press, 2017.

Holzhammer, Robert Ernest. "The Formation of the Domestic and Foreign Missionary Society." *Historical Magazine of the Protestant Episcopal Church* 40 (September 1971) 257–72.

Horne, Martha. Interview with William Sachs, April 7, 2022. Notes in the author's possession.

Howe, Daniel Walker. *What Hath God Wrought*. New York: Oxford University Press, 2007.

Howe, Reuel L. *The Miracle of Dialogue*. New York: Seabury, 1963.

In Trust Center for Theological Schools. "All People Considered: Redemptive Significance; Seminary Chapel Becomes Vaccine Clinic." *In Trust* (Summer 2021). https://intrust.org/Magazine/Issues/Summer-2021/All-People-Considered.

Iwai, Timothy. "Christianity and Japanese Culture." *Japan Missions* 6 (Winter 1956) 16–18.

Jenkins, Philip. *The Great and Holy War*. New York: HarperOne, 2015.

Jones, Richard. "From Uganda Martyrs to Sudan Ox: Notes from a Sabbatical Semester." *Virginia Seminary Journal* (2000) 18–21.

Jones, Richard J., and J. Barney Hawkins IV. Introduction to *Staying One, Remaining Open*, edited by Richard J. Jones and J. Barney Hawkins IV, 27–41. Harrisburg: Morehouse, 2010.

Journal of the 21st General Convention of the Episcopal Church. New York: Sparks, 1845.

Kesselus, Kenneth. *John E. Hines*. Austin: Episcopal Theological Seminary of the Southwest, 1995.

Kidd, Thomas S. *America's Religious History*. Grand Rapids: Zondervan, 2019.

Kimel, Alvin F., Jr. "A Confessing Faith: The Baltimore Declaration." In *Reclaiming Faith*, edited by Ephraim Radner and George R. Sumner, 272–85. Grand Rapids: Eerdmans, 1993.

King, Martin Luther, Jr. *Letter from the Birmingham Jail*. New York: HarperCollins, 1994.

Kinsolving, Lucien Lee. "The Brazilian Church in Council." *Spirit of Missions* 74 (1909) 17–20.

Krumm, John M. "Albert T. Mollegen: An Appreciation." In *Theology and Culture: Essays in Honor of Albert T. Mollegen and Clifford L. Stanley*, edited by W. Taylor Stevenson, 9–18. Evanston, IL: Anglican Theological Review, 1976.

"Leadership and Mission." Themed edition of *Virginia Theological Seminary Journal* (Fall 2010).

Lehman, Paul. Letter from Paul Lehman to J. Seymour Flinn, April 12, 1954. Seminary Archives, Virginia Theological Seminary.

LeRoy, Milton R. "Cuba in Revolution." *Seminary Journal* (March 1959) 33–34.

Lewis, Harold T. *Christian Social Witness*. Boston: Cowley, 2001.

———. *Yet with a Steady Beat*. Valley Forge, PA: Trinity, 1996.

Lin, Mei-Mei. "The Episcopal Missionaries in China, 1835–1900." PhD diss., University of Texas, 1994.

Lippy, Charles H. *Faith in America: Changes, Challenges, New Directions*. 3 vols. Westport, CT: Praeger, 2006.

Livingston, James. "Reflections on Tanzania." *Virginia Theological Seminary Journal* (Fall 2010) 28.

Lloyd, Arthur Selden. *Christianity and the Religions*. New York: Dutton, 1909.

Mabie, Hamilton W. "The Missionary as Statesman." *Spirit of Missions* 78 (November 1913) 773–75.

Markham, Ian. "Reaffirming Our Baptismal Promise to Respect the Dignity of Every Human Being." *News from the Hill* (Spring 2017) 4–5.

Marsh, Charles. *The Beloved Community*. New York: Basic Books, 2006.

Marty, Martin E. *Pilgrims in Their Own Land*. Boston: Little, Brown, 1984.

Mathews, Donald G. "The Second Great Awakening as an Organizing Process." *American Quarterly* 21 (Spring 1969) 23–43.

Meade, William. *Lectures on the Pastoral Office*. New York: Stanford and Swords, 1849.

———. *Old Churches, Ministers and Families of Virginia*. 2 vols. Philadelphia: Lippincott, 1861.

Mendez, Troy D. "A History of Mission: International Students and Virginia Theological Seminary." Independent report. Alexandria: Virginia Theological Seminary, 2008.

———. "Survey of Current International Students Attending Virginia Theological Seminary." Independent report. Alexandria: Virginia Theological Seminary, 2008.

Merrins, Edward M. "Christian Education and National Progress." *Spirit of Missions* 77 (1912) 355–60.

Micks, Marianne H., and Charles P. Price. Introduction to *Toward a New Theology of Ordination*, edited by Marianne H. Micks and Charles P. Price, ix–x. Somerville, MA: Greeno, Hadden, 1976.

Miller, Brian J. "Growing Suburbs, Relocating Churches." *JSSR* 56 (August 2017) 342–64.

Miller, Glenn T. *Piety and Profession: American Protestant Theological Education, 1870–1970*. Grand Rapids: Eerdmans, 2007.

Missionary Society. Correspondence, 1953 and 1954. Seminary Archives, Virginia Theological Seminary.

———. "Letters from Young Churches." *Virginia Theological Seminary* (1963) 1–69. Seminary Archives, Virginia Theological Seminary.

———. "Proposed Missionary Appropriations." Spring 1953. Seminary Archives, Virginia Theological Seminary.

Missionary Society of Inquiry. Minutes, June 25, 1835. Seminary Archives, Virginia Theological Seminary.

Mollegen, Albert T. *Christ and Everyman*. Washington, DC: Henderson, 1964.

———. *Christianity and Modern Man: The Crisis of Secularism.* Indianapolis: Bobbs-Merrill, 1961.

———. "Christology and Biblical Criticism in Tillich." In *The Theology of Paul Tillich,* edited by Charles W. Kegley and Robert W. Bretall, 230–47. New York: Macmillan, 1956.

———. "Evangelicalism and Christian Social Ethics." In *Anglican Evangelicalism,* edited by Alexander C. Zabriskie, 229–61. Philadelphia: Church Historical Society, 1943.

Morris, James W. "The Church's Message and Mission in Brazil." *Spirit of Missions* 73 (1908) 431–37.

Mullin, Robert Bruce. *Episcopal Vision / American Reality.* New Haven: Yale University Press, 1986.

Naoum, Hosam. Interview with William Sachs, July 17, 2022. Notes in the author's possession.

———. "Lambeth Call: Anglican Identity." Unpublished paper in the author's possession. July 2022.

Nelson, John K. *A Blessed Company: Parishes, Parsons, and Parishioners in Anglican Virginia, 1690–776.* Chapel Hill: University of North Carolina Press, 2001.

News on the Hill (2016). Alexandria: Virginia Theological Seminary.

Noll, Mark A. *America's God: From Jonathan Edwards to Abraham Lincoln.* New York: Oxford University Press, 2005.

———. *A History of Christianity in the United States and Canada.* Grand Rapids: Eerdmans, 2019.

———. *The Old Religion in a New World: The History of North American Christianity.* Grand Rapids: Eerdmans, 2002.

———. *The Rise of Evangelicalism: The Age of Edwards, Whitefield and the Wesleys.* Downers Grove: InterVarsity, 2003.

Nooteboom, Bart. *Beyond Humanism.* New York: Palgrave Macmillan. 2012.

Oast, Jennifer. *Institutional Slavery: Slaveholding Churches, Schools, Colleges, and Businesses in Virginia, 1680–1860.* Cambridge: Cambridge University Press, 2016.

Packard, Joseph. *Recollections of a Long Life.* Edited by Thomas J. Packard. Washington, DC: Byron S. Adams, 1902.

Page, Henry D. "Organization of the Church in Japan." *Spirit of Missions* 52 (1887) 186–88.

Partridge, Sidney C. "Our Mission in China." *Spirit of Missions* 50 (1895) 14–18.

Penick, Charles Clifton. Papers. 11 boxes. Richmond, VA: Library of Virginia.

Peterson, Derek R. *Ethnic Patriotism and the East African Revival.* Cambridge: Cambridge University Press, 2014.

Pippa, Norris, and Ronald Inglehart. *Cosmopolitan Communications.* Cambridge: Cambridge University Press, 2019.

Porter, Andrew. *Religion versus Empire? British Protestant Missionaries and Overseas Expansion, 1700–1914.* Manchester, UK: Manchester University Press, 2004.

Pott, F. L. Hawks. "Bishop Ingle." *Spirit of Missions* 69 (1904) 10–17.

Price, Charles P. "Clifford Leland Stanley: Teacher and Theologian." In *Theology and Culture: Essays in Honor of Albert T. Mollegen and Clifford L. Stanley,* edited by W. Taylor Stevenson, 19–30. Evanston, IL: Anglican Theological Review, 1976.

———. "The Virginia Seminary Liturgical Tradition." *Virginia Seminary Journal* 40 (November 1988) 24–26.

Price Charles P., and Louis Weil. *Liturgy for Living.* Harrisburg: Morehouse, 2000.

Prichard, Robert W. *Hail, Holy Hill: A Pictorial History of the Virginia Theological Seminary.* Alexandria, VA: River Place Communication Arts, 2012.

———. *A History of the Episcopal Church.* 3rd ed. New York: Morehouse, 2014.

———. "Latin American Anglicanism." *Virginia Seminary Journal* (1988) 30–32.

———. Letter from Robert W. Prichard to the Community Life Committee, May 16, 2000. Unpublished letter in the author's possession.

———. *The Nature of Salvation: Theological Consensus in the Episcopal Church, 1801–73.* Urbana: University of Illinois Press, 1997.

———. "The Place of Doctrine in the Episcopal Church." In *Reclaiming Faith*, edited by Ephraim Radner and George R. Sumner 13–45. Grand Rapids: Eerdmans, 1993.

———. "Virginia Seminary Since World War II." *Virginia Seminary Journal* 37 (June 1985) 33–43.

Putney, Clifford, and Paul T. Burlin, eds. *The Role of the American Board in the World.* Eugene, OR: Wipf & Stock, 2012.

Radner, Ephraim, and George R. Sumner. "Reclaiming Faith in Gratitude and Submission." Introduction to *Reclaiming Faith: Essays on Orthodoxy in the Episcopal Church and the Baltimore Declaration*, edited by Ephraim Radner and George R. Sumner, 1–10. Grand Rapids: Eerdmans, 1993.

Radner, Ephraim, and Philip Turner. *The Fate of Communion.* Grand Rapids: Eerdmans, 2006.

Reifsnider, Charles S. "The Christian College and Moral Leadership." *Spirit of Missions* 78 (April 1913) 239–40.

"Report of the Foreign Committee—China." *Spirit of Missions* 49 (1884) 605–8.

Richmond, Annette B. *The American Episcopal Church in China.* New York: Domestic and Foreign Missionary Society, 1907.

Rightor, Henry H. "The Existing Canonical Authority for Women's Ordination." In *Toward a New Theology of Ordination*, edited by Marianne H. Micks and Charles P. Price, 101–10. Somerville, MA: Greeno, Hadden, 1976.

Robert, Dana L. *Converting Colonialism.* Grand Rapids: Eerdmans, 2008.

Robertson, David M. *A Passionate Pilgrim.* New York: Vintage, 2006.

Rollins, Wallace E. "The Mission to Greece." In Goodwin, *History of the Theological Seminary in Virginia*, 2:252–70.

Sachs, William L. *Homosexuality and the Crisis of Anglicanism.* Cambridge: Cambridge University Press, 2009.

———. Introduction to *The Oxford History of Anglicanism*, vol. 5, *Global Anglicanism, c. 1910–2000*, edited by William Sachs, 1–22. Oxford: Oxford University Press, 2017.

———. "Public Theology as Religious Practice: Anglican Mission and Interreligious Encounter." *Anglican Theological Review* 102 (March 2020) 269–82.

———. "'Self-Support': The Episcopal Mission and Nationalism in Japan." *Church History* 58 (1989) 489–501.

———. "Sexuality and Anglicanism." In *The Oxford History of Anglicanism*, vol. 4, *Global Western Anglicanism, c. 1910–Present*, edited by Jeremy Morris, 93–116. Oxford: Oxford University Press, 2017.

Saloutos, Theodore. "American Missionaries in Greece: 1820–869." *Church History* 24 (June 1955) 152–74.

Santelli, Maureen Connors. *The Greek Fire.* Ithaca, NY: Cornell University Press, 2020.

Schreiter, Robert J. *Constructing Local Theologies.* Maryknoll, NY: Orbis, 2015.

————. *The New Catholicity: Theology Between the Global and the Local.* Maryknoll, NY: Orbis, 2005.

————. "What Is the Church's Enduring Mission in the World?" *Virginia Seminary Journal* (Spring 2009) 23–33.

Scott, David. "A Vision for SEAD." *SEAD* 3 (December 1993) 1–3.

————. "Concerning a Center of Anglican Theology." *Anglican Theological Review* 77 (1995) 90–95.

Scott, David A., and Harry C. Griffith. "A Christian Response to Human Sexuality." Winter Park, FL: Bible Reading Fellowship, 1987.

"Second Conference of the Chinese Mission." *Spirit of Missions* 61 (1896) 271–75.

Seminary Journal (March 1959). Alexandria: Virginia Theological Seminary.

Seminary Journal (Commencement 1961). Alexandria: Virginia Theological Seminary.

Seminary Journal (July 1963). Alexandria: Virginia Theological Seminary.

Sergel, C. H. C. "From One Generation to Another." *Spirit of Missions* 73 (1908) 180–81.

Shattuck, Gardiner. *Episcopalians and Race.* Lexington: University Press of Kentucky, 2003.

Shils, Edward. *Tradition.* Chicago: University of Chicago Press, 1981.

Shiras, Alexander. *Life and Letters of Rev. James May, D.D.* Philadelphia: Protestant Episcopal Book Society, 1865.

Southern Churchman 56 (1889). Alexandria, VA.

Southern Churchman 57 (1890). Alexandria, VA.

Southern Churchman 58 (1891). Alexandria, VA.

Spence, Jonathan D. *The Search for Modern China.* New York: Norton, 1990.

Spirit of Missions 2 (1837). New York: Swords, Stanford, 1837.

Spirit of Missions 4 (1839). New York: Swords, Stanford, 1839.

Spirit of Missions 6 (1841). New York: Board of Missions, 1841.

Spirit of Missions 11 (1846). New York: Dana, 1846.

Spirit of Missions 12 (1847). New York: Dana, 1847.

Spirit of Missions 13 (1848) New York: Dana, 1848.

Spirit of Missions 16 (1851). New York: Dana, 1851.

Spirit of Missions 20 (1855). New York: Dana, 1855.

Spirit of Missions 26 (1861). New York: John A. Gray, 1861.

Spirit of Missions 28 (1863). New York: Gray & Green, 1863.

Spirit of Missions 32 (1867). New York: Sanford, Harroun, 1867.

Spirit of Missions 33 (1868). New York: Sanford, Cushing, 1868.

Spirit of Missions 34 (1869). New York: American Church Press, 1869.

Spirit of Missions 40 (1875). New York: Board of Missions, 1875.

Spirit of Missions 49 (1884). New York: Bible House, 1884.

Spirit of Missions 60 (1895). New York: Church Missions House, 1895.

Spirit of Missions 74 (1909). New York: Church Missions House, 1909.

Spong, John Shelby. *Here I Stand.* San Francisco: HarperOne, 2001.

————. *Rescuing the Bible from Fundamentalism.* San Francisco: HarperOne, 1992.

————. *Why Christianity Must Change or Die.* San Francisco: HarperOne, 1999.

Stafford, Barbara. "The Virginia Theological Seminary Center for Anglican Communion Studies." *Virginia Seminary Journal* (June 1998) 15–19.

Stamper, James H. "Results of Survey of Missionary Interest in Junior and Middler Classes," May 1961. Seminary Archives, Virginia Theological Seminary.

———. "Study of the Missionary Society of the Virginia Theological Seminary." January 1961. Seminary Archives, Virginia Theological Seminary.

Stevenson, W. Taylor, ed. *Theology and Culture: Essays in Honor of Albert T. Mollegen and Clifford L. Stanley.* Evanston, IL: Anglican Theological Review, 1976.

Stout, Harry S. *The Divine Dramatist: George Whitefield and the Rise of Modern Evangelicalism.* Grand Rapids: Eerdmans, 1991.

Strategic Planning Committee, Virginia Theological Seminary. "Strategic Objectives for the 21st Century." Report of the Strategic Planning Committee to the Board of Trustees, Virginia Theological Seminary, November 1998. Seminary Archives, Bishop Payne Library, Virginia Theological Seminary.

Swartz, David R. *Facing West: American Evangelicals in an Age of World Christianity.* New York: Oxford University Press, 2020.

Tai, Masakazu. "A Report by the Rev. Mr. Tai." *Spirit of Missions* 62 (1897) 318–19.

Taylor, Jay. *The Generalissimo: Chiang Kai-shek and the Struggle for Modern China.* Cambridge: Belknap, 2011.

Thomas, W. M. M. "Some Children of Brazil Yesterday and To-Day." *Spirit of Missions* 74 (1909) 125–27.

Thomson, Elliott. "The Extension of Mission Work in China." *Spirit of Missions* 48 (1883) 289–94.

Thompson, Joseph. Interview with the author, September 6, 2022. Notes in the author's possession.

Tietz, Christiane. *Karl Barth: A Life in Conflict.* Oxford: Oxford University Press, 2019.

Trotter, Jesse M. "Virginia Seminary in Uganda, East Africa." *Seminary Journal* (July 1963) 1–16.

Tucker, Beverley D. Letter from Beverley D. Tucker to family and friends, May 28, 1959. BDT VII-5. Archives. Alexandria: Virginia Theological Seminary.

———. Letter from Beverley D. Tucker to Mary Dillon, July 20, 1954. BDT VII-5. Archives. Alexandria: Virginia Theological Seminary.

Tucker, H. St. George, and Alexander C. Zabriskie. "Evangelicals and Missions." In *Anglican Evangelicalism*, edited by Alexander C. Zabriskie, 187–200. Philadelphia: Church Historical Society, 1943.

Tucker, Henry St. George. *Exploring the Silent Shore of Memory.* Richmond, VA: Whittet & Shepperson, 1951.

———. *The History of the Episcopal Church in Japan.* New York: Scribner, 1938.

———. "What This Church Is Trying to Do in Her Work Abroad." *Spirit of Missions* 81 (December 1916) 853–58.

Tyng, Theodosius. "The Kind of Workers Needed in Mission." *Spirit of Missions* 50 (1895) 149–50.

"The Unfinished Business of Mission: A Symposium in Celebration of the Ministry of Richard J. Jones." *Virginia Seminary Journal* (Spring 2009) 21.

VanderWeele, Tyler J. "On the Promotion of Human Flourishing." *PNAS* 114.31 (2017) 8148–56.

Virginia Theological Seminary. "Dr. Kings—Mission Theologian on CACS." YouTube video, 1:13. Posted June 20, 2015. https://www.youtube.com/watch?v=POJlu56j7Tg.

———. "Explore Our 200 Years of History." https://vts.edu/timeline.

"Virginia Theological Seminary Awards Five Honorary Degrees." *News from the Hill* (Spring 2017) 25. https://vts.edu/wp-content/uploads/2021/01/203432_VTS_NFTH_March2017_p11.pdf.

Virginia Theological Seminary Journal (Fall 2010). Alexandria: Virginia Theological Seminary.

Wacker, Grant. "Pearl S. Buck and the Waning of the Missionary Impulse." *Church History* 72 (December 2003) 852–74.

Walker, Cornelius. *The Life and Correspondence of Rev. William Sparrow, D.D.* Philadelphia: Hammond, 1876.

Walters, Kevin L. "Beyond the Battle: Religion and American Troops in World War II." PhD diss, University of Kentucky, 2013.

Warnock, Raphael G. *The Divided Mind of the Black Church.* New York: New York University Press, 2014.

Washington National Cathedral. "Third Summit of Christian and Muslim Religious Leaders." Press Release. Episcopal News Service. December 18, 2014. https://www.episcopalnewsservice.org/pressreleases/third-summit-of-christian-and-muslim-religious-leaders/.

Wasserstrom, Jeffrey N., ed. *The Oxford History of Modern China.* Oxford: Oxford University Press, 2022.

White, Stephen L. "Two Bishops of Liberia: Race and Mission at the Dawn of the Twentieth Century." *Anglican and Episcopal History* 70 (2001) 478–97.

Wiener, Antje. "A Theory of Contestation—a Concise Summary of Its Argument and Concepts." *Polity* 49 (January 2017) 109–12.

Winner, Lauren F. *A Cheerful and Comfortable Faith: Anglican Religious Practice in the Elite Households of Eighteenth-Century Virginia.* New Haven: Yale University Press, 2010.

Wood, Gordon S. *Empire of Liberty: A History of the Early Republic, 1789–1815.* New York: Oxford, 2009.

Woodmason, Charles. "The Journal of Reverand Charles Woodmason." Private paper, 1766. https://teachingamericanhistory.org/document/the-journal-of-reverand-charles-woodmason/.

Woolverton, John Frederick. *Colonial Anglicanism in North America.* Detroit: Wayne State University Press, 1984.

Yarsiah, James T. *Early Missionary Work of the Protestant Episcopal Church (DFMS) in Liberia and Their Differential Effects.* Scotts Valley, CA: CreateSpace, 2010. Ebook.

Zabriskie, Alexander C. *Arthur Selden Lloyd.* New York: Morehouse-Gorham, 1942.

———. "No Mean Inheritance." Unpublished manuscript. Seminary Archives, Virginia Theological Seminary.

———. "The Rise and Major Characteristics of Anglican Evangelicalism." In *Anglican Evangelicalism,* edited by Alexander C. Zabriskie, 3–38. Philadelphia: Church Historical Society, 1943.

Zabriskie, Mary Tyler. "Brazil Mission Shows Forth the Christ." *Spirit of Missions* 101 (February 1936) 57–64.